Gender, Development and Social Change

Series Editor
Wendy Harcourt, The International Institute of Social Studies, Erasmus University, The Hague, The Netherlands

The *Gender, Development and Social Change* series brings together path-breaking writing from gender scholars and activist researchers who are engaged in development as a process of transformation and change. The series pinpoints where gender and development analysis and practice are creating major 'change moments'. Multidisciplinary in scope, it features some of the most important and innovative gender perspectives on development knowledge, policy and social change. The distinctive feature of the series is its dual nature: to publish both scholarly research on key issues informing the gender and development agenda as well as featuring young scholars and activists' accounts of how gender analysis and practice is shaping political and social development processes. The authors aim to capture innovative thinking on a range of hot spot gender and development debates from women's lives on the margins to high level global politics. Each book pivots around a key 'social change' moment or process conceptually envisaged from an intersectional, gender and rights based approach to development.

Minako Sakai · Amelia Fauzia

Women Entrepreneurs and Business Empowerment in Muslim Countries

palgrave
macmillan

Minako Sakai
The University of New South Wales
Canberra, ACT, Australia

Amelia Fauzia
Syarif Hidayatullah State Islamic University
Banten, Indonesia

ISSN 2730-7328 ISSN 2730-7336 (electronic)
Gender, Development and Social Change
ISBN 978-3-031-05953-7 ISBN 978-3-031-05954-4 (eBook)
https://doi.org/10.1007/978-3-031-05954-4

This Palgrave Macmillan imprint is published by the registered company Springer Nature Switzerland AG
The registered company address is: Gewerbestrasse 11, 6330 Cham, Switzerland

Acknowledgements

This research draws on discussions with inspiring Muslim women in Indonesia. We thank all of you who have shared your thoughts through countless hours of discussion throughout our journey to finish this book. In addition to those who appear in our book, many other mompreneurs shared their thoughts with us. We also met many supportive family members that stand behind great mompreneurs.

Research students and Visiting Fellows in the Asia Pacific Development Security Group, the University of New South Wales, Canberra offered valuable input at various stages of this project. Our thanks go to Dr. Bhirawa Anoraga, Dr. Ajie Saksono, Juel Kutub, Hadi Noori, Farhat Hamid, Pinkey Rani Paul and Sammy Chapman, Dr. Rafisah Mat Radzi, Dr. Stephen Sherlock for offering valuable input at various stages of this project through seminars and conference panels. Dr. Bhirawa Anoraga and Dr. Haula Noor also offered timely research assistance. Dr. Sally Burt and Melita Eagling have assisted us with the editing of the manuscript. The University of New South Wales, the State Islamic University of Jakarta and the Ford Foundation, Jakarta generously supported this project.

The idea of this book emerged at a workshop, we co-convened with Professor Samina Yasmeen on Narratives of Muslim Womanhood, held at UNSW Canberra in 2014. Our findings and arguments have been discussed and tested through presentations at other conferences, workshops and through publications. We appreciate insightful discussions with

Professor James Piscatori, Professor Azyumardi Azra, Professor Louise Edwards, Professor Kathy Robinson and Associate Professor Felix Tan that helped develop our thinking and findings.

We owe our special thanks to our family, husbands and sons, who have fully supported the writing journey of two mothers and wives over years.

January 2022

Minako Sakai
Amelia Fauzia

Contents

About the Authors

Minako Sakai is an anthropologist, and is Associate Professor and Deputy Head of School (Research) at the School of Humanities and Social Sciences at the University of New South Wales, Canberra.

Amelia Fauzia is a social historian, and is Professor and Director for Social Trust Fund at Syarif Hidayatullah State Islamic University (UIN) Jakarta. She is a Senior Visiting Fellow with the School of Humanities and Social Sciences at the University of New South Wales, Canberra.

Abbreviations

BEKRAF	Badan Ekonomi Kreatif or Creative Economy Agency
BKKBN	Badan Kependudukan dan Keluarga Berencana Nasional or National Family Planning Board
BKMT	Badan Kontak Majelis Taklim or Majelis Taklim Coordinating Body
BMT	Baitul Maal wat Tamwil, Islamic Savings and Credit Institution
BUEKA	Bina Usaha Ekonomi Keluarga Aisyiyah, Aisyiyah Family Economic Business Development Unit
GEM	Global Entrepreneurship Monitor
ICMI	Ikatan Cendekiawan Muslim Indonesia, Indonesian Association of Muslim Intellectuals
ICT	Information Communication Technology
ILO	International Labour Organization
IPB	Institut Pertanian Bogor, Bogor Agricultural Institute
IPEMI	Ikatan Pengusaha Muslimah Indonesia, Indonesian Muslim Women Entrepreneurs Association
IWAPI	Ikatan Wanita Pengusaha Indonesia, Indonesian Business Women's Association
KADIN	Kamar Dagang dan Industri Indonesia, Indonesian Chamber of Commerce and Industry
KNEKS	Komite Nasional Ekonomi dan Keuangan Syariah, Committee for Islamic Economy and Finance
LKKNU	Lembaga Kemaslahatan Keluarga NU, Nahdlatul Ulama Institute for Family Welfare
MUI	Majelis Ulama Indonesia, Indonesian Council of Islamic Scholars
NGO	Non-governmental organisation

Ojesy	Ojek Syariah, a syariah-compliant transport service for women
PKK	Pemberdayaan Kesejahteraan Keluarga, Empowerment for the Welfare of the Family. Previously known as Pendidikan Kesejahteraan Keluarga (Education for Family Welfare)
PNPM	Program Nasional Pemberdayaan Masyarakat Mandiri, National Program for Independent Community Empowerment
POSYANDU	Pos Pelayanan Terpadu or Integrated Health Station
SDGs	United Nation's Sustainable Development Goals
STEM	Science, Technology, Engineering and Mathematics
SWA	Sekolah Wirausaha Aisyiyah, Aisyiyah Entrepreneurship School
UIN	Universitas Islam Negeri, State Islamic University
UMKM	Usaha Mikro Kecil Menengah, Micro, Small and Medium Enterprises

List of Figures

List of Tables

CHAPTER 1

Women Entrepreneurs, Islam and the Middle Class

Minako Sakai and Amelia Fauzia

Abstract The emergence of middle-class Muslim women entrepreneurs known as mompreneurs is an intriguing social phenomenon. In this book, Sakai and Fauzia show that becoming a Muslim mompreneur is a considered response of middle-class Muslim women to modernity. This chapter provides theoretical discussions on middle-class entrepreneurialism and women, and our approach to examining women's agency. We focus on Indonesia as the largest Muslim-dominant country and cover other countries in the Asia–Pacific. In this book, narratives of women, social media, government policies and responses from Muslim women's organisations will be examined to analyse women's perceptions about their gender roles. The authors argue that middle-class Muslim mompreneurs are shifting the gender power balance within the framework of Islam.

Keywords Business · Gender roles · Islam · Modernity · Mompreneurs · Middle class · Role models

M. Sakai and A. Fauzia, *Women Entrepreneurs and Business Empowerment in Muslim Countries*,
Gender, Development and Social Change,
https://doi.org/10.1007/978-3-031-05954-4_1

Introducing Muslim Mompreneurs

This book is a modest attempt to examine how Muslim women perceive their life choices, and whether Islam interferes with their choice between a life of domestic care and income-generating activities. Having observed the largest Muslim-dominant country, Indonesia, over three decades, seeing Muslim female traders in markets and shops as the main workforce, a widespread perception of Islam oppressing women appears to be different from the social realities of Muslim women's choices. Our book shows that middle-class Indonesian Muslim women are drawing on their own initiatives to develop innovative interpretations of Islam that facilitate and foster their active economic role in supporting their family. We highlight that Indonesian Muslim women continue to value raising a family as their primary role, as they did in the 1980s (Woodcroft-Lee 1983), and the 1990s (Wright and Tellei 1993) but they have found a solution to the burden of juggling their office work and family through starting up and running their own home-based businesses. Entrepreneurship, in their minds, is closely associated with the widely known role of the Prophet Muhammad's first wife, Khadijah, who successfully ran a family business and raised several children, supporting her husband as a wife and fulfilling her role as a mother.

Establishing a home-based business while raising a family as a mompreneur is a growing trend in both Western and Muslim countries (Agnihotri and Bhattacharya 2020; Ali and Nekouei 2020; Breen and Leung 2020; Landour 2020; Weidhaas 2020; Yusoff 2021). Mompreneur is a term deriving from two words, mother and entrepreneur. Although the word entrepreneurship is gender neutral, men's participation in entrepreneurial activities are reportedly higher than women's (Verheul et al. 2006). Successful male entrepreneurial behaviour impacts women's participation in entrepreneurial activities, making it more difficult for women to break through (Laguía et al. 2019). Furthermore, recent scholarly findings indicate that mompreneurs are struggling to balance their work and family despite the expectations that women can manage them well (Jean and Forbes 2012; Wijaya and Layman 2018; Wilton 2017). Is a mompreneur a myth or a reality? This is the question we will explore in this book focusing on middle-class Muslim women especially from Indonesia.

The concept of mompreneurs refers to a growing number of women entrepreneurs replacing their nine-to-five office jobs with self-employment, running a business from home while raising a family. Womenpreneur is another popular term, which consists of women and entrepreneur, referring to female entrepreneurs. According to Richomme-Huet and Vial (2014), the term mompreneur has become widely used thanks to two American entrepreneurs, Patricia Cobe and Ellen H. Parlapiano. They authored two books, *Mompreneurs: A Mother's Practical Step-By-Step Guide to Work-at-Home Success* in 1996 followed by *Mompreneurs Online: Using the Internet to Build work @ Home Success* in 2001, and appeared on popular US shows such as Oprah, which resulted in increasing the visibility of mompreneurs. They also developed a dedicated website (mompreneurs online.com) to promote this model of business for mothers who are aiming to work at home.[1] As women struggle to meet the demands of raising a family and work, the number of women drawn to self-employment to seek flexibility in their time management is increasing (Cobe and Parlapiano 2002). As our chapters show, the spread of the digital economy among the urban middle class and the use of social media through mobile phones created a supportive business ecosystem for running home-based businesses.

However, mompreneurs are not found everywhere. For example, in a recently published monograph consisting of in-depth interviews with UK women, Orgad (2019) has demonstrated that university-educated middle-class Western women, who had enjoyed a successful professional career, often became stay-at-home mothers. These women can suffer from feeling a sense of failure because of the gap between their expectations of having both a successful career and a family while being supported by their partner. Despite the commonly held ideal of being a stay-at-home mother, and being among the privileged economic minority who can comfortably live on a single income, these women can still struggle with their sense of failure because they feel that they had failed to meet societal expectation that middle-class women can have it all. Orgad (2019: 39) summarises the struggles of these women as being that they felt 'disillusioned and disempowered' because they had failed in combining motherhood with an elite career, to which they had previously aspired.

The deep disappointment of these UK women demonstrates that despite their academic training and professional work experience, they experienced a lack of agency or decision-making power against what

Giddens called 'structure, consisting of rules and resources' (Giddens 1984: 377). These modern Western women agonise over a sense of guilt and failure because of the mismatch between their personal desires and the assumed idea of successful womanhood widely held in Western society and seen as a sign of gender equality. The fact that they remain economically dependent on their partner who has equal academic qualifications adds to their misery. This is because in Western countries, being a full-time mother does not generally elevate a woman's status (Wilton 2017).[2]

On the other hand, do successful career women feel satisfied with their course of life? Well-known female Australian journalist Virginia Haussegger, a long-term presenter of the national broadcaster, ABC, until 2016, is one of the familiar faces among successful career women in Australia. She admits that there are no formal barriers for women of her generation (Hausegger was born in 1964) to pursue their career choices. However, she highlighted the continued use of two labels used for women in comparison with men: mother or not. She stated that she questions her success as a woman. As a consequence of life choices she had made in her 20s and 30s, she has found herself childless at the age of 38 and with a diminishing possibility of having her own children as age-related fertility issues become a factor. In her book titled *Wonder Woman: The Myth of 'Having It All'* (Haussegger 2005) she questioned whether women were duped into believing that the premise of feminism was having it all, meaning having both a meaningful career and raising a family. In reality, she has seen the struggles mothers face to hold on to their jobs and to navigate their careers, while she, incidentally, has found herself childless as a return on the investment in her career. She says that feminists did not warn women that the biological clock would not stop, irrespective of whether they were working or not. In the process of pursuing a career, not only can women remain childless, but also often partnerless as well. The successful juggling of a career and a family remains an unresolved issue in Western countries. To illustrate the point, previewing its Global Gender Gap Report 2020, the World Economic Forum (2019) confirms that women's participation in the labour market is lagging behind men globally as illustrated by the fact that only 55% of adult women are in the labour market as opposed to 78% of men.

So, do Muslim women see Islam as depriving their agency and life choices? Is their situation worse than that of Western women? This book will show that by utilising innovative interpretations of Islam, middle-class

Muslim women are, to some degree, expanding the societal expectations of their role through the examples of Muslim mompreneurs. They combine Islam, motherhood and entrepreneurship to support their new Muslim womanhood. The findings in this book show that long-standing active economic role of women, state economic policies and emergent role models based on the interpretations of Islam—often endorsed by Muslim organisations and preachers—are creating a particular set of favourable conditions in contemporary Indonesia where there is a greater emergence of the phenomenon of Muslim mompreneurs in comparison with other Muslim-dominant countries.

As this book shows, Muslim women in Indonesia are generally eager to marry and raise their family, and raising a family while working is a matter of concern. According to the Marriage Law of 1974, earning a household income is a husband's responsibility.[3] This legal system concurs with the common Islamic and customary interpretations of gender roles (Geertz 1961; Robinson 2009; Sullivan 1994). Traditionally among the lower-class women, wives generally face financial necessity to generate additional income, as one wage is usually not enough to meet the needs of a growing family (Jellinek 1991; Murray 1991). As Indonesia's industrialisation progressed, women's work—particularly unmarried daughter's work in factories, which started to increase in the late 1980s in Indonesia—highlighted the importance of generating additional income for the family (Wolf 1992). To increase household incomes, women started to work as migrant workers and in other informal areas of the economy to increase their financial means despite the risks associated with such work (Anggraeni 2006; Mee 2016).

An interesting recent development in the Muslim world is that middle-class mothers are taking up entrepreneurial pursuits, becoming mompreneurs, as an alternative to office jobs, to create additional income. As Chapter 2 shows, the increased interest in taking up entrepreneurship among the middle class reflects the current predicants surrounding work situations in Muslim-dominant countries. In Indonesia and Malaysia, women have a long tradition of working as petty traders in markets (Alexander 1987), cottage industry producers, textile merchants and producers (Brenner 1998). As industrialisation progressed, rural women were enticed to waged work in manufacturing with a steady cash flow for supplemental incomes and also to work as housemaids and in other unskilled services in urban areas of Southeast Asia (Heyzer 1986). Yet, recent research demonstrates that wages in manufacturing remain low, and women's employment is becoming increasingly precarious (Osterreich 2020). On the other hand, public sector employment in Indonesia including teaching (preferred by university graduates as a lifetime career with prestige), without taking up positions in remote areas, causing disruptions to the family–work balance for female employees, offers low prospects of promotions. As a result, women stay at a low level in their lifetime career (Azmi et al. 2012). Furthermore, the strict quotas on new recruitment have hardly grown the number of public servants in Indonesia (Booth 2021). Private sector positions are known to be demanding with long hours of commuting in large cities. This book shows that becoming a mompreneur provides an attractive avenue for middle-class Muslim women to finding meaningful employment while raising a family and contributing to the community. Currently, Indonesian mompreneurs are at the forefront of this scene.

Modernity and Middle-Class Muslim Women

Writing this book stemmed from our shared interest in the role of Islam in Indonesia and its impact on Indonesian middle-class Muslims (Sakai and Fauzia 2014a). Our research collaborations also investigated how middle-class interpretations of Islam in Indonesia had been translated into concrete action to offer at the time of socio-economic disasters (Sakai and Fauzia 2014b). Our findings have illustrated that members of the expanding Muslim middle class, particularly university-educated Indonesian Muslims, are using their interpretations of Islam for taking social action, and conventional and new media are becoming key sources of these interpretations of Islam for them (Nisa 2018a; Rinaldo 2013; Sakai 2012: 12; Slama 2017; Smith-Hefner 2007, 2019).

Muslims are using their everyday actions as an important way to demonstrate and measure their Muslim identity and to conduct ***dakwah bil hal*** or propagate Islamic teaching by action (Meuleman 2011). In Muslim countries, the visibility of Islamic symbols in the public sphere has also generally increased in recent decades (Anderson 2018; Fealy and White 2008) along with an increase in support for conservative Islam in politics. Our initial work was based on the findings of an in-depth study of three women and found this trend reflected in Indonesia, highlighting that middle-class Muslim women are turning to interpretations of Islam to justify their womanhood and regarding it as the most important element in framing their choices of work (Sakai and Fauzia 2016).

Our initial findings were part of the workshop Sakai had convened with Professor Samina Yasmeen titled *Narratives of Muslim Womanhood* (Sakai and Yasmeen 2016) held at the University of New South Wales (UNSW), Canberra.

Following this early work, both of us became intrigued to examine whether the narratives of women's own experiences as demonstrated by recent works (Haeri 2002; Yasmeen 2016, 2017) focusing on Muslim women's agency would provide insightful accounts to answer questions. We sought to answer what strategies could foster women's empowerment, and gender equality as framed in the United Nation's Sustainable Development Goals (SDGs). We wanted to explore what Muslim women thought of gender equality with a focus on their gender role including women's economic role in Islamising Indonesia.

In this book we also explored two interrelated issues that required investigation. Firstly, we have analysed what Indonesian Muslim women are seeing as enabling factors for empowerment, and what resources are mobilised in this process of empowerment. We also wanted to explore if Muslim women have encountered any debilitating factors. Secondly, we have examined case studies from Indonesia that aim to help to identify key factors in the facilitation of Muslim women's participation in entrepreneurial activities. For this aim we have included relevant examples from Muslim-dominant countries in the Asia–Pacific region to help us analyse what is increasingly drawing Muslim women to entrepreneurial activities as mompreneurs, and what this means for our understanding of gender relations.

At times this task seemed extremely difficult. One of the reasons derives from our understanding that there is no single Muslim world. Both of us were academically trained in Australian universities and have strongly embraced the intellectual tradition of the Asian Studies in Australia. Prior to the September 11 attacks in 2001 and the Bali bombings in 2003, scholars frequently collaborated in the framework of Asian Studies that reflected very little concern about the Middle East, let alone North African Muslim countries. Because they are located on the doorstep, Indonesia and Malaysia have been the main regions of focus in Australia's Asian Studies and along with countries in Northeast Asia such as Japan and China are of great interest in terms of regional security and socio-economic development issues. After the Global War on Terror was waged, the notion of the Muslim world began to emerge. What constitutes the Muslim world is highly subjective and our book is not an exception.

What constitutes the Muslim world reflects historical and geographical understanding pertinent in the given society. This realisation was well-explained by the history of the study of Islam in Southeast Asia. As Hefner (1997) stated, Islam in Southeast Asia received limited attention from scholars in Islamic studies as they focused on textual Islam in the Middle East, and anthropologists working on Southeast Asia saw the role of Islam as marginal and an addition to the indigenous culture. Counter-balancing this history and intellectual tradition, our geographical scope of the Muslim world certainly focuses on Indonesia and other relevant countries close to the Asia–Pacific region. By doing so, we intend to avoid creating a reductionist and orientalist approach to view the Muslim world as a single entity, and to place Indonesia as the centre of the emergent phenomenon of Muslim mompreneurs.[4]

This book is informed by the scholarly discussions that have examined Muslim responses to modernity by examining the middle-class Muslim women's active choice of becoming a mompreneur. In simple words, our analysis is framed by entrepreneurialism and women's agency as a unique response to modernity of Muslim women. Our discussions on the articulations of the concept of modernity reflect the existing scholarly discussions prevalent in the Asia–Pacific.

The features of modernity have been discussed as a key concept to examine the socio-economic political transformation. The concept of modernity as pointed out by Berger (1979) and Cox (1984) assumed secularisation of the society where the role of religion becomes less significant and is replaced by other features of modernity. Although the concept draws much from Western unique experiences, the expectations are that Muslims would follow the same path. Yet, recent historical examples such as the Iranian Revolution in 1979 and the rise of the mujahideen against the Russian invasion of Afghanistan raised doubt regarding the assumption of secularisation in the concept of modernity (Casanova 2007, 2011).

Since the mid-1980s, scholars working on Asian countries have also noted that the realisation of modernity and the imaginaries of modernity are different from those of Western countries. One of the areas that attracted much scholarly attention surrounded the position of women in Muslim-dominant countries. Women's status and their use of veiling are deemed to be the guardian and the defender of moral and political imagination of the order of the Muslim society (Eickelman and Piscatori 1996: 91). Despite this assumption, which is widely shared in Muslim imagination, women's participation in the public sphere has increased. For example, opportunities for employment outside the family home to generate a handsome income increased and, alongside industrialisation and economic development, undermined male authority in Malaysia (Ong 1995) and family prestige in Bangladesh (White 1992). As a result, the politics of gender in Muslim societies has largely targeted the control of women's rights, body and sexuality that scholars have examined (Cesari and Casanova 2017). In the case of Indonesia, scholars have examined the negotiations of public and private spheres surrounding women's position and body to clearly identify the level of defending Islam in society (Brenner 2011; Smith-Hefner 2007, 2019).

Thus, the rise of Islamism and the seemingly paradoxical Muslim women's decision to support it have shown Muslims' responses to a shared notion of modernity in Muslim societies (Göle 1996, 2002, 2015; Rinaldo 2008a, b, 2013; Stivens 1991, 2002). Of importance is the growing scholarly view that women are actively negotiating and responding to social change and modernity by constructing their subjectivity based on their own embracement of Islam (Deeb 2006; Mahmood 2011).

A rapid economic development based on capitalism and the emergence of the middle-class in Asia denote another facet of significant modernity. In Southeast Asia, economic growth, accelerated by industrialisation and capitalism across the region, supported the rise of the new rich in the 1980s. The middle-class political and religious orientations did not parallel the Western experiences, but denoted specific historical contexts reflecting how capitalism developed in the region (Goodman and Robison 1996). The identity construction of the middle class in Asia, as distinct from that in the West, was accompanied by their cultural behaviour, which included a preference for extravagant luxurious goods (Kondo 1990; Pinches 1999). Furthermore, Islam has become an important part of the middle-class identity (van Klinken and Berenschot 2014; Nagata 1980; Porter 2004; Shamsul 1999; Stivens 2013). Along this rise of the urban middle class, scholars have shown the compatibility of Islam and capitalism in Malaysia (Sloane-White 2007, 2008, 2017) and Indonesia (Hoesterey 2008, 2015; Rudnyckyj 2010), for example, the consumption of *halal* goods has become more prevalent (Fischer 2008, 2011). Growing interest in developing the Islamic economy to avoid economic marginalisation of Muslims in Indonesia has fostered Islamic financial institutions (Hefner 1998, 2003; Lubis 2004; Sakai 2008, 2014).

The trend of the growing impact of Islam in regulating the everyday lives of Muslims reflected what Eickelman (1992) called the objectification of religion among middle-class Muslims in Arab countries where mass higher education introduced a new way of understanding the role of Islam in a Muslim's life. Using the examples of Egypt, Morocco and Oman, he explained that these educated Muslims turned to books as religious authority rather than traditional learned religious teachers who had mastery of the religious texts. Starrett (1998) further presented a detailed ethnographic analysis on the impact of higher education upon Egyptian religious culture where the application of Islam in everyday life has been emphasised. Alongside this change, media has become an important source of Islamic authority in the Muslim-majority countries (Eickelman and Anderson 2003), as a vehicle for Islamising the public sphere as part of the distinctive Islamic modernity (Meyer and Moors 2005). The growing appetite for knowledge among middle-class Muslims created a booming market of Islamic books in Indonesia (Watson 2005) and the acceleration of Islamisation in Southeast Asia has changed the urban outlook of Southeast Asia as reflected in the growing popularity of Islamic popular culture and consumption of halal commodities among middle-class Muslims (Fealy 2008; Heryanto 2008; Hoesterey and Clark 2012; Jones 2018).

Estimating the size of the middle-class population is not easy, yet approximately 20% of the Indonesian population or roughly 52 million people are classified as the middle class, while 45% of the population or 115 million Indonesians are the aspiring middle class (World Bank 2020).[5] Out of these, the Muslim population accounts for over 87%. We follow the definition that the Muslim middle class is 'a group of population who has both purchasing power and degree of religiosity' (Ali and Purwandi 2017: 7). Yet, it is important to highlight that multiple definitions of middle class are used across different academic disciplines, referring to financial indicators, credentials, lifestyle and social standing (Reeves et al. 2018). As this book explores middle-class Muslim women's perceptions and how these women exert their agency, we side with the views used by the majority of social scientists focusing on the analysis of social standing, income and educational attainments shaping aspirations, and associated lifestyle choices of the middle class.

Muslim Women and Ideal Womanhood

The interest in exploring women's agency to the increasing presence of conservative interpretations of Islam, including the spread of modest fashion, attracted scholarly inquiry about women's religious authority and gender roles. Islamic feminism is a branch of Islamic thought where religion and secular feminist thinking have intersected. It originally derived from the theological debates of modern reformist Islam in the twentieth century to achieve gender equality based on the interpretations the Qur'an as its foundation by exercising *ijtihad*, independent reasoning (Badran 2005, 2008). The thoughts and actors of Islamic feminism were further affected by the rise of feminism in the 1960s (Schröter 2017). Yet recent publications on Islamic feminism show that the production of knowledge framed as Islamic feminism reflects local contexts and the thoughts of Islamic feminism are diverse (Sirri 2020). In Indonesia discourses and studies of Islamic feminism are taught at university (Robinson 2006, 2018). In Malaysia Sisters in Islam, a Muslim women's NGO that was established in 1988, advocates gender equality based on the interpretations of Islam that defend women's rights (Anwar 2001). Even though the use of *ijtihad* by scholars and Islamic organisations has led to the acceptance of Islamic feminism (Saeed 1997), Indonesian Muslim women do not generally feel comfortable with the terms feminist or feminism as these terms could be seen as 'culturally inauthentic or, worse, a form of Western imperialism' (Rinaldo 2013: 8). In Kuwait, feminism associated with secular and individualistic traits is not popular among Muslim women (González 2013). In Qatar, secular feminism is regarded as alien (Golkowska 2017).

The lack of enthusiasm in the use of feminism in public debates and discourse does not mean that Muslim women do not strive for or negotiate to locate gender equality, it means they turn to Islam to strengthen their rights (González 2013). Studying the history of Islamic feminism in Indonesia, Anwar (2018) has shown that Indonesian Muslim women have acted on their interpretations of Islam in their daily life to demonstrate their agency within the framework of Islam. Focusing on Indonesia, van Doorn-Harder (2006, 2013) and Schröter (2013, 2017) have shown a grassroots form of Islamic feminism in practice in which Muslim women in Indonesia negotiated the interpretations of Islam through the study of mainstream Muslim women's organisations as affiliated with Indonesia's two largest Muslim organisations, Muhammadiyah and

Nahdlatul Ulama (NU). Islamic feminism—as presented as *ijtihad* (independent reasoning) by a younger women's affiliate of Muhammadiyah called Nasyiatul Aisyiyah—means to stand between secular feminists and Islamists (Syamsiyatun 2016). Our approach in this book aligns with this current development of research findings to examine the endeavours in achieving gender equality, and we argue that Muslim women act and disseminate their interpretations of Islam in their daily life by expanding the role of what is considered a good Muslim woman.

As embracing Islam has become important for urban middle-class Muslims, new research has highlighted the increased influence of new media where TV Muslim preachers, not necessarily linked with traditional religious authorities of Indonesia, have become influential, reflecting the fact that religious authority for Muslim women has been diffused (Baulch and Pramiyanti 2018; Beta 2014; Nisa 2018a, b; Nurlaelawati 2020; Rinaldo 2008a, b, 2013; Robinson 2018; Sakai 2019; Sakai and Fauzia 2014a). A wide range of expressions of women's agency in constructing their womanhood as illustrated by these scholarly works reflects the complexities of what it means to be a Muslim as Soares and Osella (2009: 11) have shown by *Islam mondain* or 'Islam in the present world'. It reflects the varied and complex ways Muslims express and negotiate being a proper religious self amid the uncertainties surrounding politics and economic activities as they are further faced with increased global connectivity.

In view of these discussions, this book will examine the construction of ideal womanhood among middle-class Muslim women in Indonesia through the lens of entrepreneurialism and Islam. This is particularly important in the context of Indonesia because role modelling has played a significant part in this country throughout the history of Islamisation and nation-making. Although Islam prohibits worshipping humans, Muslim preachers are widely respected as they have shown exceptional qualities and behaviour to spread Islam. For example, the first Islamic preachers of Islam across the island of Java, known as nine saints or *wali songo*, have been remembered and their names are used as part of state Islamic universities and higher education. In Islamic boarding schools, the principal male Islamic teachers known as *kiai* are role models for Muslim students (Isbah 2020). For female Muslim students, the wives of the *kiai*, known as *nyai*, are influential figures they share their dreams with and look up to. This is because a *nyai* is a capable and exemplary Muslim woman who can manage an Islamic educational institution along with her wifely and motherly obligations (Hefner 2008; Srimulyani 2007). Further role modelling occurs through Islamic popular culture such as movies and novels, which are used as an emerging source of Islamic knowledge and interpretations. Contemporary Muslim popular novelists are aiming to create new role models for Muslim youth in Indonesia (Sakai 2012).

In addition to the long-standing role-modelling tradition in Indonesia, the Indonesian government has been working steadily to collect and present national heroes, these heroes include both men and women who contributed to the making of Indonesian society through national history programs (Abdullah 2009; Pramono et al. 2021). Raden Ajeng Kartini (1879–1904), a young Javanese woman born to an aristocratic family, is known as a national hero who inspired women's education (Bijl and Chin 2020; Blackburn 2004; Hatley and Blackburn 2013; Robinson 2020). These national role models are introduced through the school curriculum, and remembered through annual celebration rituals that aim to instil what ideal Indonesian citizens should look up to and emulate and not free from contested.[6] Motherhood as part of women's role has been strongly advocated in the making of modern Indonesia (Blackburn 2004: 138–166; Suryakusuma 1996). Public servants and their wives are also expected to embody a national role model for the citizens by following the national policies.[7] Yet, one income is increasingly not enough for middle-class families in Indonesia (Robinson 2018: 316). In this context, as this book shows, looking up to Muslim female role models, particularly Khadijah, is closely linked with being middle-class Muslim entrepreneurs who have actively chosen to emulate these role models in the process of Islamisation of the middle class, particularly in Southeast Asia.

Thus, female entrepreneurship and Islam among middle-class Muslim women convey distinctive meaning. As Freeman (2007, 2014) has shown through her ethnographic analysis of Caribbean women entrepreneurs, the entrepreneurialism for the middle class is not simply a way to generate an income, but is a way of making an appropriate self, reflecting the history and local contexts associated with capitalism. She has highlighted that having flexibility in life among the Barbadians is not just the accommodation of flexibility associated with neoliberalism but is also negotiated in the cultural embeddedness of the socio-cultural tradition of the locality. Some early features of the urban middle class in Jakarta have strongly denoted consumer culture and some inclination for political democratisation in the late 1990s (van Leeuwen 2011). Yet, 20 years since the beginning of Indonesia's democratisation in 1998, the life of the urban middle class has increased in Islamic inclination. Thus, the emergent trend of choosing to become a mompreneur illustrates the 'cultural convergences', borrowing Freeman's words (2007), where the reinvented imaginaries of the wives of the Prophet Muhammad foster and support modern women's aspirations of career pursuits.

To become mompreneurs, middle-class Muslim women are embodying new discourses about ideal womanhood that are closely linked with the social imaginaries of the two well-known wives of the Prophet Muhammad, Khadijah and Aishah. Along with Fatimah, the elder daughter of the Prophet Muhammad and Khadijah, these two wives are widely respected as exemplary Muslim women in the Muslim world.

It is important to note that the wives of Prophet Muhammad, including Khadijah and Aishah, were called as *umm al-mukminin* (the title recorded in the Qur'an 33, 6) or 'the mothers of the believers' (Abbott 1942; Afsaruddin 2011; Stowasser 1992). Khadijah binti Khuwailid (555–619 AD) was born into a rich merchant family of the Quraish tribe. She inherited her family's business, was known as a successful businesswoman and employed Muhammad when he was in his early 20s. She was a widow who proposed to Muhammad and married him when he was aged 25. She is known as the first convert to Islam, and was the main comfort, protection and support for her husband's *dakwah* (propagation activities). She gave birth to four daughters; one was named Fatimah. Fatimah married the Prophet Muhammad's cousin Ali and was the mother of Hasan and Hussein, both of whom continued the lineage of the prophet and linked Shiite Muslims. Muhammad and Khadijah's marriage remained monogamous until her death (Khalafallah 2014).

After Khadijah died, Muhammad married Sawdah and Aishah as his second and third wives before he married many other widows of his supporters and political clans. Aishah (614–678) was the daughter of his close friend, Abu Bakar Shiddiq (573–634). Aishah later became an important female figure because of her contribution to the propagation of Islam through her recollection of the Prophet Muhammad's *hadith* (deeds and sayings).[8]

The importance of motherhood seems rather contradictory to the reality of Aishah's life, as she produced no children of her own. Aishah married the Prophet Muhammad when she was nine years old, and she was 12 before they lived in the same house. In a number of *hadiths*, told by Aishah and others, she asked Muhammad to give her a nickname, just as he did for his other wives. Even though she does not bear a child, Muhammad called her 'Umm 'Abdullah (Arabic: mother of Abdullah) (Ibn Hibban 1988: 55; Ibn Hanbal 2001: 99; Al-Baihaqi 2003: 522). This nickname derived from the name Abdullah ibn Zubair (the son of her sister Asma), whom 'she is said to have "adopted" and loved like her own son' (Stowasser 1994: 109). Thus, the practice of child adoption, both symbolic and legal, enables childless women to become mothers to fulfil the gender expectation found in strongly patriarchal Muslim communities. The running of orphanages by Muslim women's organisations funded by almsgivings has naturally become common. The care of orphans has been an important social service provided by Muhammadiyah and Nahdlatul Ulama (Barton 2014; Fealy and Bush 2014). For example, Muhammadiyah owns 550 orphanages, and from this 159 are under the management of Aisyiyah (Interview with Sularno, 3 October 2021). As Chapter 4 illustrates, child adoption is an appropriate practice for married women who would otherwise remain childless.

It deserves to be highlighted that the understanding of the accounts of these women has changed over the time. Scholars (El-Cheikh 2015; Stowasser 1992, 1994) have shown that earlier narratives about the wives' behaviour have been modified. For example, Stowasser (1994: 126) has analysed that trivial jealousy among the wives has been translated into women's piety and their support for the propagation of Islam, and their supportive and nurturing roles as wives and mothers became emphasised in the modern interpretations of the accounts of these women in the *hadith*. She writes (Stowasser 1994: 126):

> The transformation of the old manipulative jealousy into a positive aspect of the female psyche fits in with the widespread and increasingly influential modern Muslim typology of the prophet's wives as soldiers who fought for the establishment and also the protection of Islamic values.

This transformation of narratives has become a so-called new tradition 'constructed around and through specific discourses that constitute the social core of religious traditions' (Starrett 1998: 13). By analysing the ways such social imaginaries are reinvented and transmitted through a diverse set of sources and acted by contemporary role models to negotiate and shift the balance of authority in patriarchy, this book will show that mompreneurs are embedded in this tradition.

Narratives about Khadijah and Aishah epitomise two exemplary role models for Muslim women and the two competing narratives about ideal womanhood that exist in the Muslim imagination (Khalafallah 2014). Both are known as mother and wife, and along with their husband both strongly supported the dissemination of Islam. In the context of modernity in Muslim-dominant countries, Muslim women are increasingly identifying themselves as part of the narratives because 'creating one's identity occurs with an individual locating oneself within a narrative— that is, seeing oneself as part of a context or story— and envisioning oneself emplotted as such' (El-Cheikh 2015: 115).

In contemporary narratives of women, Khadijah provides a role model used as a validation of the practice of women seeking permission to work to support their family. She is used by Muslim feminists as a role model of Muslim women who are educated and brave (Sidani 2018: 75). Aishah, on the other hand, has also been used as a role model to support women's work outside the home involving the propagation of Islam and the development of community welfare. For example, Aishah is associated with the concept of *taqwa*, meaning piety. In Bangladesh, her association with *taqwa* also comes in the context of protecting the community—as she joined the prophet in fighting to protect her own community—inspiring Muslim women to leave their homes to engage in development projects in Bangladesh (Salehin 2016: 183).

Aishah is also respected as the mother of the whole community—along with Khadijah and others—even though she did not have her own children. Aishah's story has generally been used to support marriage at an early age and as a representation of the most loving wife in Muslim communities (Abbott 1942; Stowasser 1992). Depending on the context, the life stories of both these women have been extensively used by contemporary religious authorities and by Muslim women to justify their different life choices (Roded 2008). In Indonesia the name of the youngest wife of the prophet was well known as one of the mainstream Muslim women's organisations. Muhammadiyah, a reformist Muslim organisation in Indonesia, named its women's organisations Aisyiyah, named for the women who follow in the steps of Aishah (Syamsiyatun 2016: 77) and because Aishah assisted the prophet in disseminating Islam. The wife of K.H. Ahmad Dahlan also actively assisted her husband in disseminating reformist Islamic views to Muslim women (Ro'fah 2016: 29). Her name is associated with piety; she was a woman who assisted her husband's propagation of Islam.[9]

In our case studies of Muslim women, the increasingly frequent references to Khadijah highlight the emergent importance of her role among Muslim female entrepreneurs in Indonesia and in other Muslim-dominant countries. This is, we contend, an attempt to reverse the historical processes of the domestication of Muslim women that took place in the socio-economic changes caused by urbanisation and industrialisation. For example, the recent change from a matrilineal social structure to urbanisation and nuclear family residence in West Sumatra in Indonesia has placed women under a stronger influence of patriarchy and economic development (Schröter 2013: 16). Referring to Khadijah presents a sturdy discourse to counterbalance gender norms and expand women's role.

The traditional approach to the examination of sources of Islamic authority in Indonesia concentrates on the study of classical texts and Islamic law and legal systems (Amal 2013; Azra and Salim 2003; Hasyim 2006, 2020; Hooker 1983, 2008; Sonneveld and Lindbekk 2017), formal educational institutions (Lukens-Bull 2005, 2013; Pohl 2009; Smith and Woodward 2013; Tan 2012) and Muslim organisations (Barton and Fealy 1996; Peacock 1978). The emergent area of research focuses on women's agency in interpretating Islam and female religious authority (Arnez 2010; Kloos 2016; Kloos and Künkler 2016; van Doorn-Harder 2006). Arnez (2010) and van Doorn-Harder (2006) and highlighted the importance of women's responses to the interpretations of Islam through study groups associated with two major Muslim organisations, Muhammadiyah and Nahdlatul Ulama in Indonesia. How women respond to their Islamic faith in social change associated with modernity is an emergent area of research (Afrianty 2020, 2015; Hefner 2016, 2017; Naafs 2018; Nurmila 2009, 2016; Smith-Hefner 2005, 2007, 2018, 2019; van Wichelen 2010). Yet, the economic activities of women and Islamic authority in changing social and Islamising contexts remain to be fully explored.

This book will focus on the area of entrepreneurial activities to examine how middle-class Muslim women are responding to and creating Islamic discourses to support their activities. Their entrepreneurial being is emerging along with Indonesia's economic growth as promoted by the government, yet their subjectivity is closely associated with helping their husbands and families, and contributing widely to the community, as the wives of the prophet demonstrated. Their action, in practice, negotiates gender relations and patriarchal norms in society.

Our intention is not to pinpoint specific Islamic texts and philological evidence supporting the deeds and conduct of the two ideal women. Rather, we are more intrigued by how these two role models, as social images, subconsciously guide and inspire Muslim women in contemporary contexts. It is important to note that with a strong upholding of nationalism in Indonesia, the images of ideal womanhood are not only limited to Muslim women in Indonesia but also to those women who have widely contributed to the making of Indonesian society. Thus, adherence to interpretations of Islam is usually framed as a contribution to the making of Indonesian society, which the Indonesian state strongly encourages, as shown in Chapter 3.[10] In comparison with other Muslim-dominant countries, the combination of these factors has resulted in Indonesia becoming a leader in its support of Muslim mompreneurs.

Analysing Women's Voices and Empowerment

This book analyses how Muslim women are empowered by entrepreneurship and what women's economic empowerment entails for them. The word empowerment has been widely used by both scholars and development practitioners (Buvinic and O'Donnel 2021; Kabeer 2005). Definitions and interpretations of the concept of empowerment, however, vary greatly (Parpart et al. 2002). In light of the discursive nature of scholarly debates about the meaning of this concept, we engage with the following scholarly debates in this book.

Firstly, in a widely cited cornerstone work Naila Kabeer (2002: 435) defines that 'women's empowerment is the process by which those who have been denied the ability to make strategic life choices acquire such an ability'. This understanding proposes that women's work participation alone should not be equated with economic empowerment if this does not lead to the possibility of control over a woman's life choices (Kabeer 2019).

Secondly, when discussing giving women access to resources for empowerment, economic resources, particularly microfinancing, have been the common focus. Yet, while women's access to microfinance has received wide recognition, as highlighted by the achievements of the Grameen Bank in Bangladesh and Muhammad Yunus, co-awardees of the Nobel Peace Prize in 2006, feminist scholars have criticised the longer-term impacts on women of access to microfinance (Kar 2018; Karim 2008; Schuler et al. 1998). These scholars argue that women's agency in managing their businesses was limited within the existing patriarchy and that domestic violence against women increased as this agency was obtained. Yet, the emergent scholarly findings demonstrate that it is essential to focus on women's own voices and perceptions (Khan and Khan 2016). This understanding needs to be emphasised, as in some societies social transformation and change may take a different path, reflecting the specific conditions of that society. In Muslim-dominant societies, as discussed earlier, secularisation of religion and the position of women have always been contested.

Thirdly, we side with recent studies that highlight the importance of cultural contexts that affect the meaning of empowerment (Kabeer and Khan 2014; Porter 2007, 2013; Rozario 2006). Without cultural changes that support women's subjective wellbeing, gender norms may not change for the better and women do not feel validated in their new role when transcending the existing gender norms (De Hoop et al. 2014). As Porter (2013: 2) states, 'understandings of empowerment differ according to cultural contexts, and thus strategies to foster empowerment must be locally driven'. Following this contention, with a focus on middle-class Muslim women in Indonesia, this book examines localised strategies used to foster Muslim women's empowerment.

This book's findings concur with the emergent scholarly literature that focuses on Islam as an important element in Muslim women's economic empowerment (Samani and Marinova 2020; Tlaiss 2014, 2015; Tlaiss and McAdam 2021). Our empirical findings in this book also support the emergent development project framework to highlight that women's economic empowerment can be attained when they are free to make decisions and their subjective wellbeing is safeguarded and supported by the community (De Hoop 2021; De Hoop et al. 2014; Kabeer and Khan 2014).

Our approach focuses on women's own perceptions and understanding of the nature of Islamic authority, and how Muslim women utilise it to enable them to pursue entrepreneurial activities alongside their family life. Traditionally, theological and inherently normative interpretations of gender roles dominated the study of Muslim women's position in society. While legal sources constitute an important source of Islamic interpretation, gender norms and rights may be very different in reality. A leading anthropologist, Lila Abu-Lughod (2013), has rightly stated that various institutions, both local and national, and state and non-state, influence the way Muslim women's rights are negotiated and practised Thus, the analysis of Muslim women's roles and their views of empowerment needs to be done in the context of lived experience (Mee 2016: 164). As the authors of this book, both of us have research experience in Indonesia over three decades on the issues of Islam and social development. For data collection of this book, Sakai spent considerable time with the informants and communicated with them in Indonesian. As Sakai had cultivated these research associations over a long period of time, the informants were able to lead conversations surrounding the issues of work and family.[11]

In analysing the concept of modern ideal Muslim womanhood, we side with the established views provided by Robinson (2009) and Tickamyer and Kusujiarti (2012) that gender relations have been evolving along with social change. Our unique contribution is to focus on social change and the spread of diverse Islamic interpretations in Indonesia, in comparison with other Muslim-dominant countries, with a specific focus on the female economic role approximately after the 1980s when the effects of Islamisation started to increase in Southeast Asia. Women's economic roles attracted scholarly attention and solid ethnographic work, but this has focused on women's roles as small traders (Alexander 1987), and small business owners (Brenner 1998; Sullivan 1994). However, research examining women's economic activities using empirical studies of small trades has received less attention over the last two decades (Tambunan 2016). This may be due to the socio-economic change in Indonesia that has led to women having an equal level of primary and secondary education as men and trading in dirty traditional markets is now deemed an old-fashioned livelihood (Suryadarma et al. 2007). Furthermore, women now find employment in new areas, such as manufacturing and services (Ford and Parker 2008), through overseas work (Anggraeni 2006) and opportunities in the civil service, all of which are seen as more stable sources of income. However, recent research on women's work shows that their participation in formal structured employment has stalled, as women struggle with raising families and rigid office-work employment conditions (Cameron et al. 2019). Despite starting new entrepreneurial businesses, their financial security remains unstable (Sakai and Anoraga 2020).

What these Muslim women are aiming for is centrality in the family and community to be recognised as an important Muslim principle, which we contend is one of the appropriate ways to promote gender equality in Muslim-dominant communities. Becoming marginal to the family system with insecure employment poses a graver risk to Muslim women than simply gaining individual autonomy (Kabeer 2001; Salway et al. 2005; White 1992). This book shows that middle-class Muslim women are strengthening their position in the family and their Muslim community, thus differentiating themselves from profit-driven small traders.

In analysing Muslim women's work participation, we have taken into account relevant conditions that need to be achieved to enable women to participate in the waged workforce presented by Nadia Hijab (1988). In her seminal work, *Womanpower: The Arab Debate on Women at Work*, she identified needs, opportunity and ability as key factors that must be met at both the state and individual levels.

Since the publication of Hijab's book, important developments in this field have occurred, including the international development frameworks that have impacted gender empowerment policymaking and implementation processes. For example, the United Nations' Fourth World Conference on Women in Beijing in 1995 produced the Beijing Declaration and Platform for Action (Afkhami and Friedl 1997), which was subsequently incorporated into the UN-led Millennium Development Goals and Sustainable Development Goals (SDGs). The current guiding framework, the SDGs, have Gender Equality listed as one of the specific goals (goal number 5). Muslim countries, including Indonesia, are thus expected to integrate this goal into their policies relating to women's role in society.

Hijab's framework was further refined by Spierings (2015: 55–58) in his comparative study of Muslim women's work participation, in which he adjusted categories to account for the realities facing Muslim women. To illustrate, he firstly redefined needs to mean 'what *must* be done?' (Spierings 2015: 55). He expanded women's needs to reflect material needs and care needs. The care needs are of particular relevance to the work choices of Muslim women. Secondly, he expanded the notion of opportunities to mean 'what *can* be done?' (Spierings 2015: 56). To explore suitable conditions, he focuses on analysing the presence of suitable jobs for women's qualifications, which have changed over time in each country. Thirdly, he presented the notion of values as a reference to 'what *should* be done?', instead of meaning the woman's abilities. In particular he emphasised the importance of two sets of values affecting women's employment as being the 'general role of women in the public sphere' and 'the specific values about the existence and extent of complementary roles of men and women' (Spierings 2015: 57). In simple terms, he argues that women are more likely to be accepted into work in feminised job sectors (Spierings 2015: 107) as these are deemed to be appropriate for female employment. To address recent developments, he also expanded Hijab's simple dichotomy of the state and popular into five conceptual levels that affect women's agency and their choice to participate in work that include individual, household, community, country and global levels.

Our position reflects these scholarly debates as we analyse empirical case studies of Indonesian Muslim women's small businesses and entrepreneurship. We will examine how women's wholistic needs and opportunities interact with personal aspirations. In other words, we will examine women's own aspirations for empowering themselves within patriarchal Muslim societies and structures. In doing so, we identify religious authority and women's agency as key factors supporting Muslim women's empowerment. Case studies from Indonesia will examine how women perceive and negotiate the gender norms to empower themselves and the community in everyday life. Whether women see Islam as enabling or restricting women's economic empowerment is our focus of concern.

Overview of Indonesia

While this book encompasses other Muslim communities, the geographical focus and ethnographic material derives from Indonesia. With a population of 270.2 million in 2020, Indonesia's population consists of 87% (234 million) Muslims while about half of the population is female. Indonesia has the largest Muslim population in the world. It is followed by Pakistan, India and Bangladesh, though the Pew Research Centre (2011) predicts Pakistan will surpass it in 2030. Socio-politically, Islam is the dominant religion in Indonesia. Despite the significance of the Muslim population, since its independence declaration in 1945, Indonesia has been governed under a secular democracy based on a Republican presidential system. Indonesia has embraced the national philosophy of Pancasila (Five Principles), rather than forming an Islamic state. One of the principles is that citizens should follow an acknowledged world religion, with Islam being one of these official religions. Under 'unity in diversity' as its motto, all the citizens—irrespective of ethnicity and religion—are guaranteed the freedom of the choice of religion under the law, but challenges of religious intolerance remain (Kersten 2015, 2017). Indonesia adheres to civil law but acknowledges both religious and customary laws. Islamic law can be used alongside national laws to manage personal affairs such as marriage and inheritance. According to the 1974 Indonesian Marriage Law, earning a livelihood for the family is the responsibility of the husband as the head of the household, while the wife is expected to manage other household matters. This law is applicable for all citizens irrespective of their religious background. This legal context creates a sensitive but discursive environment where women need to negotiate their pursuit of economic activities in contemporary Indonesia. Women are generally expected to manage financial matters by making ends meet, but generating a supplementary income is considered normal for women in Indonesia to help achieve this end (Cameron and Contreras Suarez 2017; Utomo 2004). Traditionally, Indonesian women have worked in small trades and cottage industries for this supplementary income.

Islam arrived and gradually spread across the Nusantara archipelago between the seventh and ninth centuries. The northern tip of Sumatra was among the earliest areas to develop strong Muslim communities and in the thirteenth century had established Islamic kingdoms. Prior to the arrival of Islam, the local population adhered to Buddhism, Hinduism as epitomised by the Sriwijaya Kingdom (seventh to thirteenth centuries) and the Majapahit Kingdom (thirteenth to sixteenth centuries), and animist beliefs. After the thirteenth century, Islamic kingdoms grew and achieved their peak between the sixteenth and nineteenth centuries, in conjunction with the period of European arrival as traders and later colonial rulers, which brought Catholicism and Protestantism to the archipelago. Most Islamic kingdoms then weakened and disappeared, and the population was governed under secular Dutch rule, which crystallised in the twentieth century under the name Indonesia.

Despite deepening and widening Islamisation in the country (Ricklefs 2012), gender roles were not significantly affected. Since its early modern period, Indonesia, as part of Southeast Asia, has offered a relatively favourable space for women (Andaya 2007, 2008; Reid 1988). Social and political changes brought by foreign traders during the early modern period did not significantly affect the robust role of female traders and merchants who had worked in traditional markets (Andaya 2008: 123–125). This phenomenon has continued to present.

Indonesian nationalism has been forged through the struggle to achieve independence from Dutch colonialism (Elson 2008). The struggle for independence brought secular nationalist forces and Islamic forces into contest within Indonesian society, and this resulted in the principles of the Pancasila guiding the development of Indonesian nationalism (Kersten 2015, 2017; Pringle 2010). Further bolstering Indonesian nationalism, the implementation of national education provided an important vehicle to teach the national language of Bahasa Indonesian and forge the Indonesian identity.

The majority of the Indonesian population adheres to the Sunni Shafi'i schools of Islam and the Ghazali Sufi mystic tradition. This has led to the emergence of Islamic boarding schools with centralised Islamic authority guiding Islamic scholars, and was based on the subsuming of local customs and traditions into Islamic practices. From the early twentieth century, Muslim social, economic and religious organisations were established and have played an important role as civil society organisations in the country ever since.

The different sides of the Islamisation of Indonesia can be seen in the establishment of two mainstream Muslim organisations. Nahdlatul Ulama is a loosely organised network of Islamic boarding schools known as *pesantren* and leaders known as *kiai*. It was established in 1926. Muhammadiyah, which is a modernist and reformist Islamic organisation, was formed in 1912. Contrary to NU, Muhammadiyah pushed an agenda of purifying Islam by renouncing local and syncretic practices of Islam. Muhammadiyah has focused on establishing day schools and has increased its membership base across Indonesia. In 2010, Muhammadiyah owned 11,666 social, economic and educational institutions, and this does not include its 12,068 mosques (Fauzia 2016: 213). To date, Nahdlatul Ulama reportedly has 60 million members, while Muhammadiyah has 40 million, together accounting for over 35% of the Muslim population of Indonesia between the two organisations (Nashrullah 2019). Both organisations have women's affiliates that form part of the official organisation, (Aisyiyah-Muhammadiyah and Muslimat- Nahdlatul Ulama). Since the fall of Suharto's authoritarian government known as the New Order (1966–1998), Islamisation expanded the population of both Islamists and Salafis as democratisation progressed. Salafi Muslims are Sunni adherents who follow Salafism. Salafism is named to reflect the traditions carried out by a pious pioneer of this faith (Hasan 2007; Wagemakers 2016). Salafism idealises the pure tradition of Islamic teachings as practised by the Prophet Muhammad and his companions in the early days of Islam. Islamist organisations, both national and transnational, have strengthened the formation of women's organisations to expand their influence over women. However, in 2017 the state banned the Hizbut Tahrir Indonesia (HTI), a transnational political movement seeking to establish a global Islamic polity, to curtail their influence because it undermined the unity of Indonesia.

The role of Islam and religious authority is relatively fluid because there are multiple sources of Islamic authority in Indonesia. For example, in Indonesia two dominant Muslim social organisations, Nahdlatul Ulama and Muhammadiyah, and the Indonesian Council of Islamic Scholars (MUI) are deemed as important sources of Islamic authority directing appropriate Muslim behaviour. The Ministry of Religious Affairs manages Islamic education from primary to higher education in institutions such as State Islamic Universities (UIN) and supervises religious practices for Indonesian citizens. Adhering to *fatwa*, or a legal opinion issued by the MUI council, however, is voluntary.

Ethnic identities have become blurred as urbanisation and outward migration have become increasingly common, resulting in the decline of the practice of traditions associated with customary laws and identity. In the meantime, the syncretic practice of Islam has declined (Hefner 2011; Sakai 2017) and has been replaced with more orthodox practices of Islam for urban middle-class Muslims (Kuipers and Askuri 2017).

Since the 1970s, Indonesia has successfully industrialised and since the 2000s, increased its Gross Domestic Product (GDP) at an average of approximately 4.48% per annum (Trading Economics 2021). Assisted by this strong economic growth, Indonesia has developed as a lower middle-income country, and as one of the significant world economies is now a member country of the G20. In this economic landscape, small and medium enterprises are integral elements of the Indonesian economy. Indeed, these enterprises helped revive the Indonesian economy following both the 1998 and 2008 financial crises (Ministry of Cooperatives and Small and Medium Enterprises 2001; Tambunan 2020) Some reports, including that of the World Bank (2016), have attempted to calculate the percentage of small enterprises run or owned by women. These estimates have ranged from 40 to 80%.[12]

Indonesia is developing the use of the internet for a digital economy. The World Bank (2021) estimates that internet connectivity has progressed to around 50% of the adult population in 2021, with the younger population (aged 16–25) being the most active users. Another data source reports that 73.7% of the population had access to the internet in January 2021, with 61.8% of the population in January 2021 being social media users (Kemp 2021). While the digital divide exists, the Widodo government has been encouraging Indonesians to become digital entrepreneurs and create start-ups, capitalising on the enthusiasm of internet and social media users (Jurriëns and Tapsell 2017).

As Indonesia industrialised, women started to work in new areas such as factories, and the retail and service industries. However, more recently, the participation rate of Indonesian women in the workforce has stalled. Cameron et al. (2019) highlight the fact that women who take time off after childbirth and begin raising a family face significant difficulties in returning to work; it is much easier for younger unmarried women to find work. The case studies of middle-class Indonesian Muslim women presented demonstrate this demographic's everyday struggles and the negotiations that allow them to initiate, develop and grow their businesses as Muslim mompreneurs while also respecting their faith. Through their efforts, these middle-class Muslim women are disseminating a new role model in Islamising Indonesia.

The Scope of This Book

This book draws on published research material, the internet and in-depth interviews and observations of Muslim women and relevant organisations that are involved in promoting women's economic activities in Indonesia. Sakai has collaborated with Fauzia since 2012, using UNSW internal grants to undertake and disseminate this research. The UIN Jakarta has sponsored this research in Indonesia in partnership with UNSW. The Ford Foundation Grant on Muslim women's economic empowerment managed by the Social Trust Fund at UIN Jakarta also supported this project. The final stage of writing up was facilitated by a study leave period for Sakai in 2021.

The scope of the interviewees was formed and influenced by the networks of Muslim businesswomen and the existing research networks Fauzia and Sakai have established for other research projects since 2006. The interviews conducted in Indonesian as approved by UNSW Human Ethics Approval HC17241 explore women's own views on the ideal balance between work, family and community demands. The Indonesian language has been mainly used for data collection and analysis. The narratives were translated by authors and pseudonyms were used for some individuals to protect their privacy. Consequently, although we endeavoured to reflect regional socio-economic diversity of Muslim women in

Indonesia, our informants are mainly Muslim women from Indonesia's main island of Java and the region of Greater Jakarta. There is a long history of female entrepreneurship across Java, including in the region of Greater Jakarta, and our research contacts in these areas were extensive. Since empirical research and in-depth interviews are based on trust and interest from the interviewees and organisations, we hold the view that our analysis of narratives demonstrates significant socio-cultural changes taking place in Indonesia nationally. A series of meetings and discussions were held at UIN Syarif Hidayatullah Jakarta, UIN Sunan Ampel Surabaya and Gadjah Mada University between 2017 and 2019, and it was Sakai who mainly conducted fieldwork using Indonesian, and this division of labour reflected the authorship of each chapter. In writing this book, the authors regularly discussed in person and online to bring together our collaborative findings.

Notes

1. This website is no longer accessible at the time of writing in April 2021.
2. We hold the view that economic action is embedded in the social structure (Granovetter 1985) and the meaning of entrepreneurship varies.
3. The revision of this law was passed in No. 16/2019, preventing early marriage. The amendment raised the age of marriage to 19 years old for both men and women.
4. For example, a similar concern was raised by Sidani (2018: 12) who stated that the use of over-arching categories such as Arab or Islamic countries risk reducing regional diversity into orientalist reductionism.
5. The middle class is defined as economically secured class of society that has certain life style refers to income and expenditure between USD 2.00 to USD 20 per day. The World Bank (2020) views that lower middle class is referred to as aspiring middle class. With the above calculation, Muslim women middle class is between 22.6 and 72 million from total of 135 Indonesian women.
6. For example, since 2015, every Kartini Day celebration, pictures of Kartini wearing a Muslim headscarf and a text stating that she was a *santri* of *kiai* Sholeh Darat, an Islamic scholar, has been widely circulated. This is an attempt to Islamise the portrait of Kartini.
7. See Chapter 3 for women's organisations.
8. After Muhammad's death, Aishah contributed as a *hadith* transmitter for Islam.
9. See Chapter 3 for Muslim women's organisations in Indonesia.
10. This does not mean that Islam and nationalism have always been compatible.

11. Recent anthropological works have shown that it is effective for the female informants to lead the conversation to enable them to highlight important aspects. See Abu-Lughod (2013) and Haeri (2002).
12. See Chapter 3 for further discussions.

References

Abbott, Nabia. 1942. *Aishah, the Beloved of Mohammed: A Biography*. Chicago: University of Chicago Press.

Abdullah, Taufik. 2009. *Indonesia: Towards Democracy*. Singapore: ISEAS Publishing.

Abu-Lughod, Lila. 2013. *Do Muslim Women Need Saving?* Cambridge, MA and London, England: Harvard University Press.

Afkhami, Mahnaz, and Erika Friedl. 1997. *Muslim Women and the Politics of Participation: Implementing the Beijing Platform*. Syracuse, NY: Syracuse University Press.

Afrianty, Dina. 2015. *Women and Sharia Law in Northern Indonesia: Local Women's Ngos and the Reform of Islamic Law in Aceh*. Abingdon, Oxon, New York: Routledge.

Afrianty, Dina. 2020. Rising Public Piety and the Status of Women in Indonesia Two Decades after Reformasi. *TRaNS: Trans-Regional and-National Studies of Southeast Asia* 8 (1): 65–80.

Afsaruddin, Asma. 2011. Early Women Exemplars and the Construction of Gendered Space. In *Booth, Marilyn*, ed. Harem Histories, 21–48. North Carolina: Duke University Press.

Agnihotri, Arpita, and Saurabh Bhattacharya. 2020. Drivers of Mompreneurship: Evidence from India. *Society and Business Review* 15 (4): 373–396. https://doi.org/10.1108/sbr-01-2020-0016.

Al-Baihaqi, Ahmad ibn Hasan. 2003. *Sunan Al-Kubra*. Beirut: Dar Al Kutub Al Ilmiah.

Alexander, Jennifer. 1987. *Trade, Traders and Trading in Rural Java*. Oxford: Oxford University Press.

Ali, Hasanuddin, and Lilik Purwandi. 2017. Indonesia Middle Class Muslim: Religiosity and Consumerism, February 2017. Alvara Research Center.

Ali, Yumna, and Naghmeh Nekouei. 2020. Motherhood and Entrepreneurship: Exploring the Entrepreneurial Identity of 'Mompreneurs' in the Middle East. Masters Thesis, Linneaus University, Sweden.

Amal, Andi Sri Suriati. 2013. *Role Juggling: Perempuan Sebagai Muslimah, Ibu, dan Istri*. Jakarta: Gramedia Pustaka Utama.

Andaya, Barbara Watson. 2007. Studying Women and Gender in Southeast Asia. *International Journal of Asian Studies* 4 (1): 113–136. https://doi.org/10.1017/S147959140700054X.

Andaya, Barbara Watson. 2008. *The Flaming Womb: Repositioning Women in Early Modern Southeast Asia*. Honolulu: University of Hawai'i Press.

Anderson, Jon W. 2018. The Internet and Islam's New Interpreters. In *Religion and the Internet: Mapping the Rise of the Study of Religious Practice Online*, ed. Heidi Campbell, 52–65. London and New York: Routledge.

Anggraeni, Dewi. 2006. *Dreamseekers: Indonesian Women as Domestic Workers in Asia*. Jakarta: Equinox Publishing.

Anwar, Etin. 2018. *A Genealogy of Islamic Feminism: Pattern and Change in Indonesia*. Abingdon and New York: Routledge, Taylor and Francis Group.

Anwar, Zainah. 2001. What Islam, Whose Islam? Sisters in Islam and the Struggle for Women's Rights. In *The Politics of Multiculturalism: Pluralism and Citizenship in Malaysia, Singapore, and Indonesia*, ed. Robert W. Hefner, 227–254. Honolulu: University of Hawaii Press.

Arnez, Monika. 2010. Empowering Women through Islam: Fatayat NU between Tradition and Change. *Journal of Islamic Studies* 21 (1): 59–88.

Azmi, Ilhaamie Abdul Ghani, Sharifah Hayaati Syed Ismail, and Siti Arni Basir. 2012. Women Career Advancement in Public Service: A Study in Indonesia. *Procedia-Social and Behavioral Sciences* 58: 298–306.

Azra, Azyumardi, and Arskal Salim. 2003. *Shari'a and Politics in Modern Indonesia*. Singapore: ISEAS Publishing.

Badran, Margot. 2005. Between Secular and Islamic Feminism/s: Reflections on the Middle East and Beyond. *Journal of Middle East Women's Studies* 1 (1): 6–28.

Badran, Margot. 2008. Between Muslim Women and the Muslimwoman. *Journal of Feminist Studies in Religion* 24 (1): 101–106.

Barton, Greg. 2014. The Gulen Movement, Muhammadiyah and Nahdlatul Ulama: Progressive Islamic Thought, Religious Philanthropy and Civil Society in Turkey and Indonesia. *Islam and Christian-Muslim Relations* 25 (3): 207–301. https://doi.org/10.1080/09596410.2014.916124.

Barton, Greg, and Greg Fealy. 1996. *Nahdlatul Ulama, Traditional Islam and Modernity in Indonesia*. Clayton: Monash Asia Institute, Monash University.

Baulch, Emma, and Alila Pramiyanti. 2018. Hijabers on Instagram: Using Visual Social Media to Construct the Ideal Muslim Woman. *Social Media + Society* 4 (4): 2056305118800308.

Berger, Peter L. 1979. *Facing up to Modernity: Excursions in Society, Politics, and Religion*. Harmondsworth: Penguin.

Beta, Annisa R. 2014. Hijabers: How Young Urban Muslim Women Redefine Themselves in Indonesia. *International Communication Gazette* 76 (4–5): 377–389.

Bijl, Paul, and Grace V.S. Chin. eds. 2020. *Appropriating Kartini: Colonial, National and Transnational Memories of an Indonesian Icon*. Singapore: ISEAS-Yusof Ishak Institute.

Blackburn, Susan. 2004. *Women and the State in Modern Indonesia*. New York: Cambridge University Press.

Booth, Anne. 2021. A Diagnostic Study of the Civil Service in Indonesia. *Bulletin of Indonesian Economic Studies* 57 (2): 257–259. https://doi.org/10.1080/00074918.2021.1956406.

Breen, Rebecca Hudson, and Aegean Leung. 2020. Choosing Mothering and Entrepreneurship: A Relational Career-Life Process. *International Journal of Gender and Entrepreneurship* 12 (3): 253–271.

Brenner, Suzanne April. 1998. *The Domestication of Desire: Women, Wealth, and Modernity in Java*. Princeton, NJ: Princeton University Press.

Brenner, Suzanne April. 2011. Private Moralities in the Public Sphere: Democratization, Islam, and Gender in Indonesia. *American Anthropologist* 113 (3): 478–490.

Buvinic, Marra, and Megan O'Donnel. 2021. Measuring Women's Economic Empowerment: 5 Takeaways from Researchers and Practitioners. https://oxfamapps.org/fp2p/measuring-womens-economic-empowerment-5-takeaways-from-researchers-and-practitioners/. Accessed 13 Oct 2021.

Cameron, Lisa, and Diana Contreras Suarez. 2017. Women's Economic Participation in Indonesia: A Study of Gender Inequality in Employment, Entrepreneurship, and Key Enablers for Change, 91. Available at: https://www.monash.edu/business/cdes/research/publications/publications2/Womens-economic-participation-in-Indonesia-June-2017.pdf.

Cameron, Lisa, Diana Contreras Suarez, and William Rowell. 2019. Female Labour Force Participation in Indonesia: Why Has It Stalled? *Bulletin of Indonesian Economic Studies* 55 (2): 157–192. https://doi.org/10.1080/00074918.2018.1530727.

Casanova, José. 2007. Rethinking Secularization: A Global Comparative Perspective. In *Religion, Globalization, and Culture*, eds. Peter Beyer and Lori Beaman, 101–120. Leiden: Brill.

Casanova, José. 2011. *Public Religions in the Modern World*. Chicago: University of Chicago Press.

Cesari, Jocelyne, and José Casanova. 2017. *Islam, Gender, and Democracy in Comparative Perspective*. Oxford: Oxford University Press.

Cobe, Patricia, and Ellen H. Parlapiano. 2001. *Mompreneurs Online: Using the Internet to Build Work@ Home Success*. Perigee Trade.

Cobe, Patricia, and Ellen H. Parlapiano. 2002. *Mompreneurs: A Mother's Practical Step-by-Step Guide to Work-at-Home Success*. New York: TarcherPerigee.

Cox, Harvey Gallagher. 1984. *Religion in the Secular City: Toward a Postmodern Theology*. New York: Simon and Schuster.

De Hoop, Thomas. 2021. Guidelines to Standardize Women's Economic Empowerment Measurement across a Portfolio of Evaluations. Paper presented at the Evidence Consortium on Women's Groups (ECWG), USA, July 15.

De Hoop, Thomas, Luuk van Kempen, Rik Linssen, and Anouka van Eerdewijk. 2014. Women's Autonomy and Subjective Well-Being: How Gender Norms Shape the Impact of Self-Help Groups in Odisha, India. *Feminist Economics* 20 (3): 103–135.

Deeb, Lara. 2006. *An Enchanted Modern: Gender and Public Piety in Shi'i Lebanon*. Princeton, NJ: Princeton University Press.

Eickelman, Dale F. 1992. Mass Higher Education and the Religious Imagination in Contemporary Arab Societies. *American Ethnologist* 19 (4): 643–655.

Eickelman, Dale F., and Jon W. Anderson. 2003. *New Media in the Muslim World: The Emerging Public Sphere*. Bloomington: Indiana University Press.

Eickelman, Dale F., and James Piscatori. 1996. *Muslim Politics*. Princeton, New Jersey: Princeton University Press.

El-Cheikh, Nadia Maria. 2015. *Women, Islam, and Abbasid Identity*. Cambridge, Massachusetts: Harvard University Press.

Elson, Robert E. 2008. *The Idea of Indonesia: A History*. Cambridge: Cambridge University Press.

Fauzia, Amelia. 2016. *Filantropi Islam, Sejarah dan Kontestasi Masyarakat Sipil dan Negara di Indonesia*. Yogyakarta: Gading.

Fealy, Greg. 2008. Consuming Islam: Commodified Religion and Aspirational Pietism in Contemporary Indonesia. In *Expressing Islam: Religious Life and Politics in Indonesia*, eds. Greg Fealy and Sally White, 15–39. Singapore: ISEAS Publishing.

Fealy, Greg, and Robin Bush. 2014. The Political Decline of Traditional Ulama in Indonesia. *Asian Journal of Social Science* 42 (5): 536–560. https://doi.org/10.1163/15685314-04205004.

Fealy, Greg, and Sally White. 2008. *Expressing Islam: Religious Life and Politics in Indonesia*. Singapore: Institute of Southeast Asian Studies.

Fischer, Johan. 2008. *Proper Islamic Consumption: Shopping among the Malays in Modern Malaysia*. Copenhagen: NIAS Press.

Fischer, Johan. 2011. *The Halal Frontier: Muslim Consumers in a Globalized Market*. New York: Palgrave Macmillan.

Ford, Michele, and Lyn Parker. 2008. *Women and Work in Indonesia*. Oxon and New York: Routledge.

Freeman, Carla. 2007. The "Reputation" of Neoliberalism. *American Ethnologist* 34 (2): 252–267. https://doi.org/10.1525/ae.2007.34.2.252.

Freeman, Carla. 2014. *Entrepreneurial Selves: Neoliberal Respectability and the Making of a Caribbean Middle Class*. Durham: Duke University Press.

Geertz, Clifford. 1961. Studies in Peasant Life: Community and Society. *Biennial Review of Anthropology* 2: 1–41.

Giddens, Anthony. 1984. *The Constitution of Society: Outline of the Theory of Structuration*. Berkeley: University of California Press.
Göle, Nilüfer. 1996. *The Forbidden modern: Civilization and Veiling*. Ann Arbor: University of Michigan Press.
Göle, Nilüfer. 2002. Islam in Public: New Visibilities and New Imaginaries. *Public Culture* 14 (1): 173–190.
Göle, Nilüfer. 2015. The Gendered Nature of the Public Sphere. In *Islam and Secularity: The Future of Europe's Public Sphere*, ed. Nilüfer Göle, 103–134. Durham: Duke University Press.
Golkowska, Krystyna. 2017. Qatari Women Navigating Gendered Space. *Social Sciences MDPI* 6 (4): 123.
González, Alexandra. 2013. *Islamic Feminism in Kuwait: The Politics and Paradoxes*. New York: Palgrave Macmillan.
Goodman, David, and Richard Robison. 1996. The New Rich in Asia: Economic Development, Social Status and Political Consciousness. In *The New Rich in Asia: Mobile Phones, Mcdonald's and Middle Class Revolution*, eds. David Goodman and Richard Robison, 1–16. London: Routledge.
Granovetter, Mark. 1985. Economic Action and Social Structure: The Problem of Embeddedness. *American Journal of Sociology* 91 (3): 481–510.
Haeri, Shahla. 2002. *No Shame for the Sun: Lives of Professional Pakistani Women*. Syracuse, New York: Syracuse University Press.
Hasan, Noorhaidi. 2007. The Salafi Movement in Indonesia: Transnational Dynamics and Local Development. *Comparative Studies of South Asia, Africa and the Middle East* 27 (1): 83–94.
Hasyim, Syafiq. 2006. *Understanding Women in Islam: An Indonesian Perspective*. Jakarta and Singapore: Equinox Publishing.
Hasyim, Syafiq. 2020. Fatwas and Democracy: Majelis Ulama Indonesia (MUI, Indonesian Ulema Council) and Rising Conservatism in Indonesian Islam. *TRaNS: Trans-Regional and-National Studies of Southeast Asia* 8 (1): 21–35.
Hatley, Barbara, and Susan Blackburn. 2013. Representations of Women's Roles in Household and Society in Indonesian Women's Writing of the 1930s. In *Women and Households in Indonesia. Cultural Notions and Social Practices*, eds. Juliette Koning, Marleen Nolten, Janet Rodenburg, and Ratna Saptari, 59–81. London: Routledge. https://doi.org/10.4324/9781315027791.
Haussegger, Virginia. 2005. *Wonder Woman: The Myth of 'Having It All'*. Crows Nest: Allen & Unwin.
Hefner, Claire-Marie. 2016. Models of Achievement: Muslim Girls and Religious Authority in a Modernist Islamic Boarding School in Indonesia. *Asian Studies Review* 40 (4): 564–582.
Hefner, Claire-Marie. 2017. Aspiration, Piety, and Traditionalism among Indonesian Islamic Boarding school Girls. *Anthropological Perspectives on Student Futures*, 69–81. New York: Palgrave Macmillan.

Hefner, Robert W. 1997. *Islam in an Era of Nation-States Politics and Religious Renewal in Muslim Southeast Asia*. University of Hawaii Press.
Hefner, Robert W. 1998. Markets and Justice for Muslim Indonesians. In *Market Cultures: Society and Morality in the New Asian Capitalism*, ed. Robert W. Hefner, 224–250. Colorado: Westview Press.
Hefner, Robert W. 2003. Islamizing Capitalism: On the Founding of Indonesia's First Islamic Bank. In *Shari'a and Politics in Modern Indonesia*, eds. Azyumardi Azra and Arskal Salim, 148–167. Singapore: ISEAS Publishing.
Hefner, Robert W. 2008. Islamic Schools, Social Movements, and Democracy in Indonesia. In *Making Modern Muslims: The Politics of Islamic Education in Southeast Asia*, ed. Robert W. Hefner, 55–105. Honolulu: University of Hawaii Press. https://doi.org/10.1515/9780824863463.
Hefner, Robert W. 2011. Where Have All the Abangan Gone? Religionization and the Decline of Non-Standard Islam in Contemporary Indonesia. In *The Politics of Religion in Indonesia: Syncretism, Orthodoxy, and Religious Contention in Java and Bali*, eds. Michel Picard and Rémy Madinier, 86–106. London: Routledge. https://doi.org/10.4324/9780203817049.
Heryanto, Ariel. 2008. *Popular Culture in Indonesia: Fluid Identities in Post-Authoritarian Politics*. New York: Routledge.
Heyzer, Noeleen. 1986. *Working Women in South-East Asia: Development, Subordination, and Emancipation*. Milton Keynes [Buckinghamshire] Philadelphia: Open University Press.
Hijab, Nadia. 1988. *Womanpower: The Arab Debate on Women at Work*. Cambridge: Cambridge University Press.
Hoesterey, James Bourk. 2008. Marketing Morality: The Rise, Fall and Rebranding of Aa Gym. In *Expressing Islam: Religious Life and Politics in Indonesia*, eds. Greg Fealy and Sally White, 95–112. Singapore: ISEAS Publishing.
Hoesterey, James Bourk. 2015. *Rebranding Islam: Piety, Prosperity, and a Self-Help Guru*. Stanford: Stanford University Press.
Hoesterey, James Bourk, and Marshall Clark. 2012. Film Islami: Gender, Piety and Pop Culture in Post-Authoritarian Indonesia. *Asian Studies Review* 36 (2): 207–226. https://doi.org/10.1080/10357823.2012.685925.
Hooker, Michael Barry. 1983. *Islam in South-East Asia*. Leiden: Brill Archive.
Hooker, Michael Barry. 2008. *Indonesian Syariah: Defining a National School of Islamic Law*. Singapore: Institute of Southeast Asian Studies.
Ibn Hanbal, Abu Abdullah Ahmad ibn Muhammad. 2001. *Musnad Al Imam Ahmad Ibn Hanbal*. Bairut: Muassasah al Risalah.
Ibn Hibban, Muhammad. 1988. *Al Ikhsan Fi Taqribi Shahihi Ibn Hibban*. Bairut: Muassasah al Risalah.

Isbah, M. Falikul. 2020. Pesantren in the Changing Indonesian Context: History and Current Developments. *Qudus International Journal of Islamic Studies (QIJIS)* 8 (1): 65–106.

Jean, Melissa, and Caroline S. Forbes. 2012. An Exploration of the Motivations and Expectation Gaps of Mompreneurs. *Journal of Business Diversity* 12 (2): 112–130.

Jellinek, Lea. 1991. *The Wheel of Fortune: The History of a Poor Community in Jakarta.* Honolulu: University of Hawaii Press.

Jones, Carla. 2018. Consumption and the New Middle Classes. In *Routledge Handbook of Contemporary Indonesia*, ed. Robert W. Hefner, 187–196. Routledge. https://doi.org/10.4324/9781315628837-15.

Jurriëns, Edwin, and Ross Tapsell. 2017. Challenges and Opportunities of the Digital 'Revolution' in Indonesia. In *Digital Indonesia*, eds. Edwin Jurriëns and Ross Tapsell, 1–18. Singapore: ISEAS-Yusof Ishak Institute.

Kabeer, Naila. 2001. Conflicts over Credit: Re-evaluating the Empowerment Potential of Loans to Women in Rural Bangladesh. *World Development* 29 (1): 63–84.

Kabeer, Naila. 2002. *The Power to Choose: Bangladeshi Women and Labor Market Decisions in London and Dhaka.* London: Verso.

Kabeer, Naila. 2005. Gender Equality and Women's Empowerment: A Critical Analysis of the Third Millennium Development Goal. *Gender & Development* 13 (1): 13–24.

Kabeer, Naila. 2019. Women's Empowerment and the Question of Choice. *Journal of International Affairs* 72 (2): 209–214.

Kabeer, Naila, and Ayesha Khan. 2014. Cultural Values or Universal Rights? Women's Narratives of Compliance and Contestation in Urban Afghanistan. *Feminist Economics* 20 (3): 1–24. https://doi.org/10.1080/13545701.2014.926558.

Kar, Sohini. 2018. *Financializing Poverty: Labor and Risk in Indian Microfinance.* Stanford: Stanford University Press.

Karim, Lamia. 2008. Demystifying Micro-Credit: The Grameen Bank, Ngos, and Neoliberalism in Bangladesh. *Cultural Dynamics* 20 (1): 5–29.

Kemp, Simon. 2021. Digital 2021: Indonesia. We Are Social and Hootsuite. https://datareportal.com/reports/digital-2021-indonesia. Accessed 18 Aug 2021.

Kersten, Carool. 2015. *Islam in Indonesia: The Contest for Society, Ideas and Values.* London and New York: Hurst & Co. and Oxford University Press.

Kersten, Carool. 2017. *A History of Islam in Indonesia: Unity in Diversity.* Edinburgh: Edinburgh University Press.

Khalafallah, Haifaa G. 2014. Precedent and Perception: Muslim Records That Contradict Narratives on Women. *Hawwa* 11 (2–3): 108–132. https://doi.org/10.1163/15692086-12341244.

Khan, Shahrukh Rafi, and Shaheen Rafi Khan. 2016. Microcredit in South Asia: Privileging Women's Perceptions and Voices. *Progress in Development Studies* 16 (1): 65–80. https://doi.org/10.1177/1464993415608083.

Kloos, David. 2016. The Salience of Gender: Female Islamic Authority in Aceh, Indonesia. *Asian Studies Review* 40 (4): 527–544.

Kloos, David, and Mirjam Künkler. 2016. Studying Female Islamic Authority: From Top-Down to Bottom-up Modes of Certification. *Asian Studies Review* 40 (4): 479–490.

Kondo, Dorinne K. 1990. *Crafting Selves: Power, Gender, and Discourses of Identity in a Japanese Workplace*. Chicago: University of Chicago Press.

Kuipers, Joel C., and Askuri. 2017. Islamization and Identity in Indonesia: The Case of Arabic Names in Java. *Indonesia* 103: 25–49.

Laguía, Ana, Cristina García-Ael, Dominika Wach, and Juan A. Moriano. 2019. "Think Entrepreneur - Think Male": A Task and Relationship Scale to Measure Gender Stereotypes in Entrepreneurship. *International Entrepreneurship and Management Journal* 15 (3): 749–772. https://doi.org/10.1007/s11365-018-0553-0.

Landour, Julie. 2020. Mompreneurs. Economics, Parenting and Identity. *Travail et Emploi* (Hors-série): 121–142. https://doi.org/10.4000/travailemploi.10041.

Lubis, Nur Ahmad Fadhil. 2004. Financial Activism among Indonesian Muslims. In *Islamic Perspectives on the New Millennium*, eds. Virginia Hooker and Amin Saikal, 91–112. Singapore: ISEAS Publishing.

Lukens-Bull, Ronald. 2005. *A Peaceful Jihad: Negotiating Identity and Modernity in Muslim Java*. New York: Palgrave Macmillan.

Lukens-Bull, Ronald. 2013. *Islamic Higher Education in Indonesia: Continuity and Conflict*. New York: Palgrave Macmillan.

Mahmood, Saba. 2011. *Politics of Piety. The Islamic Revival and the Feminist Subject*. Princeton and Oxford: Princeton University Press.

Mee, Wendy. 2016. The Social Lives of Gender and Religion: Implications for Development Policy. *Sustainable Development* 24 (3): 163–171.

Meuleman, Johan. 2011. Dakwah, Competition for Authority, and Development. *Bijdragen Tot De Taal-, Land-En Volkenkunde/journal of the Humanities and Social Sciences of Southeast Asia* 167 (2–3): 236–269.

Meyer, Birgit, and Annelies Moors. eds. 2005. *Religion, Media, and the Public Sphere*. Bloomington: Indiana University Press.

Ministry of Cooperatives and Small and Medium Enterprises. 2001. Co-Operative and Small/Medium Enterprises development in Indonesia. *Journal of Economic Cooperation and Development* 22 (3): 1–26. https://jecd.sesric.org/pdf.php?file=ART01040101-2.pdf.

Murray, Alison J. 1991. *No Money No Honey: A Study of Street Traders and Prostitutes in Jakarta*. Singapore: Oxford University Press.

Naafs, Suzanne. 2018. Youth Aspirations and Employment in Provincial Indonesia: A View from the Lower Middle Classes. *Children's Geographies* 16 (1): 53–65. https://doi.org/10.1080/14733285.2017.1350634.

Nagata, Judith. 1980. Religious Ideology and Social Change: The Islamic Revival in Malaysia. *Pacific Affairs* 53 (3): 405–439.

Nashrullah, Nashih. 2019. Peran NU dan Muhammadiyah Diapresiasi Eropa. https://khazanah.republika.co.id/berita/dunia-islam/islam-nusantara/pthnnu320/peran-nu-dan-muhammadiyah-diapresiasi-di-eropa. Accessed 18 Aug 2021.

Nisa, Eva F. 2018a. Creative and Lucrative Daʿwa: The Visual Culture of Instagram Amongst Female Muslim Youth in Indonesia. *Asiascape: Digital Asia* 5 (1–2): 68–99.

Nisa, Eva F. 2018b. Social Media and the Birth of an Islamic Social Movement: Odoj (One Day One Juz) in Contemporary Indonesia. *Indonesia and the Malay World* 46 (134): 24–43.

Nurlaelawati, Euis. 2020. Muslim Female Authorities in Indonesia: Conservatism and Legal Notion of Women Preachers on Familial Issues. In *New Santri: Challenges to Traditional Religious Authority in Indonesia*, eds. Norshahril Saat and Ahmad Najib Burhani, 83–104. Singapore: ISEAS Publishing.

Nurmila, Nina. 2009. *Women, Islam and Everyday Life Renegotiating Polygamy in Indonesia*. Milton Park, Abingdon, Oxon, New York: Routledge.

Nurmila, Nina. 2016. Polygamous Marriages in Indonesia and Their Impacts on Women's Access to Income and Property. *Al-Jami'ah: Journal of Islamic Studies* 54 (2): 427–446.

Ong, Aihwa. 1995. State Versus Islam: Malay Families, Women's Bodies, and the Body Politic in Malaysia. In *Bewitching Women, Pious Men: Gender and Body Politics in Southeast Asia*, eds. Aihwa Ong and Michael Gates Peletz, 135–162. Berkeley: University of California Press.

Orgad, Shani. 2019. *Heading Home: Motherhood, Work, and the Failed Promise of Equality*. New York: Columbia University Press.

Osterreich, Shaianne T. 2020. Gender, Decent Work, and Global Production Sharing in Indonesian Manufacturing. *Journal of Economic Issues* 54 (1): 54–76. https://doi.org/10.1080/00213624.2020.1720563.

Parpart, Jane L., Shirin M. Rai, and Kathleen A. Staudt. 2002. Rethinking Em(Power)Ment: Gender and Development an Introduction. In *Rethinking Empowerment. Gender and Development in a Global/Local World*, eds. Jane L. Parpart, Shirin M. Rai, and Kathleen A. Staudt, 3–21. London: Routledge.

Peacock, James L. 1978. *Purifying the Faith: The Muhammadijah Movement in Indonesian Islam*. Menlo Park, CA: Benjamin/Cummings Pub. Co.

Pew Research Centre. 2011. The Future Global Muslim Population Projections for 2010–2030. January 2011. Pew Research Center Forum on Religion &

Public Life. Available at: https://www.pewforum.org/wp-content/uploads/sites/7/2011/01/FutureGlobalMuslimPopulation-WebPDF-Feb10.pdf.

Pinches, Michael, ed. 1999. *Culture and Privilege in Capitalist Asia*. London, New York: Routledge.

Pohl, Florian. 2009. *Islamic Education and the Public Sphere*. Münster: Waxmann Verlag.

Porter, Donald. 2004. *Managing Politics and Islam in Indonesia*. London, New York: Routledge.

Porter, Elisabeth. 2007. *Peacebuilding: Women in International Perspective*. London: Routledge.

Porter, Elisabeth. 2013. Rethinking Women's Empowerment. *Journal of Peacebuilding & Development* 8 (1): 1–14. https://doi.org/10.1080/15423166.2013.785657.

Pramono, Suwito Eko, T.A. Ahmad, and P.A. Wijayati. 2021. Mapping the National Heroes in Indonesia to Strengthen National Identity in History Learning. *IOP Conference Series: Earth and Environmental Science* 747 (1). https://doi.org/10.1088/1755-1315/747/1/012072.

Pringle, Robert. 2010. *Understanding Indonesian Islam: Politics and Diversity*. Honolulu: University of Hawaii Press.

Reeves, Richard V., Katherine Guyot, and Eleanor Krause. 2018. Defining the Middle Class: Cash, Credentials, or Culture? https://www.brookings.edu/research/defining-the-middle-class-cash-credentials-or-culture/. Accessed 08 Aug 2021.

Reid, Anthony. 1988. Female Roles in Pre-Colonial Southeast Asia. *Modern Asian Studies* 22 (3): 629–645. https://doi.org/10.1017/S0026749X00009720.

Richomme-Huet, Katia, and Virginie Vial. 2014. Business Lessons from a "Mompreneurs" Network. *Global Business and Organizational Excellence* 33 (4): 18–27. https://doi.org/10.1002/joe.21550.

Ricklefs, M.C. 2012. *Islamisation and Its Opponents in Java: A Political, Social, Cultural and Religious History, C. 1930 to Present*. Singapore: NUS Press.

Rinaldo, Rachel. 2008a. Envisioning the Nation: Women Activists, Religion and the Public Sphere in Indonesia. *Social Forces* 86 (4): 1781–1804.

Rinaldo, Rachel. 2008b. Muslim Women, Middle Class Habitus, and Modernity in Indonesia. *Contemporary Islam* 2 (1): 23–39.

Rinaldo, Rachel. 2013. *Mobilizing Piety: Islam and Feminism in Indonesia*. Oxford and New York: Oxford University Press.

Ro'fah. 2016. *Posisi dan Jatidiri 'Aisyiyah: Perubahan dan Perkembangan*. Yogyakarta: Suara Muhammadiyah.

Robinson, Kathryn. 2006. Islamic Influences on Indonesian Feminism. *Social Analysis* 50 (1): 171–177. https://doi.org/10.3167/015597706780886012.

Robinson, Kathryn. 2009. *Gender, Islam, and Democracy in Indonesia*. Oxon and New York: Routledge.

Robinson, Kathryn. 2018. Gender Culture and Politics in Post–New Order Indonesia. In *Routledge Handbook of Contemporary Indonesia*, ed. Robert W. Hefner. London and New York: Routledge. https://doi.org/10.4324/9781315628837-25.

Robinson, Kathryn. 2020. Appropriating Kartini: Colonial, National and Transnational Memories of an Indonesian Icon. In *Call Me Kartini? Kartini as a Floating Signifier in Indonesian History*, eds. Bijl Paul and V.S. Chin Grace, 131–156. Singapore: ISEAS Publishing. https://doi.org/10.1355/9789814843928-008.

Roded, Ruth. 2008. Recreating Fatima, Aisha and Marginalized Women in the Early Years of Islam: Assia Djebar's Far from Medina (1991). *Hawwa: Journal of Women of the Middle East and the Islamic World* 6 (3): 225–253.

Rozario, Santi. 2006. The New Burqa in Bangladesh: Empowerment or Violation of Women's Rights? *Women's Studies International Forum* 29 (4): 368–380.

Rudnyckyj, Daromir. 2010. *Spiritual Economies: Islam, Globalisation, and the Afterlife of Development*. Ithaca, NY: Cornell University Press.

Saeed, Abdullah. 1997. *Ijtihad* and Innovation in Neo-Modernist Islamic Thought in Indonesia. *Islam and Christian-Muslim Relations* 8 (3): 279–295. https://doi.org/10.1080/09596419708721127.

Sakai, Minako. 2008. Community Development through Islamic Microfinance: Serving the Financial Needs of the Poor in a Viable Way. In *Expressing Islam: Religious Life and Politics in Indonesia*, eds. Greg Fealy and Sally White, 267–286. Singapore: ISEAS Publishing. https://doi.org/10.1355/9789812308528.

Sakai, Minako. 2012. Preaching to Muslim Youth in Indonesia: The 'Dakwah' Activities of Habiburrahman El Shirazy. *RIMA: Review of Indonesian and Malaysian Affairs* 46 (1): 9–31.

Sakai, Minako. 2014. Establishing Social Justice through Financial Inclusivity: Islamic Propagation by Islamic Savings and Credit Cooperatives in Indonesia. *TRaNS: Trans-Regional and-National Studies of Southeast Asia* 2 (2): 201–222.

Sakai, Minako. 2017. *Kacang Tidak Lupa Kulitnya: Identitas Gumay, Islam, dan Merantau di Sumatra Selatan*. Jakarta: Yayasan Pustaka Obor Indonesia.

Sakai, Minako. 2019. Embracing Islam, Work and Family: Women's Economic Empowerment in Islamising Indonesia. *Intersections: Gender and Sexuality in Asia and the Pacific* 43 (July). http://intersections.anu.edu.au/issue43/sakai2.html#n18.

Sakai, Minako, and Bhirawa Anoraga. 2020. Education, Digital Enterprise and Islam in the Indonesian Modern Embedded Economy. In *Muslim Women in the Economy: Development, Faith and Globalisation*, eds. Shamim Samani and

Dora Marinova, 214–228. Oxon and New York: Routledge. https://doi.org/10.4324/9780429263194.

Sakai, Minako, and Amelia Fauzia. 2014a. Islamic Orientations in Contemporary Indonesia: Islamism on the Rise? *Asian Ethnicity* 15 (1): 41–61. https://doi.org/10.1080/14631369.2013.784513.

Sakai, Minako, and Amelia Fauzia. 2014b. Key Factors for Capacity-Building of Disaster Relief Operations: Indonesian Examples. In *Disaster Relief in Asia Pacific*, eds. Minako Sakai, Edwin Jurriëns, Jian Zhang, and Alec Thornton, 35–51. London and New York: Routldege.

Sakai, Minako, and Amelia Fauzia. 2016. Performing Muslim Womanhood: Muslim Business Women Moderating Islamic Practices in Contemporary Indonesia. *Islam and Christian-Muslim Relations* 27 (3): 229–249. https://doi.org/10.1080/09596410.2015.1114243.

Sakai, Minako, and Samina Yasmeen. 2016. Narratives of Muslim Womanhood and Women's Agency. *Islam and Christian-Muslim Relations* 27 (4): 371–377. https://doi.org/10.1080/09596410.2016.1227046.

Salehin, Mohammad Musfequs. 2016. Piety, Gender Relations and Muslim Women's Empowerment: The Case of Islamic Ngos in Bangladesh. In *Islam and Development: Exploring the Invisible Aid Economy*, eds. Matthew Clarke and David Tittensor, 183–206. London: Routledge. https://doi.org/10.4324/9781315589893.

Salway, Sarah, Sonia Jesmin, and Shahana Rahman. 2005. Women's Employment in Urban Bangladesh: A Challenge to Gender Identity? *Development and Change* 36 (2): 317–349. https://doi.org/10.1111/j.0012-155X.2005.00413.x.

Samani, Shamim, and Dora Marinova, eds. 2020. *Muslim Women in the Economy: Development, Faith and Globalisation*. London and New York: Routledge.

Schröter, Susanne. 2013. Gender and Islam in Southeast Asia: An Overview. In *Gender and Islam in Southeast Asia: Women's Rights Movements, Religious Resurgence and Local Traditions*, ed. Susanne Schröter, 7–52. Leiden: Brill.

Schröter, Susanne. 2017. Islamic Feminism, national and Transnational Dimensions. In *Islam, Gender and Democracy in Comparative Perspective*, eds. Jocelyne Cesari and José Casanova, 113–136. Oxford Scholarship Online. https://doi.org/10.1093/oso/9780198788553.001.0001.

Schuler, Sidney Ruth, Syed M. Hashemi, and Shamsul Huda Badal. 1998. Men's Violence against Women in Rural Bangladesh: Undermined or Exacerbated by Microcredit Programmes? *Development in Practice* 8 (2): 148–157.

Shamsul, Amri Baharuddin. 1999. From Orang Kaya Baru to Melayu Baru. In *Culture and Privilege and Capitalist Asia*, ed. Michael Pinches, 87–111. London: Routledge.

Sidani, Yusuf. 2018. *Muslim Women at Work: Religious Discourses in Arab Society*. New York: Springer.

Sirri, Lana. 2020. *Islamic Feminism: Discourses on Gender and Sexuality in Contemporary Islam*. Milton: Routledge.

Slama, Martin. 2017. Social Media and Islamic Practice: Indonesian Ways of Being Digitally Pious. In *Digital Indonesia: Connectivity and Divergence. Singapore: Iseas Publishing*, eds. Edwin Jurriëns and Ross Tapsell, 146–162. Singapore: ISEAS—Yusof Ishak Institute.

Sloane-White, Patricia. 2007. Why Malays Travel: Middle-Class Tourism and the Creation of Social Difference and Global Belonging. *Crossroads (De Kalb, Ill.)* 18 (2): 5–28.

Sloane-White, Patricia. 2008. The Ethnography of Failure: Middle-Class Malays Producing Capitalism in an 'Asian Miracle' Economy. *Journal of Southeast Asian Studies* 39 (3): 455–482. https://doi.org/10.1017/S0022463408000362.

Sloane-White, Patricia. 2017. *Corporate Islam: Sharia and the Modern Workplace*. Cambridge: Cambridge University Press.

Smith-Hefner, Nancy J. 2005. The New Muslim Romance: Changing Patterns of Courtship and Marriage among Educated Javanese Youth. *Journal of Southeast Asian Studies* 36 (3): 441–459. https://doi.org/10.1017/S002246340500024X.

Smith-Hefner, Nancy J. 2007. Javanese Women and the Veil in Post-Soeharto Indonesia. *Journal of Asian Studies* 66 (2): 389–420. https://doi.org/10.1017/S0021911807000575.

Smith-Hefner, Nancy J. 2018. Courtship and Marriage in Indonesia's New Muslim Middle Class. In *Routledge Handbook of Contemporary Indonesia*, ed. Robert W. Hefner, 335–345. London and New York: Routledge. https://doi.org/10.4324/9781315628837-27.

Smith-Hefner, Nancy J. 2019. *Islamizing Intimacies: Youth, Sexuality, and Gender in Contemporary Indonesia*. Honolulu: University of Hawai'i Press.

Smith, Bianca J., and Mark Woodward. 2013. *Gender and Power in Indonesian Islam: Leaders, Feminists, Sufis and Pesantren Selves*. Abingdon, Oxon, New York: Routledge.

Soares, Benjamin, and Filippo Osella. 2009. Islam, Politics, Anthropology. *Journal of the Royal Anthropological Institute* 15: S1–S23.

Sonneveld, Nadia, and Monika Lindbekk. 2017. *Women Judges in the Muslim World : A Comparative Study of Discourse and Practice*. Leiden and Boston: Brill.

Spierings, Niels. 2015. *Women's Employment in Muslim Countries: Patterns of Diversity*. New York: Springer.

Srimulyani, Eka. 2007. Muslim Women and Education in Indonesia: The Pondok Pesantren Experience. *Asia Pacific Journal of Education* 27 (1): 85–99.

Starrett, Gregory. 1998. *Putting Islam to Work: Education, Politics, and Religious Transformation in Egypt*. Berkeley: University of California Press.

Stivens, Maila. 1991. *Why Gender Matters in Southeast Asian Politics*. Clayton: Centre for Southeast Asian Studies, Monash University.

Stivens, Maila. 2002. Theorising Gender, Power and Modernity in Affluent Asia. In *Gender and Power in Affluent Asia*, eds. Krishna Sen and Maila Stivens, 1–34. London: Routledge.

Stivens, Maila. 2013. 'Family Values' and Islamic Revival: Gender, Rights and State Moral Projects in Malaysia. In *Gender and Islam in Southeast Asia: Women's Rights Movements, Religious Resurgence and Local Traditions*, ed. Susanne Schröter, 143–168. Leiden: Brill.

Stowasser, Barbara. 1992. The Mothers of the Believers in the Hadith. *The Muslim World* LXXXII: 1–36.

Stowasser, Barbara. 1994. *Women in the Qur'an, Traditions, and Interpretation*. New York, Oxford: Oxford University Press.

Sullivan, Norma. 1994. *Masters and Managers: A Study of Gender Relations in Urban Java*. Crows Nest, NSW: Allen & Unwin.

Suryadarma, Daniel, Adri Poesoro, Sri Budiyati, and Meuthia Rosfadhila. 2007. *Impact of Supermarkets on Traditional Markets and Retailers in Indonesia's Urban Centers*. SMERU Research Institute.

Suryakusuma, Julia I. 1996. The State and Sexuality in New Order Indonesia. In *Fantasizing the Feminine in Indonesia*, ed. Laurie J. Sears, 92–119. New York: Duke University Press.

Syamsiyatun, Siti. 2016. *Pergolakan Putri Islam: Perkembangan Wacana Gender dalam Nasyiatul 'Aisyiyah*. Yogyakarta: Suara Muhammadiyah.

Tambunan, Tulus. 2016. Barriers to Women's Entrepreneurship. In *Routledge Handbook of Entrepreneurship in Developing Economies*, ed. Colin C. Williams and Anjula Gurtoo, 260–277. London: Routledge. https://doi.org/10.4324/9781315725826.ch21.

Tambunan, Tulus. 2020. MSMEs in Times of Crisis: Evidence from Indonesia. *Journal of Developing Economies* 5 (2): 89–102.

Tan, Charlene. 2012. *Islamic Education and Indoctrination: The Case in Indonesia*. New York: Routledge.

Tickamyer, Ann R., and Siti Kusujiarti. 2012. *Power, Change, and Gender Relations in Rural Java: A Tale of Two Villages*. Athens: Ohio University Press.

Tlaiss, Hayfaa A. 2015. Entrepreneurial Motivations of Women: Evidence from the United Arab Emirates. *International Small Business Journal* 33 (5): 562–581.

Tlaiss, Hayfaa A., and Maura McAdam. 2021. Unexpected Lives: The Intersection of Islam and Arab Women's Entrepreneurship. *Journal of Business Ethics* 171 (2): 253–272.

Tlaiss, Hayfaa A. 2014. Women's Entrepreneurship, Barriers and Culture: Insights from the United Arab Emirates. *The Journal of Entrepreneurship* 23 (2): 289–320. https://doi.org/10.1177/0971355714535307.

Trading Economics. 2021. Indonesia GDP Annual Growth Rate. https://tradingeconomics.com/indonesia/gdp-growth-annual. Accessed 20 Oct 2021.

Utomo, Ariane J. 2004. Women as Equal Partners and Secondary Earners: Gendered Expectations on Career and Family Formation in Modern Indonesia. In *12th Biennial Conference of the Australian Population Association.* Canberra: Australian Population Association.

van Doorn-Harder, Nelly. 2006. *Women Shaping Islam : Indonesian Women Reading the Qur'an.* Urbana: University of Illinois Press.

van Doorn-Harder, Nelly. 2013. Polygamy and Harmonious Families: Indonesian Debates on Gender and Marriage. In *Gender and Islam in Southeast Asia: Women's Rights Movements, Religious Resurgence and Local Traditions*, ed. Susanne Schröter, 55–71. Leiden: Brill.

van Klinken, Gerry, and Ward Berenschot. 2014. *In Search of Middle Indonesia: Middle Classes in Provincial Towns.* Leiden and Boston: Brill.

van Leeuwen, Lizzy. 2011. *Lost in Mall: An Ethnography of Middle-Class Jakarta in the 1990s.* Leiden: KITLV Press.

van Wichelen, Sonja. 2010. *Religion, Politics and Gender in Indonesia: Disputing the Muslim Body.* London & New York: Routledge.

Verheul, Ingrid, André van Stel, and Roy Thurik. 2006. Explaining Female and Male Entrepreneurship at the Country Level. *Entrepreneurship and Regional Development* 18 (2): 151–183. https://doi.org/10.1080/08985620500532053.

Wagemakers, Joas. 2016. *Salafism in Jordan: Political Islam in a Quietist Community.* Cambridge: Cambridge University Press.

Watson, Conrad William. 2005. Islamic Books and Their Publishers: Notes on the Contemporary Indonesian Scene. *Journal of Islamic Studies* 16 (2): 177–210.

Weidhaas, Allison. 2020. Mompreneur: Is This a Real Job? In *Mothering and Entrepreneurship: Global Perspectives, Identities and Complexities*, eds. Talia Esnard and Melanie Knight, 72–104. Ontario: Demeter.

White, Sarah C. 1992. *Arguing with the Crocodile: Gender and Class in Bangladesh.* London: Zed Books.

Wijaya, Lindawati, and Chrisanty Victoria Layman. 2018. How Do Mompreneurs Achieve Work-Life Balance? [Evidence from Small Business in Tangerang, Indonesia]. *Journal of Business and Entrepreneurship* 6 (2): 1–12. https://doi.org/10.46273/job&e.v6i2.40.

Wilton, Shauna. 2017. Mompreneurs, Leaning in and Opting Out: Work/Family Choices under Neo-Liberalism. *Atlantis: Critical Studies in Gender, Culture & Social Justice* 38 (2): 191–204.

Wolf, Diane L. 1992. *Factory Daughters: Gender, Household Dynamics, and Rural Industrialization in Java*. Berkeley: University of California Press.

Woodcroft-Lee, Carlien Patricia. 1983. Separate but Equal: Indonesian Muslim Perceptions on the Roles of Women. In *Women's Work and Women's Roles: Economics and Everyday Life in Indonesia, Malaysia and Singapore*, ed. Lenore Manderson, 173–192. Canberra: The Australian National University.

World Bank. 2016. Women Entrepreneurs in Indonesia: A Pathway to Increasing Shared Prosperity. World Bank. https://openknowledge.worldbank.org/handle/10986/24751. Accessed 7 April 2021.

World Bank. 2020. Aspiring Indonesia-Expanding the Middle Class. https://www.worldbank.org/en/country/indonesia/publication/aspiring-indonesia-expanding-the-middle-class. Accessed 10 August 2021.

World Bank. 2021. Beyond Unicorns: Harnessing Digital Technologies for Inclusion in Indonesia. World Bank. https://elibrary.worldbank.org/doi/abs/10.1596/36018. Accessed 10 Aug 2021.

World Economic Forum. 2019. The Global Gender Gap report 2020. World Economic Forum. https://www.weforum.org/reports/gender-gap-2020-report-100-years-pay-equality/digest. Accessed 10 Apr 2021.

Wright, Lorna, and Virginia Crockett Tellei. 1993. Women in Management in Indonesia. *International Studies of Management & Organization* 23 (4): 19–45.

Yasmeen, Samina. 2016. Pakistan, Muslim Womanhood and Social Jihad: Narratives of Umm Abd Muneeb. *Islam and Christian-Muslim Relations* 27 (3): 251–265.

Yasmeen, Samina. 2017. *Jihad and Dawah: Evolving Narratives of Lashkar-E-Taiba and Jamat Ud Dawah*. London: C. Hurst & Co., Publishers Ltd.

Yusoff, Syarah Syahira Mohd. 2021. Financial Literacy and the Impact of Movement Control Order (Mco) among the Muslim Mompreneurs: A Qualitative Study. *Turkish Journal of Islamic Economics* 8 (Special Issue): 377–386. https://doi.org/10.26414/A2373.

CHAPTER 2

Women and Entrepreneurship in Muslim Countries

Minako Sakai

Abstract What are the significant factors motivating Muslim women to become mompreneurs in Muslim-dominant countries? Sakai answers this question by analysing the subregional trend in Muslim-dominant regions of the Gulf countries, South Asia and Southeast Asia. This chapter examines commonly identified influences on Muslim women's choices about work participation, education policy, state economic policies and Islam. This chapter shows that the increasing interest that middle-class Muslim women are showing in entrepreneurship is a result of a diverse range of factors arising from specific local contexts, with Indonesia leading this field. This chapter proposes that female entrepreneurship in Muslim-dominant countries grows when it is supported by state policies, existing entrepreneurial tradition and gender norms. Women who engage in entrepreneurial activities are supported by key stakeholders.

Keywords Bangladesh · Education · Empowerment · Entrepreneurship · Indonesia · Malaysia · Saudi Arabia · Social policy · Women

M. Sakai and A. Fauzia, *Women Entrepreneurs and Business Empowerment in Muslim Countries*,
Gender, Development and Social Change,
https://doi.org/10.1007/978-3-031-05954-4_2

Introduction

This chapter will explore female entrepreneurship in the Middle East, South Asia and Southeast Asia to analyse the diversity of women's involvement in entrepreneurship activities in Muslim-dominant patriarchal societies. It will examine the socio-cultural structures of these societies, including kinship and religious authority as important factors influencing the popularity of female entrepreneurship. The cases of Saudi Arabia, Bangladesh, Indonesia and Malaysia are analysed with the aim of identifying specific conditions that have fostered the emergence of Indonesian Muslim mompreneurs. Some of the exemplary profiles of women entrepreneurs have been provided as highlights. This chapter will also provide an analysis of the reasons for Indonesia's emergence as a supportive environment for Muslim mompreneurs.

Tables 2.1 and 2.2 show some recent figures related to the growth of female entrepreneurs in Muslim-dominant countries, highlighting that the number of Indonesian women entrepreneurs is higher there than in other Muslim countries.

Table 2.1 Women entrepreneurs ranking and work participation rate

Country	*Ranking 2020*	*Ranking 2019*	*% Change from 2019 to 2020*	*Women's work participation rate (% of population ages 15+ (2018)*
Bangladesh	58	57	−1	36
Indonesia	17	22	5	52
Malaysia	26	26	0	51
Saudi Arabia	53	55	2	23

Source The Mastercard (2020: 13) and the World Bank (2019)

Table 2.2 Economic participation and opportunity ranking

Country and year	*2006*	*2020*
Bangladesh	111	133
Indonesia	67	68
Malaysia	68	97
Saudi Arabia	115	148

Source World Economic Forum (2019)

As women's role in the economy and gender relations vary across Muslim countries and over the time, this chapter will focus on and analyse post-independence Muslim-dominant countries and emergent subregional trends surrounding the rise of women's interest in running small businesses. In doing so, this chapter will examine commonly identified influences on Muslim women's decisions about work participation. Recent research indicates that in Indonesia, Malaysia, the United Arab Emirates and Saudi Arabia, women entrepreneurs' motivations to start businesses are predominantly fostered by business opportunities (Global Entrepreneurship Monitor 2019: 23).[1] This overview does not intend to provide a comprehensive coverage of the Muslim-dominant countries, but rather highlights the distinctive features to compare against the Indonesian cases where the rise of mompreneurs has become prominent. It will demonstrate that Indonesian Muslim women have benefited from strong underlying socio-economic conditions that support female entrepreneurship in Muslim communities.

Middle East: Saudi Arabia and Women's Entrepreneurship

The Gulf Cooperation Council (GCC) states consist of leading oil-producing countries including Bahrain, Kuwait, Oman, Qatar, Saudi Arabia and the UAE. Economic development based on oil production in these countries has resulted in the rise of non-traded sectors such as construction and services, incidentally limiting women's work participation (Ross 2008). Yet, in view of the future decline of fossil fuels, the GCC countries started to prepare for a drastic socio-economic transformation. The governments of these countries have all identified entrepreneurship and market innovation as part of their economic diversification plans for developing post-oil economies, and to create jobs in the private sector for educated women (Ennis 2019; Langworthy and Warnecke 2021). Three Gulf states—the UAE, Saudi Arabia and Oman—are demonstrating 'a quiet revolution', a term coined by Forster (2017) that refers to social transformation of gender roles being led by university-educated professional women. The UAE is a thriving business hub for entrepreneurs from a wide range of nationalities, and nearly half of the globe's female entrepreneurs are based in there (IFC 2007). For example, Huda Beauty, established by Iraqi–American sisters Huda, Mona and Alya Kattan, and with annual sales of USD 250 million in 2020, is based there

(Forbes Middle East 2021). Huda Kattan, educated at the University of Michigan, is the face of the brand. Furthermore, 73% of businesswomen surveyed in the UAE have an undergraduate or postgraduate degree.

As an illustration of this emergent change in the Gulf states, let us explore the case of Saudi Arabia and how its university-educated women are seizing on entrepreneurship as a way to challenge the existing patriarchal norms. In 2008, the unemployment rate of Saudi women was the highest in the Gulf states at 45.8% (AlMunajjed and Sabbagh 2011). The 2020 World Bank data set titled Women, Business and the Law (2020) shows that Saudi women are the most constrained among the GCC states in terms of their mobility and employment or ability to start a business. Islam originated in Saudi Arabia and the royal family is the backbone of its government. The holy city of Mecca is located in Saudi Arabia and Muslim pilgrims visit the holy city as one of their devotional acts.

The Saudi economy developed rapidly after the discovery of oil in 1935. Oil production changed Saudi Arabia from having an economy based on animal herding and agriculture to one that is reliant on oil production and the wealth that has flowed from this transition. The economic role of females in Saudi Arabia was marginal before oil production became the focus; they could offer only supplementary assistance to men's income. The subsequent rapid economic change has affected the labour force and available jobs in the country as the development of the oil sector and resultant urban development needed labour skills suitable for this new economy. These needs could not be filled by Saudi citizens alone and consequently expatriates and migrant workers have been filling the gap in the labour force. Saudi Arabia has 16% of the world's proven petroleum reserves and is the largest exporter of oil (CIA 2021). In 2016, however, the country introduced a new economic policy to diversify its economy, named Saudi Vision 2030. It is a vision for transforming Saudi Arabia's oil economy to one that can develop non-oil manufacturing industries and tourism (Esmail 2018), and also one that encourages women to actively participate in the economy (Alshahrani et al. 2020).

While boys had access to a general education from 1926, it wasn't until 1959 that girl's education, called *Katatib*, was offered at home or in private institutions with a focus on Islamic studies (Jamjoom and Kelly 2013). Women began attending university as part-time students in 1961/1962 and gradually increased in number across the country. Princess Noura Bint Abdulrahman University is the main tertiary institution offering education to women, and in 2007 the University was allowed to offer degrees in science, IT, business management and pharmacy. Due to this rapid change, enrolment in tertiary education now has gender parity; in 2017, 68% of women and 69% of men attended university and women exceeded men in the tertiary completion rate (women 42% and men 28%) (World Bank 2019). Capitalising on this oil economy and education, the middle class have emerged in Saudi Arabia. They are professionally and technically skilled and have some disposable income with strong preferences for Western luxurious consumerism (Assad 2007).

The delayed access to education and traditionally lower economic position of women arising from the pre-oil economy has affected female participation in work in Saudi Arabia. Women's work participation rate has not changed significantly since 2000 being 16% in 2000, and 23% in 2017. This is in contrast to men's work participation rate being 76% in 2000 and 79% in 2017 (World Bank 2019: 182). The employment-to-population rate of women in 2017 lagged significantly behind men (women 19% and men 77%), and the female unemployment rate was higher than for men at 20%, compared to the male unemployment rate of 3%. Female employment was concentrated in the service sector with 98% of employed women being engaged in this sector in 2017. Women are currently legally allowed to work in an area deemed suitable for women. The appropriateness of an occupation is subject to interpretation, yet Saudi Vision 2030 strongly supports Saudi women to work in the new tourism and private sectors (Alasgah and Rizk 2021).

This pattern of female work participation reflects traditional gender roles that are shared widely across the Arab culture. Women's main role is that of wife and mother, with men being the breadwinners (Al-Ahmadi 2011; Langworthy and Warnecke 2021). This perception, however, is changing among young Gulf-state women aged 15–24 years old. In 2011, only 22% of the surveyed women in this age bracket agreed with this traditional view of gender roles in 2011, while 59% of the men surveyed agreed (AlMunajjed and Sabbagh 2011), showing the gender perception gap taking place in the region.

State-endorsed Islamic discourses that promote Wahhabism also emphasise that women should stay at home unless their participation in the workforce is necessary economically (Sidani 2018: 18). Divorced women and widows who need to find a job to support themselves are drawn to entrepreneurship (Alkhaled and Berglund 2018). In general, in this socio-economic context in Saudi Arabia, women's economic choices have been severely restricted. One major obstacle for women's agency in decision-making is the requirement of male guardianship for all adult women (Syed et al. 2018: 164). This is not written law but organisations, such as employers, can impose the need for consent from a male guardian as a condition of women's movements.

The Saudi government's vision to develop young entrepreneurs as part of their wider economic vision provided entrepreneurship training opportunities to both men and women, and charities provided low-fee loans to widows and divorced women to help them start their own businesses. Recent research (Abou-Moghli and Al-Abdallah 2019; Zamberi Ahmad 2011) showed that Saudi Arabian women entrepreneurs are drawn to entrepreneurship by their family's support. It is understandable that they needed support from their male guardian to start a business because, for example, until 2005, bank loans required permission from a male guardian (Zamberi Ahmad 2011). Dissatisfaction with office jobs, market opportunities and the flexibility of work arrangements also influence women's decision to start their own businesses (Fallatah 2012). They will also start-up businesses offering services such as female-only shopping to cater for the needs of other women. Yet women remain in the minority of business leaders, making up less than 6–15% of business owners (Mastercard 2020: 7).

Along with the changes to women's access to education and employment, women are delaying marriage in Saudi Arabia. For example, in 2016, more than 5.26 million people in Saudi Arabia were reported to be unmarried (Arabiya 2020). They choose to pursue their education and a professional career before starting a family, despite the fact that finding a suitable job in Saudi Arabia remains difficult.[2] Furthermore, the perception of gender roles between men and women as mentioned earlier could also contribute to a difficulty in matching marriage expectations. Domestic chores among middle-class households have been significantly eased with the availability of female domestic maids from South and Southeast Asia since the 1980s and Saudi Arabia is among sought-after destinations for Indonesian and Bangladeshi Muslim female migrant workers (Silvey 2006). In 2015 Saudi Arabia employed 3.16 million domestic migrant workers (ILO 2018).[3]

Islamic clerics in Saudi Arabia traditionally adhere to Wahhabism, which advocates gender segregation and conservative interpretations of gender roles (Vogel 2011). Women in Saudi Arabia and neighbouring countries advocating equality by directly challenging Islamic authority and patriarchal norms in society attract severe criticism. For example, In

New York in 2005, Aminah Wadud, a female Muslim scholar who worked closely with Sisters in Islam in Malaysia and is known as an Islamic feminist, gave a sermon on a Friday prayer with a mixed congregation of men and women, resulting in the need for heightened security surrounding the venue. She viewed that the role of a prayer leader is functional and everyone is equal to God (MomentMag 2013). Responding to this, the Mufti of the Saudi Arabia's Grand Mosque and another leading Islamic scholar, aligning with Islamic leaders from Qatar and Egypt, strongly criticised her actions (Assyaukanie 2009; Ferguson 2005). Generally Muslim scholars hold the view that women are not allowed to lead mixed congregations. At marriage ceremonies and social events, men and women sit separately in Saudi Arabia. Sex segregation has underpinned the development of the national economy, enabling women to work in appropriate women-only work spaces (Le Renard 2008). As a result of this segregation of genders and the rules imposed by conservative interpretations of Islam, women suffer from a lack of professional and business networks and social capital (Abalkhail and Allan 2015).

When the Saudi Arabian government launched its new Saudi Vision 2030 framework, it aimed to diversify and to prepare for a post-fossil fuel economy (Arabia 2021). To achieve the vision, the government, under the Crown Prince Mohammed bin Salman (popularly known as MBS), has been leading social change by giving more rights to women while simultaneously subduing the dissident voices of women's activists and conservative Islamic scholars. In 2018, women were granted permission to drive a car by themselves, and were no longer forced to wear an abaya, or loose black robe with a headscarf, in public; they are now only required to wear decent clothing. They are also now free to move around society without a male guardian from their household. Yet from 2018 to 2019 the Saudi government arrested women's rights activists, including some who challenged male guardianship and who fought the ban on women driving (Human Right Watch 2018). Prior to that, female activists used social media to attract support for women's rights (Mellor and Rinnawi 2016: 131). The state is also curtailing the dissenting voices of Islamic clerics and women's rights activists under MBS's leadership (Dadouch 2021).[4]

To promote entrepreneurship, in 2016 the private Prince Mohammad Bin Salman College of Business and Entrepreneurship was established as a co-educational tertiary institution. Entrepreneurial activities are an enabler of the new vision, and that vision includes female entrepreneurs.

The development of women's entrepreneurship is one of the focus areas of the College's research agenda (MBSC 2020). Women are taking up opportunities to study in the college and overseas, and it is reported that women's entrepreneurship has increased, accounting for 39% of all Saudi entrepreneurship in 2018 (Michaelson 2019). Most of the women engage in entrepreneurship activities because they prefer working for themselves rather than with male strangers, thus balancing their own work, family and family responsibilities (Bin Dahari et al. 2019). Gender interactions of this kind could be deemed unethical in a conservative Islamic community, despite the recent policy changes made to promote gender equality.

Women are also engaging in entrepreneurship to capitalise on female-only business opportunities and run home-based businesses (Alhothali 2020). Despite wearing a black robe, Arab women wear expensive tailor-made dresses at weddings, where men and women are segregated, so enabling women to wear expensive garments (Redvers 2016). High-end fashion and an increase in the prevalence of luxurious malls create opportunities for Arab women to explore entrepreneurial opportunities. Along with the emergence of the middle-class population in Saudi Arabia and the Gulf countries, demands for women's clothing, footwear and cosmetics are increasing, promoting business opportunities for middle-class women's lifestyle choices (Assad 2007).

As the social context of society in Saudi Arabia presents significant challenges to women, female entrepreneurship in the country is still in its infancy. For example, the World Economic Forum (2019) ranks Saudi Arabia as 148 out of 153 countries for gender equality, nearly at the bottom of the table. The potential growth of female entrepreneurship also depends on the implementation of government policies to support women Abou-Moghli and Al-Abdallah (2019), yet gender norms surrounding their economic role remain very influential (Basaffar et al. 2018). University-educated Saudi women appear to be at the forefront of female entrepreneurs in Saudi Arabia (Fallatah 2012). They have typically received their degrees from top Western universities and can effectively use social media (Iqbal 2020). In addition, they usually have support from a key male guardian to develop a business related to the needs of women such as fashion designs, arts and handicrafts, and food (Alhothali 2020), or to engage in their family business.

In other words, capitalising on university education, the ability to effectively use social media to cultivate their business market, and having support from male guardians in patriarchal societies do play a role in women's entrepreneurship. Yet, as women initiate their informal home-based businesses, these businesses do not always transition to be officially registered due to lack of resources (Ahmad 2011; Mehtap et al. 2019; Sadi and Al-Ghazali 2012).

Razan Alazzouni is a young, high-end fashion designer based in Saudi Arabia. Alazzouni, whose fashion designs include high-end wedding dresses and fashion jewellery, has Hollywood celebrities such as Paris Hilton and a Kardashian sister among her patrons (Altuwaijri 2013). Razan's fashion business was established during the final year of her undergraduate education at Tufts University, in the USA, where she majored in fine arts, sculpture and papermaking. In addition to her interest in the fine arts, she also loves feminine fashion with embroideries. In the final year of her degree, 2008, she made a dress from paper that she had produced, and the dress was worn at a party. It received a great deal of attention and the idea to start her own business was born. She called her father from the USA to tell him that she wanted to return to Saudi Arabia to start her fashion design company. Her father told her to finish her study first and offered to assist her with whatever she wanted (Sharma and Ahmed 2020). She received full support from her entire family including her siblings and parents when she started her business from home (Bazaar Staff 2012). She was busy building her business when in 2018 she married Sulaiman Al Mukhaizeem, a businessman from Oman. Her stunning wedding was featured in Vogue Arabia (Ghanem 2018). She was also featured as number one in *Forbes* magazine's list of 10 most successful Saudi women entrepreneurs and assisted with the campaign to promote Saudi Vision 2030 (AMEinfo Staff 2020).

The women featured in the *Forbes* list (Forbes Middle East 2021) all work in feminised sectors; five of the women's businesses are in fashion and two in jewellery design, two are in footwear and one is a fitness instructor. Razan's career sums up a new pathway to a being a successful Muslim womanpreneur in Saudi Arabia: a Western-university education with the full support of male guardians and other family members to develop a business, combined with encouraging government policy to assist with the business's success. While feminists criticise women's entrepreneurship in the Gulf state as a reflection of the subjugation of women by a top-down state-led enterprise development (Ennis 2019; Langworthy and Warnecke 2021), Arab women's own voices, like that of Razan, illustrate that middle-class Arab women are positively responding to emergent entrepreneurial opportunities to realise their aspirations.

Yet, how marriage may affect women entrepreneurs as they attempt to balance their work and family remains to be seen in the Saudi Arabian context. On this point, the socio-economic structure of the Gulf states means that the reliance on domestic helpers in fact supports the pursuits of middle-class women. For example, in Oman, another country sharing Arab culture and one of the GCC states, 60% of the 25 women entrepreneurs surveyed did not struggle to balance work and family because they all had domestic helpers or housemaids (McElwee and Al-Riyami 2003). In this survey 84% of the women had a bachelor's degree. Similar results are indicated by a more recent study (Ghouse et al. 2019) that involved 142 women entrepreneurs in which 32.4% of women cited struggle to balance their time or approval from their family. These studies indicate the majority of women entrepreneurs are coping with balancing family and work, thanks to the common use of domestic helpers or housemaids from South Asia and Southeast Asian countries. The Gulf states have been attracting a large number of migrant workers over decades (Gardner 2011, 2012; Kamrava and Babar 2012). This situation is likely to provide much-needed support to middle-class Muslim women to balance their work and family, support which mothers in Western countries have little access to.

South Asia and Women Entrepreneurship: Bangladesh

In South Asia, Bangladesh is emerging as one of the most economically successful countries, ahead of both Pakistan and India in 2020 (Sharma 2021). Table 2.3 shows the economic development based on GDP and the gender gap in economic participation and opportunity in Muslim-dominant countries in the scope of this chapter. Bangladesh gained independence from Pakistan in 1971, when Pakistan's GDP was far larger. Bangladesh has grown its economy at an average of 5.5% annually over the two decades since 2000, but women's economic contribution is lower than it could be due to the fact that women generally work in informal sectors and agriculture (Raihan and Bidisha 2018: 2). In Bangladesh, girls are traditionally deemed to be a burden as after marriage their ties with their parents are severed by the payment of a dowry and they start to live with their husband's family under the authority of the male family members (Cain et al. 1979). The tradition of early marriages

Table 2.3 GDP per capita comparison in 2020 and gender gap in economic participation in 2020

Countries	*GDP (USD)*	*Economic participation and opportunity ranking (out of 153 countries)*
Afghanistan	508.8	N/A
Bangladesh	1968.80	141
India	1900.70	149
Indonesia	3869.60	68
Malaysia	10,401.80	97
Pakistan	1193.70	150
Saudi Arabia	20,110.30	148

Sources The World Bank (2021)

generally deprives them of opportunities to gain an education except in adulthood.

To challenge these patriarchal norms, the Constitution of Bangladesh ensures gender equality and so women have gained access to education and the ability to progress into higher education. Female students' enrolment in primary education is 93%, while male students' enrolment is 88% (World Bank 2019). The secondary completion rate also shows the same trend for women completing their education at a higher rate (84%) in comparison to male students (59%) (World Bank 2019). The comparison between Bangladesh and Pakistan with similar patriarchal gender norms demonstrates that the Bangladesh government effectively provides girls with educational opportunities (see Table 2.4). Scholars credit the Stipend Program (FSP) introduced in 1982 along with the Education for All (EFA) in Bangladesh as an effective policy as it was designed to educate girls by delaying the common Bangladeshi practice of early child marriage (Hahn et al. 2018; Mahmud 2003). As a result of gender equality policies in education, girls in Bangladesh are outnumbering boys in education and are making strong inroads into STEM areas, which have been traditionally dominated by male students (Table 2.5).

Yet, statistics show that access to education for girls has not automatically translated into a higher work participation rate for women. This is because of the structural constraints within Pakistan.[5] For example, the female work participation rate of 36% lags well behind that of males, which was 81% in 2017 (World Bank 2019). This could be attributed to the fact that women's gender role in a classic patriarchal society like

Table 2.4 Bangladesh's educational statistics

	Girls (%)	*Boys (%)*
2017 Primary education enrolment	93	88
2017 Secondary education enrolment	67	57
Female students in STEM areas	20	N/A
Youth literacy	94	92

Source The World Bank (2019)

Table 2.5 Pakistan's educational statistics

	Girls (%)	*Boys (%)*
2017 Primary education enrolment	71	82
2017 Secondary education enrolment	40	49
Female students in STEM areas	N/A	N/A
Youth literacy	66	80

Source The World Bank (2019)

Bangladesh (Kandiyoti 1988, 1993) determines that a woman's main role is to care for men after her marriage, leaving fewer incentives for women to generate an income. The more educated women thus opt for professional jobs, such as primary school teaching and government administration, that can accommodate the gender norms in their society rather than working in highly competitive and challenging business environments (Sharma and Ahmed 2020). Furthermore, in Pakistan women's work in markets is seen as a threat to the family honour and as unsuitable for reputable families, and work environments in public service administration do not offer enough flexibility for married women with children to balance their work and family (Faisal 2010).

The delay in changing women's role in society is attributed to several factors including the role of religion, which guides family structure. A joint family common in Bangladesh consists of the family with a married son and his wife. This family system has become less common as the Bangladesh economy has industrialised and become part of globalisation. The traditional practice of *purdah*, or seclusion of women from the public, was compromised when women started to work in urban garment factories. This change in the economic role of women is seen as a challenge for patriarchy and the moral order that has been the foundation for family structure (White 2012). Furthermore, because the family structure is such that a father should be succeeded by a son, childless women suffer significantly if they remain barren despite medical treatment, irrespective of whether they have a professional career of not. Recent research shows that in Bangladesh, women's main role includes producing offspring, particularly sons (Nahar and Richters 2011).

Support for Islamic fundamentalism is intertwined with national politics and international migration. Bangladeshi nationalism combines Bengali ethnic secular nationalism and Islamic nationalism. Political tension in Bangladeshi society has increased people's need to strengthen their Islamic identity and the orthodox practices of Islam. Increased migration of Islamic workers into Bangladesh has also contributed to this process. Migrant workers have become an important source of labour in Bangladesh (ILO 2021) with 400,000 migrants arriving annually and sending their remittances back to their home countries. Migrant workers are often exposed to fundamentalism at their workplace and this strengthens their Muslim identity (Mohsina and Ranjan 2019).

Gender norms in Bangladesh are thus being contested and negotiated between the secular state policies and Islamic family norms determined by the rise of religious fundamentalism. This is because all citizens are guaranteed the same rights in the Constitution, except when it comes to issues related to family, marriage and property. These areas are governed by personal laws, largely influenced by religion (Marshall 2017: 145). Although women's efforts to reinterpret gender equality in Islam along the line of Islamic feminism has been ongoing, the efficacy of these efforts remains to be seen. Women's rights activists promote secularism to promote equal rights for women.

The status of women in Bangladesh has also been affected by the high rates of use of microfinance. As highlighted by the 2006 Nobel Prize laureates, Muhammad Yunus and Grameen Bank, microfinance for poor women who have no collateral against which to loan money has been adopted as one of the main poverty eradication strategies in South Asia. Yet, recent research has identified that women are loaner in name only, and the impact of microcredit to reduce poverty and to empower women has not been as successful as has been reported elsewhere (Karim 2008). Women are also using microcredit to pay their dowry instead of using it for business purposes (Mallick 2002). Recent research (Heintz et al. 2018) also shows that for working women in paid employment, microfinance has become a popular way to borrow. This indicates that microfinance is not entirely focused on developing women's entrepreneurship.[6]

In this context, scholars (Goetz and Gupta 1996; Karim 2011; Montgomery et al. 1996; Rahman 1999) show that women receive microfinance loans because their financial position is vulnerable and precarious but the management of their loans is often controlled by men. As personal law is guided by religion, and the elevated status of women with access to education and microcredit is seen to directly challenge patriarchy, this situation has created an impetus for religious authorities to adopt fundamental interpretations of Islam that focus on the subordinate position of women in society (Marshall 2017: 157). Women's primary role in Bangladesh is to look after their parents-in-law, with the decision-making power resting with the father-in-law. Yet, this situation is changing as NGOs have brought women into the capital market. For example, in rural areas Bangladesh Rural Advancement Committee (BRAC), a leading Bangladesh NGO, offers women the opportunity to be involved in luxury fashion items from Aarong, an ethical fashion brand that capitalises on the long tradition of handicraft and textile production by women (Khan 2019).

Research indicates that women living in rural areas perceive microcredit being offered by secular NGOs for women to generate an income ignores Islamic codes of conduct and destroys the traditional family structure. Muslim women are more inclined to join Islamic NGOs as their values align, and so it protects the community and shows they are good Muslims (Salehin 2016).

As a result, female economic participation and opportunity in Bangladesh is ranked 141 out of 153 countries, according to the WEF Gender Gap Report in 2020 (World Economic Forum 2019). Similarly, the Mastercard Index of Women Entrepreneurs 2020 report lists Bangladesh at the bottom of the table as indicated in Table 2.1. In Bangladesh, entrepreneurial activities are closely associated with men (Ahmed and Hyndman-Rizk 2020). In 2010, about 77% of available jobs were in informal work with unpaid family labour being the responsibility of women (Asian Development Bank and Statistics 2012).

Despite the strong patriarchal nature of society in Bangladesh, the emergence of professional urban middle-class families is changing the country's gender roles to some degree. Research shows that by bringing additional income to contribute to the accumulation of family wealth, the daughters-in-law are negotiating the expected gender roles by gaining support from mothers-in-law (Hussein 2017). Although these professional middle-class women are assisted by domestic helpers in everyday life, they are expected to display the respectability of their household by attending and socialising at family functions. Thus, these middle-class women are modern by being educated and working as professionals, yet they need to maintain the traditional values of being a wife, mother and daughter-in-law (Hussein 2018).

Women entrepreneurs in Bangladesh thus reflect two trajectories of development policies affecting women. The first refers to urban Bangladeshi women who are highly educated—including higher or specialised education from overseas institutions—and running their businesses to capitalise on their training and international networks. As long working hours are notorious and draw criticisms from in-laws and families, it is highly plausible that women entrepreneurs turn to entrepreneurship to balance their work and family obligations. They use ICT and social media, which are becoming available in urban areas of Bangladesh. The references to religion are not significant to them. Women with bachelor's and master's degrees who can use social media are emerging as leaders in female society (Sultan and Sharmin 2020). They make use of mobile phones, electricity and capital to lead entrepreneurship activities (Heintz et al. 2018). For example, Maliha M. Quadir is the founding managing director of Shohoz.com. Shohoz.com is an application that allows people to rideshare and book transport and also offers transport booking services, including for public transport, holiday bookings and deliveries of food and other goods. Before Quadir developed this application in Bangladesh, Maliha studied computer science and economics at Smith College, in the USA and obtained a master's degree from Harvard Business School (World Economic Forum, n.d.-b). She also worked for large companies such as Nokia, Morgan Stanley and Standard Chartered Bank. The World Economic Forum credits her contributions as Shohoz.com has achieved breakthrough work in digitising the disorganised and male-dominated transportation industry in Bangladesh (World Economic Forum, n.d.-b).

Bibi Russell a former international supermodel for top fashion magazines such as *Vogue*, *Cosmopolitan* and *Harper's Bazaar* is another example. She graduated from the London College of Fashion in 1976, and worked as a model for two decades before returning to Bangladesh in the 1990s to start her fashion company working with craft producers in Bangladesh (World Economic Forum, n.d.-a). Her company—with the motto 'Fashion for Development'—is aimed at reviving handicrafts including weaving textiles and creating fashion (Startup 2013). She has worked with UNESCO to promote weaving from Bangladesh. Her company's mission is to save and revive the crafts and support the craftspeople, while raising their awareness about the importance of education and health (Pikkat and Šopova 2018). Her company works with village craftspeople across Bangladesh to allow them to earn a living for their family and to ensure that traditional Bangladeshi craftwork skills are retained.

Although not part of the middle class (Fischer 2012), another type of woman entrepreneur is emerging. Women are running small and mainly informal businesses in rural areas where financial necessity compels those who are divorced or widowed to generate their own income. Women running stalls in rural areas was once uncommon due to the traditional gender norms and expectations of society until numerous NGOs, such as BRAC, began to offer resources for women who needed to be financially independent (Mridha 2015). In 2011, government agencies also launched a Women Entrepreneurship Development Program in Bangladesh, supported by the Prime Minister, Sheikh Hasina. Three years after the implementation of this program by the Department of Women Affairs, the Joyeeta Foundation was established to continue the program as an NGO. This foundation provides infrastructural facilities and business training coupled with the provision of loans (*Daily Observer* 2020). Women in financial need, therefore, are starting small businesses as a means to a reliable source of income to support themselves. While entrepreneurialism associated with the informal economy remains fragile, and home-based businesswomen may be burdened with both caring for the family and business responsibilities (Boeri 2018), creating a business, small or large, is an area in which women may see emergent opportunities to gain meaningful employment.[7] In summary, the references to Islam in Bangladeshi contexts to promote women's entrepreneurship appear to be limited.

Southeast Asia and Women's Entrepreneurship

Southeast Asia is the home of two Muslim-dominant countries, Indonesia and Malaysia. Indonesia has the largest Muslim population in the world. Compared with Saudi Arabia, South Asia and Malaysia, in 2017 Indonesia's female work participation rate was the highest at 52% (the male work participation rate was 82% in 2018), followed by the Malaysian rate at 51%, as shown in Table 2.1.

Indonesia

The Indonesian government has used education as an instrument to forge a sense of nationalism among its citizens (Shiraishi 1995). Schools teach the national language of Bahasa Indonesia as the official language and this promotes national unity, as does the promotion of the state philosophy of Pancasila. The state has seen education as instrumental in modernising its economy. Educating the workforce attracts direct foreign investment (Hill 1988; Wie 2002) and so secular national education in Indonesia has gained a good reputation. Yet the government has also modernised Islamic education and institutions (Azra 2015) by offering a combination curriculum of 70% secular education and 30% Islamic education. As a result, Indonesia's lower secondary completion rate for women in 2017 was 93%, and this was stronger than the male completion rate of 88% (World Bank 2019). The percentage of female graduates in STEM disciplines was 37% in 2017, indicating women's commitment to studying in technology-related areas. The graduates aim to become specialists in engineering and technology.[8]

To strengthen the national unity based on nationalism, the Suharto government also co-opted large Muslim organisations to support government social development programs, such as family planning and community health. Steady economic growth coupled with strong socio-political control has led to Islamic organisations supporting the government's agenda. The Suharto government established the Department of Religious Affairs whose role includes supervision of matters related to Islamic courts, education and religious affairs. In 1975, Majelis Ulama Indonesia or the Indonesian Council of Islamic Scholars (MUI) was established by the Suharto government with the remit to regulate public expressions of Islam and to co-opt the Islamic constituency to support the government's development agenda (Sirry 2013). In the early 1990s, the government also supported the creation of the Ikatan Cendekiawan Muslim Indonesia (ICMI) as an umbrella organisation for intellectual Muslims, accommodating Muslims educated at secular universities who work as professionals, such as doctors, journalists and engineers.

Undertaking good deeds to assist in realising the state policies is seen as *dakwah bil hal* or a propagation strategy using real examples

(Meuleman 2011). As a result, Indonesian Muslims, particularly middle-class Muslims, have become used to using Islam as a guiding principle in their lives and seeking advice from multiple sources of Islamic authority as explained in the following chapters of this book. We have observed that a common topic for discussion at women's Islamic study groups in mosques, neighbourhoods and other Indonesian community venues is how women are embracing prominent role models of Muslim women as represented by Khadijah and Aishah to influence their main responsibilities. The content of these discussions is often disseminated in social media platforms to other women for sharing.[9]

An important enabler for Indonesian Muslim women, entrepreneurship is a long-standing custom; they are expected to manage the household finances as part of their traditional gender role (Geertz 1961; Sullivan 1994). Even though men are expected to be the primary breadwinner, as fits with a patriarchal society, women are expected to manage household expenditure and to earn additional income for the family if needed. This norm is particularly prevalent in Java where running small family businesses has been a feminised job for Indonesian women for some time. Women work in traditional markets selling goods they produce and buying the goods of others. As Chapter 3 shows, the government policy to create jobs through small businesses, though not directly intended, benefited many women who were already owners of small businesses. Further, women's wifely and motherly obligations, as disseminated through women's organisations such as Dharma Wanita and PKK (Guidance for the Family Welfare), necessitated them to acquire basic skills in developing and running small businesses.[10] For example, in 2013, female ownership of formal SMEs in Indonesia was estimated to be 43% (IFC 2016). Yet, further analysis of these statistics indicates that in Indonesia, the self-employment rates for women were lower than those for men. Moreover, according to the statistics, women who were university graduates were not actively involved in start-up businesses in Indonesia (Global Entrepreneurship Monitor 2019). Yet, university-educated women tend to resume work using their qualifications at certain points after childbirth (Cameron et al. 2019; Cameron and Contreras Suarez 2019).

Previous research findings indicate that women were pulled into self-employment and entrepreneurship out of financial necessity (Tambunan 2008, 2009, 2015, 2016, 2017). Yet it is important to note that a new trend of women's entrepreneurship is emerging among those who are university-educated and are inspired by the success stories of friends running businesses (Hani et al. 2012). Women tend to operate in the feminised sectors such as food and beverages, garments and textiles and leather and handbag sectors and are motivated by personal aspirations (Rafiki and Nasution 2019). The growing interest in taking up entrepreneurship can be attributed to the university-led youth entrepreneurship at campus.[11] University-educated women's preference for taking up office or more formal jobs after completing their qualifications, seeing the practice of women running small businesses in Indonesia as a less attractive employment option, is gradually changing. This environment does facilitate the emergence of Muslim mompreneurs among Indonesia's middle class.

In middle-class households, the wife's responsibility is increasingly associated with managerial skills to keep the moral order of the house rather than undertaking the physical tasks of domestic chores (Jones 2004). The ideal woman should be able to manage household chores and present a neat and tidy environment—where children can grow healthily and receive a good education—while contributing to the community through her business expertise (Sakai and Fauzia 2016). She would also be an affectionate companion for her husband. Having an extra income to support her family's welfare, to contribute, for example, to education costs, spacious housing and funds towards an obligatory pilgrimage, is closely associated with the wellbeing of women (Larson et al. 2021). As this book shows, becoming a Muslim mompreneur is a way to bring extra funds to contribute to the household and raise a good Muslim family. Consequently, Muslim women are gaining centrality in the household by showing they have the skills to successfully manage their family in line with their gender roles. This makes Muslim mompreneurs valued in the community, which they are proud of. In Indonesia, there is a long tradition of hiring domestic assistance for daily chores, or relying on assistance from extended members at times. Domestic assistance is thus frequently utilised by middle-class women in Indonesia and indeed allows them to use their time to generate an income. In addition, the accelerating spread of a digital economy and social media in Indonesia has created new opportunities for women who can utilise and capitalise on Muslim consumer markets (Sakai and Anoraga 2020). The profiles of the two Muslim women, Pamella Sunardi Syahuri and Nurhayati Subakat, featured in Chapter 5 illustrate modern Muslim wives and mothers who are committed to their families, businesses and communities. They contribute to the community through socially oriented programs to assist the needy and the disadvantaged. This could be attributed to middle-class Muslims who feel uneasy with accumulating excessive wealth (Jones 2018).

Interest in entrepreneurship, then, comes from two directions. Firstly, women who have been exposed to running a family business through their family's tradition and secondly, university-educated women trying to balance their work and family commitments and seeing the increasing market opportunities for small enterprises. Divorced women with children are also in need of supporting themselves by taking up small businesses. Localised empirical research among Muslim women in Medan, North Sumatra (Rafiki and Nasution 2019) confirms that emerging successful businesswomen generally have at least diploma-level education. While we acknowledge the struggles of Muslim women as they challenge the existing gender norms in Indonesia, Indonesia consistently ranks well among the Muslim-dominant countries in terms of supporting women's entrepreneurship, as shown in Table 2.1. As we explain in Chapters 3 and 6, this is, in part, due to government policies focused on fostering the concept of the 'People's Economy', including recent efforts to support entrepreneurship among women and youth in Indonesia's partnership with Muslim NGOs. The transition from informal to formal and registered businesses remains a matter of concern (Babbitt et al. 2015) as home-based businesses remain invisible in statistics (Chen et al. 1999) and are prone to missing out on business opportunities.

Malaysia

Malaysia positions Islam as its state religion and operates as a constitutional monarchy. Malaysian society is strongly influenced by its colonial history in terms of the development of ethnicity and economic opportunities. In 2019, Malays and the indigenous population accounted for 69.3% of the population, while ethnic Chinese accounted for 22.8% and ethnic Indians accounted for 6.9%. Malays, with their cultural identity based on Islam and its customs, often hold positions in government and the public service. Ethnic Chinese, on the other hand, dominate commerce and trade, and ethnic Indians are associated with supplying labour in plantations and mining and growing small businesses (Department of Statistics Malaysia 2021).

Ethnic divisions in Malaysia resulted in the 1969 riots that undermined Malaysian unity. As a result of the riots, the government implemented the New Economic Policy in 1970 and subsequently the New Development Policy in 1990 to actively reduce poverty, particularly among the Malays (Sundaram 1989). As part of these policies the government promoted access to education for Malay Muslim women whose education lagged behind that of the other ethnic groups. Through these policies, Malay women also gained access to higher education (Shah 2018). Consequently, in 1987 women gained higher rates of completion of secondary education (87%) than men (83%) (World Bank 2019). In 2017, the percentage of Malaysian female graduates in STEM disciplines was 39%, 2% higher than the figure in Indonesia (World Bank 2019).

In the 1970s the campus-based Islamic propagation (*dakwah*) movements started in Malaysia. These activities were aimed at strengthening the faith of Muslims to build a strong society based on Islam and were supported by the increasing number of Malay university students (Nagata 1980; Frisk 2009; Shamsul 1997). With this development, the politics of Malaysia has centred on the issue of Islam in society and two main parties, UMNO and PAS, competed to strengthen the position of Islam in Malaysia. As a result, the government has mandated Islamic practices in Malaysia and the influence of Wahhabism has increased over time (Ghoshal 2010; Moser 2012; Mubarok and Hamid 2018). The increased influence of Islam in Malaysia has created opportunities for new businesses such as the production of halal consumer goods (Fischer 2008, 2011), Islamic fashion and Islamic finance and corporate management (Rudnyckyj 2013; Sloane-White 2017). Women have taken an active role in embracing Islam by participating in women's Islamic study groups (Frisk 2009). New female Muslim preachers in Malaysia are gaining popularity among Muslim women but their interpretations of gender norms remain relatively conservative and in line with the country's current Islamic discourses (Kloos 2019, 2021).

In 1992 the Malaysian government launched an economic plan known as Vision 2020 to promote economic modernisation and industrialisation (Hooker 2003). As part of this plan, the government attempted to support the growth of women entrepreneurs by establishing relevant ministries (Ming-Yen and Siong-Choy 2007). Despite Malaysia's educational advancement of women, recent research indicates that women do not feel supported when they pursue entrepreneurship activities because of the Islamic patriarchal gender norms (Choy Chong and Ming Yen Teoh 2014). Along with the enhanced Islamisation, the public spaces—such as workplace and corporate management culture—have embraced the Islamic gender norms that women's primary role is to be a good wife and mother (Sloane-White 2018b). Although Muslim women's organisations such as Sisters in Islam have been actively advocating Muslim women's rights, women still feel confined to their domesticated gender role and submissive to their husband's authority (Choy Chong and Ming Yen Teoh 2014).

Muslim women's entrepreneurship is supported by the government's policy as part of the New Economic Model to grow entrepreneurship in Malaysia. However, research shows that women are obliged to follow their husband's direction and raise their family, and this must take priority over having a professional career (Shah 2018). This is attributed to the imposition of gender norms linked with the use of Islamic moral order at workplace (Sloane-White 2018a, b). A lack of spousal support undermines women's business aspirations and employment (Choy Chong and Ming Yen Teoh 2014). The existing view of ideal manhood in Malay cultures across Indonesia and Malaysia, where men are not expected to assume any household chores, often precludes the husband's support of their wife working outside the home. Malay Muslim women, therefore, are often torn between their household chores and work responsibilities if they grow their businesses or climb the career ladder, and accept that the top jobs are suitable for men (Sloane-White 2018b). Middle-class professional women are apprehensive about the impact of Islamisation in Malaysia and the expected use of Muslim clothing, including headscarfs, which was not entirely customary in Malaysia (Olivier 2016).

Amid the contested impact of Islam on Malaysian women, younger generations appear to be comfortable with seeing Islam, including the use of Muslim headscarfs, as a way of life. Particularly appropriate Islamic consumption is closely associated with the lifestyle of the Malaysian middle class (Fischer 2017). The increase in taking up entrepreneurship among the middle class reflects this social trend. To illustrate, younger world-class university-educated Muslim women are taking up entrepreneurship as a means to achieve their aspirations in life. Vivy Sofinas Yusof, born in 1987, is one such young, Muslim mompreneur from Malaysia. She is an entrepreneur, a wife and the mother of three children. She is clad with stylishly but modest Malaysian fashion (Fig. 2.1). She gained publicity through blogging when she was studying at the London School of Economics. Her father, Dato' Yusof Jusoh, received his education at the University of Malaya, Harvard and Oxford. He worked

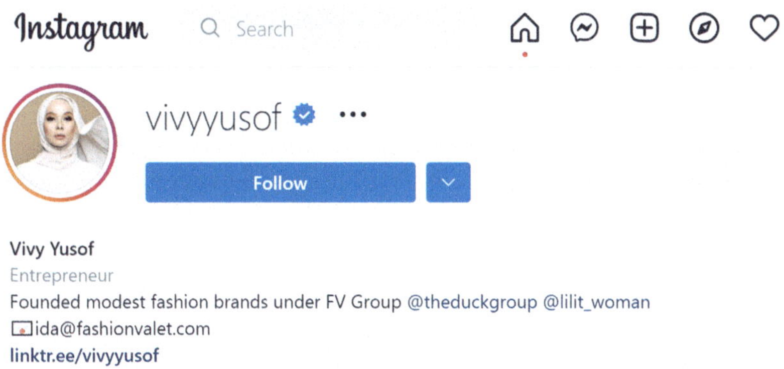

Fig. 2.1 Vivy Yusof Instagram profile (*Source* Instagram profile of Vivy Yusof [@Vivyyusof])

as a business consultant for the government and became an entrepreneur himself (Malaysia Academia Industry Network).

Vivy blogs in English (http://www.proudduck.com/) and her posts feature her student life, aspirational goals, and she has gained many followers. On her website she recounts that she originally blogged anonymously as she was afraid of her father who wanted to control her activities in London. Yet, he had known about her blog and had followed it to monitor her activities. On her graduation day, he endorsed her blogging and activities by stating, 'Continue writing. You have a gift'. She took this as his full support for her public life. Since then, with her husband, Fadzarudin Anuar (Fadza), Vivy has established herself as a Malaysian fashion icon, making Muslim clothing, particularly the veil, trendy. She runs her fashion businesses with her husband and it includes the multimillion dollar online Fashion Valet that sells more than 300 brands across Southeast Asia (Ram 2016). Her businesses include a cosmetics line called dUCk Cosmetics and in 2017 she expanded into selling halal beauty products targeting Muslim women (Global Cosmetic Industry 2017). The products are priced for everyday middle-class Muslim consumers, catering for their fashion needs (Endeavor Malaysia 2019).

As Vivy acknowledges, her public life and businesses started with social media blogging. She has extensive social media platforms with which to engage her followers and promote her businesses. Her YouTube channel named Vivy Yusof (2011) lists a series of popular tutorials, including one titled 'My Everyday Hijab Tutorial (Three Simple Styles)' (Yusof 2019), which at the time of writing has been viewed 1,504,520 times. The idea of producing fashionable headscarves and clothing came when she started to wear the veil in 2013 and became the mother to her first child. A that time, she could not find any item of clothing appealing to professional Malay Muslim women (Mayberry 2015). Continuing her work as a Muslim mompreneur, Vivy started her company dUCk in 2014. Also around 2014, another modest Malaysian fashion brand, Naelofar Hijab was launched by a single Muslim woman entrepreneur, Noor Neelofa binti Mohd Noor. Noor is a university-educated actress and former beauty queen who eventually became an entrepreneur. She is an active user of Instagram with over six million followers (Ying 2019).

To promote modest fashion, Vivy appears in her video instructing viewers on how to wear a veil in a stylish and practical way. Her business capitalises on her young professional Muslim lifestyle that engages her followers in a friendly way. On her YouTube account, she states, 'I'll be sharing exclusive and personal content on all things Family, Fashion, Business & Beauty'.

Vivy's social media—YouTube, Instagram and blogs—highlight the important moments in her life, including those of her family. She highlights the joy of being a Muslim mother of three and married to her husband while running her businesses as a Muslim mompreneur. As a result, she is known as a celebrity woman entrepreneur, receiving the full support of her family.

Discussions: Muslim Mompreneurs in Modern Patriarchal Societies

In discussing the socio-economic contexts surrounding women's entrepreneurship in Muslim-dominant countries, it is important to note how socio-economic conditions and embedded social perceptions of ideal Muslim womanhood have affected the trajectories of female entrepreneurship and small business development in a range of patriarchal societies.

In Muslim communities, the concept of patriarchy is closely associated with the practice of Islam. The practice of patriarchy, male dominance, however, differs significantly across the region. Kandiyoti (1988, 1993) advocated the need to challenge an unqualified notion of patriarchy and put forward two patriarchal models: Sub-Saharan patriarchy and classic patriarchy (Kandiyoti 1988, 2008). In Sub-Saharan patriarchy, insecurities arising from polygamy drive women to reduce their economic dependence upon their husbands. Women need to prepare to support themselves economically.[12] On the other hand, Kandiyoti describes classic patriarchy as being the situation in which women are subordinate, even to their in-laws. This type of patriarchy has been practised in the Middle East, South Asia and East Asia.[13] In a recent study of Muslim women and female workforce participation in Middle East and North African countries, Solati (2017) shows that the dominant view, that a Muslim woman's main purpose is to raise a family, discourages governments from allocating resources to enable women to work outside their homes. Furthermore, certain jobs, particularly involving labour, are allocated only to men, making it difficult for women to obtain paid employment.

The discussions in this chapter show that the structural economic changes needed to grow economy are creating favourable conditions that support women's work, particularly entrepreneurship. The recent GCC economic policy change to promote entrepreneurship including for women is certainly encouraging for the growth of mompreneurs. Its success, however, depends on the capacity of women to expand their businesses while they are raising families and is subject to suitable family-friendly policy implementations to overcome existing impediments. Yet the references to Islam among Muslim women do not appear to be as prominent as in Southeast Asia.

The Southeast Asian case studies have shown a different style of patriarchy to those identified in the models above. In Southeast Asian Muslim societies, the marriage and kinship systems are generally bilateral,[14] while different kinship systems across the Malay–Indonesian archipelago affect gender relations (Robinson 2009: 12–32) including the high-profile matrilineal and matrilocal kinship system used among the Minangkabau people in West Sumatra. Yet, along with urbanisation and job and education opportunities in urban areas, the nuclear family setting has become a norm in urban areas and larger towns (Fanany and Fanany 2019; Murray 1991). This highlights the understanding that the husband is the head of the household, as instructed in the 1974 Marriage Law in Indonesia.[15] Despite this change in fostering patriarchal gender norms, in reality the wife is expected to supplement the family's income as needed. This is because the married couple, who would ordinarily be living in a small nuclear family unit, is expected to be responsible for working together to find an abode and start a nuclear family (Papanek and Schwede 1988:

75). This enables women to strengthen their position in the family and community. Younger women, particularly university-educated women, are more likely to work than older women (Cameron et al. 2019). The fact that women can play a greater economic role in Southeast Asia strengthens the status of women in society (Booth 2016). As we explore in this book, we see that these younger women make up a significant segment of women who are turning to entrepreneurship to balance their work and family based on their interpretations of living as good Muslim women.

Finally, the increasing social connection of Muslim women in Indonesia provides a favourable environment for women's entrepreneurship. As our case studies show, the mobility of Muslim women in Southeast Asian communities is traditionally less constrained than that of women in classic patriarchal societies in South Asia (Andaya 2008). Recently, the use of mobile phones and social media, including YouTube, among tertiary-educated women has provided further opportunities for women to learn from other successful women entrepreneurs, which motivates them to start their own businesses (Rafiki and Nasution 2019). In Indonesia, women are negotiating patriarchy through economic empowerment. They are using specific strategies to address the barriers specific to their local social context.

Conclusion

This chapter has analysed the range of conditions that affect women's decisions to work and, in particular, to take up entrepreneurship across patriarchal countries in the Middle East, South and Southeast Asia. Across these regions, elite university-educated women are turning to entrepreneurship for meaningful employment. Women entrepreneurs are emerging predominantly in feminised sectors relating to fashion and beauty. State policies are supportive of women entrepreneurs as they contribute to solving unemployment issues by creating jobs. The use of social media and international media coverage is strongly associated with the success of women entrepreneurs. Women entrepreneurs highlight the importance of approval and support from their important male guardians—particularly fathers for single women and husbands and families for married women—to their pursuit of their entrepreneurial aspirations, aspirations that help them to strengthen family welfare and contribute to their community. The rise of middle-class Muslim mompreneurs in Indonesia and Malaysia reflects the way Islam and modernity intersect, and how this intersection is negotiated and articulated. The middle-class professional women of Bangladesh are also likely to pursue mompreneurship to balance their work and family expectations.

The following chapters will focus on the cases of Indonesia where the detailed analysis of Islam and modernity will be explored. Chapter 3 will examine the state policies related to small businesses and responses from mainstream Muslim organisations towards women's economic roles.

Notes

1. Bangladesh was not included in this report.
2. See Chapter 4 for the predicament of unmarried professional Muslim women.
3. Although decent work conditions are stated by the Saudi government, ill treatment of domestic workers has been widely reported in media (Johnson 2011).
4. For the recent fragmentation of religious authority and Saudi politics, see Ismail (2018).
5. For an analysis of Pakistani professional middle-class women's life accounts, see Haeri (2002).
6. Yet an empirical study of Pakistani women using microcredit shows that women's self-esteem in the community and household welfare has improved. See Khan and Khan (2016).
7. Research on informal entrepreneurship in India (Gurtoo and Williams 2009; Williams and Gurtoo 2011; Williams and Nadin 2010; Williams 2018) shows that financial necessity is not the only reason to push people to take up informal entrepreneurship, but the active choice driven by opportunities plays a key role in entrepreneurship.
8. See Chapter 6.
9. See Chapter 5.
10. See Chapter 3.
11. See Chapter 6.
12. The recent study on the motivations of women starting businesses in the Sub-Saharan region confirms this view. GEM (2019: 23) states that in the Sub-Saharan region that women entrepreneurs are '64% more likely to report necessity motives than men entrepreneurs'.
13. The typical example of male dominance in classic patriarchy entails young women cutting ties with their own family at the time of their marriage and young brides becoming a member of their husband's family headed by their husband's father. Young women are also controlled by their mothers-in-law, and security in their old age is ensured by their producing a son

to continue the family lineage. In this structure, women are subordinate to their husbands as well as their parents-in-law and their role is strongly associated with the production of sons to continue the family line.

14. The bilateral nature of kinship in Indonesia is symbolically expressed during the wedding ceremony. The ritual of *suap-suapan* illustrates the parents' last feeding of the newly wed couple, followed by the couple themselves feeding each other for the first time. This ritual shows that the parents are no longer financially responsible for the couple, and the couple should look to provide for themselves (Yulianti 2011).
15. In West Sumatra, matrilocal and matrilineal systems are traditionally used, following *adat* (local customs) but as the nuclear family has increasingly become the preferred focus, this system is being contested (Benda-Beckmann and Benda-Beckmann 2013) by patrilineal interpretations of family influenced by Islamic law and the government's discourses of the ideal gender roles (Blackwood 1995, 2000; Schröter 2013). There are reports that along with the Islamisation of the society and nuclear-residential practice, the husband's role in the nuclear family has become increasingly emphasised over the practice of matrilineal local customs.

References

@Vivyyusof '[Instagram Profile] Vivy Yusof' Yusof, Vivy. Instagram. Available at https://www.instagram.com/vivyyusof/.

Abalkhail, Jouharah M., and Barbara Allan. 2015. Women's Career Advancement: Mentoring and Networking in Saudi Arabia and the UK. *Human Resource Development International* 18 (2): 153–168. https://doi.org/10.1080/13678868.2015.1026548.

Abou-Moghli, Azzam A., and Ghaith M. Al-Abdallah. 2019. A Systematic Review of Women Entrepreneurs Opportunities and Challenges in Saudi Arabia. *Journal of Entrepreneurship Education* 22 (6): 1–14.

Ahmad, Syed Zamberi. 2011. Businesswomen in the Kingdom of Saudi Arabia: Characteristic, Growth Patterns and Progression in a Regional Context. *Equality, Diversity and Inclusion: An International Journal* 30 (7): 610–614. https://doi.org/10.1108/02610151111167052.

Ahmed, Rumana, and Nelia Hyndman-Rizk. 2020. The Higher Education Paradox: Towards Improving Women's Empowerment, Agency Development and Labour Force Participation in Bangladesh. *Gender and Education* 32 (4): 447–465. https://doi.org/10.1080/09540253.2018.1471452.

Al-Ahmadi, Hanan. 2011. Challenges Facing Women Leaders in Saudi Arabia. *Human Resource Development International* 14 (2): 149–166. https://doi.org/10.1080/13678868.2011.558311.

Alasgah, Amnah A.A., and Eman S.I. Rizk. 2021. Empowering Saudi Women in the Tourism and Management Sectors According to the Kingdom's 2030 Vision. *Journal of Sustainable Finance & Investment*: 1–27. https://doi.org/10.1080/20430795.2021.1874217.

Alhothali, Ghada Talat. 2020. Challenges Facing Women Entrepreneurs Running Home-Based Business in Saudi Arabia. *Periodicals of Engineering and Natural Sciences (PEN)* 8 (3): 1386–1397.

Alkhaled, Sophie, and Karin Berglund. 2018. "And Now I'm Free": Women's Empowerment and Emancipation through Entrepreneurship in Saudi Arabia and Sweden. *Entrepreneurship and Regional Development* 30 (7–8): 877–900. https://doi.org/10.1080/08985626.2018.1500645.

AlMunajjed, Mona, and Karim Sabbagh. 2011. *Youth in GCC Countries Meeting the Challenge*. Abu Dhabi: Booz & Company. Available at https://www.youthpolicy.org/library/wp-content/uploads/library/2011_Youth_GCC_Countries_Meeting_Challenge_Eng.pdf.

Alshahrani, Abeer, Shamim Samani, and Dora Marinova. 2020. Gender Parity through the Saudi Vision 2030: Female Representation in English as a Foreign Language Textbooks. In *Muslim Women in the Economy: Development, Faith and Globalisation*, eds. Shamim Samani and Dora Marinova, 32–47. Oxon and New York: Routledge.

Altuwaijri, Nada. 2013. Saudi Fashionista Who Dressed Paris Hilton Looks to Bridge East and West. Al Arabiya News. https://english.alarabiya.net/life-style/fashion-and-beauty/2013/10/21/Saudi-fashion-designer-who-dressed-Paris-Hilton-looks-to-bridge-East-and-West. Accessed 18 Aug 2021.

AMEinfo Staff. 2020. Forbes Middle East Reveals the Top 10 Women Behind Middle Eastern Brands List—Middle East & Gulf News | Ame Info. AMEInfonews. https://www.ameinfo.com/business/female-entrepreneurs-excel-behind-the-middle-easts-most-loved-brands/. Accessed 17 Oct 2021.

Andaya, Barbara Watson. 2008. *The Flaming Womb: Repositioning Women in Early Modern Southeast Asia*. Honolulu: University of Hawai'i Press.

Arabia, Kingdom of Saudi. 2021. Vision 2030. https://www.vision2030.gov.sa/. Accessed 18 Aug 2021.

Arabiya, Al. 2020. Over 5.6 Million Saudis Remain Unmarried Past Marriage Age, Survey Shows. https://english.alarabiya.net/features/2017/01/13/Over-5-6-million-Saudis-remain-unmarried-past-marriage-age-survey-shows. Accessed 18 Aug 2021.

Asian Development Bank, ADB, & Statistics, Bureau of Bangladesh. 2012. *The Informal Sector and Informal Employment in Bangladesh*. Phillippines: Asian Development Bank (ADB).

Assad, Soraya W. 2007. The Rise of Consumerism in Saudi Arabian Society. *International Journal of Commerce and Management* 17 (1/2): 73–104. https://doi.org/10.1108/10569210710774767.

Assyaukanie, Luthfi. 2009. *Amina Wadud's Breakthrough*. Qantara.de. https://en.qantara.de/content/luthfi-assyaukanie-amina-waduds-breakthrough. Accessed 18 Aug 2021.

Azra, Azyumardi. 2015. Genealogy of Indonesian Islamic Education: Roles in the Modernization of Muslim Society. *Heritage of Nusantara: International Journal of Religious Literature and Heritage* 4 (1): 85–114.

Babbitt, Laura G., Drusilla Brown, and Nimah Mazaheri. 2015. Gender, Entrepreneurship, and the Formal-Informal Dilemma: Evidence from Indonesia. *World Development* 72: 163–174.

Basaffar, Amal A., Linda S. Niehm, and Robert Bosselman. 2018. Saudi Arabian Women in Entrepreneurship: Challenges, Opportunities and Potential. *Journal of Developmental Entrepreneurship* 23 (2): 1850013 (20 pages).

Bazaar Staff. 2012. *Razan Alazzouni: Feminine Charm*. Bazaar.magazine.com. https://bazaar.town/razan-alazzouni/. Accessed 10 Aug 2021.

von Benda-Beckmann, Franz, and Keebet von Benda-Beckmann. 2013. *Political and Legal Transformations of an Indonesian Polity: The Nagari from Colonisation to Decentralisation*. Cambridge: Cambridge University Press.

Bin Dahari Zainurin, Abdul Rahim Abu Bakar, and Sahar Al-Gosaibi. 2019. Key Success Factors of Home-Based Business among Female Entrepreneur in Saudi Arabia. *Asia Pacific Journal of Business Review* 3 (2): 43–66.

Blackwood, Evelyn. 1995. Senior Women, Model Mothers, and Dutiful Wives: Managing Gender Contradictions in a Minangkabau Village. In *Bewitching Women, Pious Men: Gender and Body Politics in Southeast Asia*, eds. Aihwa Ong and Michael G. Peletz, 124–158. Berkeley: University of California Press.

Blackwood, Evelyn. 2000. *Webs of Power: Women, Kin, and Community in a Sumatran Village*. New York and Oxford: Rowman & Littlefield Publishers.

Boeri, Natascia. 2018. Challenging the Gendered Entrepreneurial Subject: Gender, Development, and the Informal Economy in India. *Gender & Society* 32 (2): 157–179. https://doi.org/10.1177/0891243217750119.

Booth, Anne. 2016. Women, Work and the Family: Is Southeast Asia Different? *Economic History of Developing Regions* 31 (1): 167–197. https://doi.org/10.1080/20780389.2015.1132624.

Cain, Mead, Syeda Rokeya Khanam, and Shamsun Nahar. 1979. Class, Patriarchy, and Women's Work in Bangladesh. *Population and Development Review* 5: 405–438.

Cameron, Lisa, and Diana Contreras Suarez. 2019. Why Do Millions of Indonesian Women Still Quit Work After Marriage and Kids? Indonesia at Melbourne. https://indonesiaatmelbourne.unimelb.edu.au/why-do-millions-of-indonesian-women-still-quit-work-after-marriage-and-kids/. Accessed 10 Aug 2021.

Cameron, Lisa, Diana Contreras Suarez, and William Rowell. 2019. Female Labour Force Participation in Indonesia: Why Has It Stalled? *Bulletin of*

Indonesian Economic Studies 55 (2): 157–192. https://doi.org/10.1080/00074918.2018.1530727.

Chen, Martha, Jennefer Sebstad, and Lesley O'Connell. 1999. Counting the Invisible Workforce: The Case of Homebased Workers. *World Development* 27 (3): 603–610. https://doi.org/10.1016/S0305-750X(98)00154-5.

Choy Chong, Siong, and Wendy Ming Yen Teoh. 2014. Towards Strengthening the Development of Women Entrepreneurship in Malaysia. *Gender in Management: An International Journal* 29 (7): 432–453. https://doi.org/10.1108/gm-10-2013-0122.

CIA. 2021. The World Factbook: Saudi Arabia https://www.cia.gov/the-world-factbook/countries/saudi-arabia/#economy. Accessed 18 Aug 2021.

Dadouch, Sarah. 2021. Saudi Crown Prince Mohammed Seeks to Reduce Influential Clerics' Power. *The Washington Post*. https://www.washingtonpost.com/world/middle_east/saudi-clerics-crown-prince-mohammed/2021/08/02/9ae796a0-e3ed-11eb-88c5-4fd6382c47cb_story.html. Accessed 18 Aug 2021.

Daily Observer. 2020. Joyeeta a Pioneer for Propping up Women entrepreneurs. *Daily Observer*. https://www.observerbd.com/news.php?id=289013. Accessed 10 Aug 2021.

Department of Statistics Malaysia. 2021. *Demographic Statistics Malaysia Second Quarter 2021*. Department of Statistics Malaysia, Prime Minister's Department. https://www.dosm.gov.my/v1/index.php?r=column/cthemeByCat&cat=430&bul_id=eGtwdjd4amZJb1JmcFFkYXBKNHg3dz09&menu_id=L0pheU43NWJwRWVSZklWdzQ4TlhUUT09. Accessed 14 Aug 2021.

Endeavor Malaysia. 2019. Endeavor Entrepreneurs Vivy Yusof, Fashionvalet. https://www.endeavormalaysia.org/people/Vivy-Yusof. Accessed 10 Aug 2021.

Ennis, Crystal A. 2019. The Gendered Complexities of Promoting Female Entrepreneurship in the Gulf. *New Political Economy* 24 (3): 365–384. https://doi.org/10.1080/13563467.2018.1457019.

Esmail, H. 2018. Economic Growth of Saudi Arabia Between Present and Future According to 2030 Vision. *Asian Social Science* 14 (12): 192.

Faisal, Farida. 2010. Measuring Perceptions of Work Environment Among Educated Female Public Servants in Pakistan. *Pakistan Economic and Social Review* 48: 135–165.

Fallatah, Haifa. 2012. *Women Entrepreneurs in Saudi Arabia: Investigating Strategies Used by Successful Saudi Women Entrepreneurs*. Master Thesis, Business Management, Lincoln University. http://researcharchive.lincoln.ac.nz/handle/10182/4795.

Fanany, Rebecca, and Ismet Fanany. 2019. *The Elderly Must Endure: Ageing in the Minangkabau Community in Modern Indonesia*. Singapore: ISEAS-Yusof Ishak Institute.

Ferguson, Barbara. 2005. Woman Imam Raises Mixed Emotions. *Arab News*. https://www.arabnews.com/node/264005. Accessed 19 Aug 2021.

Fischer, Johan. 2008. *Proper Islamic Consumption: Shopping among the Malays in Modern Malaysia*. Copenhagen: NIAS Press.

Fischer, Johan. 2011. *The Halal Frontier: Muslim Consumers in a Globalized Market*. New York: Palgrave Macmillan.

Fischer, Johan. 2012. Branding Halal: A Photographic Essay on Global Muslim Markets. *Anthropology Today* 28 (4): 18–21. https://doi.org/10.1111/j.1467-8322.2012.00886.x.

Fischer, Johan. 2017. Middle-Class Projects in Modern Malaysia. *Asian Anthropology* 16 (1): 54–69. https://doi.org/10.1080/1683478X.2016.1270030.

Forbes Middle East. 2021. 40 Women Behind Middle Eastern Brands 2021. *Forbes*. https://www.forbesmiddleeast.com/lists/40-women-behind-middle-eastern-brands-2021/huda-mona-kattan/. Accessed 10 Aug 2021.

Forster, Nick. 2017. *A Quiet Revolution? The Rise of Women Managers, Business Owners and Leaders in the Arabian Gulf States*. Cambridge, UK: Cambridge University Press.

Frisk, Sylva. 2009. *Submitting to God: Women and Islam in Urban Malaysia*. Copenhagen: NIAS Press.

Future Startup. 2013. *Face to Face with Bibi Russell, Founder, Bibi Productions*. Future Startup. http://futurestartup.com/2013/07/27/face-to-face-with-bibi-russell-founder-bibi-productions/. Accessed 18 Aug 2021.

Gardner, Andrew. 2011. Gulf Migration and the Family. *Journal of Arabian Studies* 1 (1): 3–25. https://doi.org/10.1080/21534764.2011.576043.

Gardner, Andrew. 2012. Why Do They Keep Coming? Labor Migrants in the Gulf States. In *Migrant Labour in the Persian Gulf*, eds. Mehran Kamrava and Zahra Babar, 41–58. London: Hurst.

Geertz, Clifford. 1961. Studies in Peasant Life: Community and Society. *Biennial Review of Anthropology* 2: 1–41.

Ghanem, Khaoula. 2018. "My Dress Was a True Reflection of Myself:" Inside Razan Alazzouni's Breathtaking Beirut Wedding. *Vogue*. https://en.vogue.me/fashion/inside-razan-alazzounis-breathtaking-beirut-wedding/. Accessed 18 Aug 2021.

Ghoshal, Baladas. 2010. Arabization: The Changing Face of Islam in Asia. *India Quarterly* 66 (1): 69–89.

Ghouse, Suhail M., Gerard McElwee, and Omar Durrah. 2019. Entrepreneurial Success of Cottage-Based Women Entrepreneurs in Oman. *International Journal of Entrepreneurial Behavior & Research* 25: 480–498.

Global Cosmetic Industry. 2017. dUCk Expands to Halal Cosmetics. *Global Cosmetics Industry Magazine*. https://www.gcimagazine.com/marketstrends/segments/cosmetics/dUCk-Expands-to-Halal-Cosmetics-448725863.html. Accessed 18 Aug 2021.

Global Entrepreneurship Monitor. 2019. *Gem 2018/2019 Women's Entrepreneurship Report*. London, UK: Babson College, Smith College, and the Global Entrepreneurship Research Association (GERA). Available athttps://www.gemconsortium.org/report/gem-20182019-womens-entrepreneurship-report.

Goetz, Anne Marie, and Rina Sen Gupta. 1996. Who Takes the Credit? Gender, Power, and Control over Loan Use in Rural Credit Programs in Bangladesh. *World Development* 24 (1): 45–63. https://doi.org/10.1016/0305-750X(95)00124-U.

Gurtoo, Anjula, and Colin C. Williams. 2009. Entrepreneurship and the Informal Sector: Some Lessons from India. *Entrepreneurship and Innovation* 10 (1): 1–8.

Haeri, Shahla. 2002. *No Shame for the Sun: Lives of Professional Pakistani Women*. Syracuse, NY: Syracuse University Press.

Hahn, Youjin, Asadul Islam, Kanti Nuzhat, Russell Smyth, and Hee-Seung. Yang. 2018. Education, Marriage, and Fertility: Long-Term Evidence from a Female Stipend Program in Bangladesh. *Economic Development and Cultural Change* 66 (2): 383–415.

Hani, Ummu, Ilma Nurul Rachmania, Santi Setyaningsih, and Rucita Cahyawati Putri. 2012. Patterns of Indonesian Women Entrepreneurship. *Procedia Economics and Finance* 4: 274–285.

Heintz, James, Naila Kabeer, and Simeen Mahmud. 2018. Cultural Norms, Economic Incentives and Women's Labour Market Behaviour: Empirical Insights from Bangladesh. *Oxford Development Studies* 46 (2): 266–289.

Hill, Hal. 1988. *Foreign Investment and Industrialization in Indonesia*. Oxford: Oxford University Press.

Hooker, Virginia. 2003. Malaysia: Still "Islam and Politics" but Now Enmeshed in a Global Web. In *Malaysia: Islam, Society and Politics*, eds. Virginia Hooker and Norani Othman, 16–34. Singapore: ISEAS Publishing.

Human Right Watch, HRW. 2018. *Saudi Arabia: Detained Women Reported Tortured*. Human Right Watch (HRW). https://www.hrw.org/news/2018/11/20/saudi-arabia-detained-women-reported-tortured. Accessed 18 Aug 2021.

Hussein, Nazia. 2017. Negotiating Middle-Class Respectable Femininity: Bangladeshi Women and Their Families. *South Asia Multidisciplinary Academic Journal* 16: 1–17. https://doi.org/10.4000/samaj.4397.

Hussein, Nazia. 2018. Bangladeshi New Women's 'Smart' Dressing: Negotiating Class, Culture, and Religion. In *Rethinking New Womanhood: Practices of Gender, Class, Culture and Religion in South Asia*, ed. Nazia Hussein, 97–121. Cham, Switzerland: Palgrave Macmillan. https://doi.org/10.1007/978-3-319-67900-6_5.

IFC, International Finance Corporation. 2007. *Women Entrepreneurs in the Middle East and North Africa: Characteristics, Contributions and Challenges*. USA & Tunisia: International Finance Corporation (IFC), Center of Arab Women for Training and Research (CAWTAR). Available at https://www.ifc.org/wps/wcm/connect/topics_ext_content/ifc_external_corporate_site/sustainability-at-ifc/publications/publications_report_womenentrepreneurs-mena__wci__1319577511913.

IFC, International Finance Corporation. 2016. *Women-Owned SMEs in Indonesia: A Golden Opportunity for Local Financial Institutions*. International Finance Corporation (IFC), USAID. Available at https://openknowledge.worldbank.org/handle/10986/25403.

ILO. 2018. Domestic Workers and Employers in the Arab States. Available at https://www.ilo.org/beirut/publications/WCMS_619661/lang--en/index.htm

ILO. 2021. *Labour Migration in Bangladesh*. International Labour Organization (ILO). Available at https://www.ilo.org/dhaka/Areasofwork/labour-migration/lang--en/index.htm.

Iqbal, Tahir. 2020. Understanding the Perception of Women Entrepreneurs and Their Adoption of Social Media: Strategies and Challenges in the Kingdom of Saudi Arabia. *Journal of Entrepreneurship Education* 23 (5): 1–21.

Ismail, Raihan. 2018. The Power of Saudi Arabia's Clerics and the Struggle for Religious Authority ABC. https://www.abc.net.au/religion/power-of-saudi-clerics/10451284. Accessed 19 Aug 2021.

Jamjoom, Fatima B., and Philippa Kelly. 2013. Higher Education for Women in the Kingdom of Saudi Arabia. In *Higher Education in Saudi Arabia*, eds. Smith L., and A. Abouammoh, 117–125. Springer. https://doi.org/10.1007/978-94-007-6321-0_11.

Johnson, Mark. 2011. Freelancing in the Kingdom: Filipino Migrant Domestic Workers Crafting Agency in Saudi Arabia. *Asian and Pacific Migration Journal* 20 (3–4): 459–478.

Jones, Carla. 2004. Whose Stress? Emotion Work in Middle-Class Javanese Homes. *Ethnos* 69 (4): 509–528.

Jones, Carla. 2018. Consumption and the New Middle Classes. In *Routledge Handbook of Contemporary Indonesia*, ed. Robert W. Hefner, 187–196. Routledge. https://doi.org/10.4324/9781315628837-15.

Kamrava, Mehran, and Zahra Babar. 2012. *Migrant Labor in the Persian Gulf*. London: Hurst.

Kandiyoti, Deniz. 1988. Bargaining with Patriarchy. *Gender & Society* 2 (3): 274–290.

Kandiyoti, Deniz. 1993. Islam and Patriarchy: A Comparative Perspective. In *Women in Middle Eastern History: Shifting Boundaries in Sex and Gender*, eds. Nikki R. Keddie and Beth Baron, 23–42. New Haven: Yale University Press.

Kandiyoti, Deniz. 2008. Islam and Patriarchy: A Comparative Perspective. In *Women in Middle Eastern History*, eds. Nikki R. Keddie and Beth Baron, 23–42. Yale University Press.

Karim, Lamia. 2008. Demystifying Micro-Credit: The Grameen Bank, NGOs, and Neoliberalism in Bangladesh. *Cultural Dynamics* 20 (1): 5–29.

Karim, Lamia. 2011. *Microfinance and Its Discontents: Women in Debt in Bangladesh*. Minneapolis: University of Minnesota Press.

Khan, Rimi. 2019. 'Be Creative' in Bangladesh? Mobility, Empowerment and Precarity in Ethical Fashion Enterprise. *Cultural Studies* 33 (6): 1029–1049.

Khan, Shahrukh Rafi, and Shaheen Rafi Khan. 2016. Microcredit in South Asia: Privileging Women's Perceptions and Voices. *Progress in Development Studies* 16 (1): 65–80. https://doi.org/10.1177/1464993415608083.

Kloos, David. 2019. Experts Beyond Discourse: Women, Islamic Authority, and the Performance of Professionalism in Malaysia. *American Ethnologist* 46 (2): 162–175.

Kloos, David. 2021. Risky Appearances, Skillful Performances: Female Islamic Preachers and Professional Style in Malaysia. *American Anthropologist*. https://doi.org/10.1111/aman.13556.

Langworthy, Melissa, and Tonia Warnecke. 2021. "Top-Down" Enterprise Development and Covid-19 Impacts on Gulf Women. *Journal of Economic Issues* 55 (2): 325–333. https://doi.org/10.1080/00213624.2021.1908085.

Larson, Silva, Natalie Stoeckl, Mardiana E. Fachry, Dalvi Mustafa, Lapong Muhammad, Purnomo Imran, Agus Heri, et al. 2021. Women's Well-Being and Household Benefits from Seaweed Farming in Indonesia. *Aquaculture* 530: 735711. https://doi.org/10.1016/j.aquaculture.2020.735711.

Le Renard, Amélie. 2008. "Only for Women:" Women, the State, and Reform in Saudi Arabia. *The Middle East Journal* 62 (4): 610–629.

Mahmud, Simeen. 2003. *Female Secondary School Stipend Programme in Bangladesh: A Critical Assessment*. EFA Global Monitoring Report 2003/2004, The Leap to Equality. Available at https://unesdoc.unesco.org/ark:/48223/pf0000146803.

Malaysia Academia Industry Network Ceo's Biodata: Dato' Yusof Jusoh. Malaysia Academia Industry Network. http://ceo.myain.my/ceo/18. Accessed 10 Apr 2021.

Mallick, Ross. 2002. Implementing and Evaluating Microcredit in Bangladesh. *Development in Practice* 12 (2): 153–163.

Marshall, Katherine. 2017. Gender Roles and Political, Social, and Economic Change in Bangladesh and Senegal. In *Islam, Gender, and Democracy in*

Comparative Perspective, eds. Jocelyne Cesari and José Casanova, 139–159. Oxford: Oxford University Press.

Mastercard. 2020. The Mastercard Index of Women Entrepreneurs. Available at https://www.mastercard.com/news/media/1ulpy5at/ma_miwe-report-2020.pdf.

Mayberry, Kate. 2015. *How Muslim Headscarves Became a Fashion Empire*. @BBC_Worklife. https://www.bbc.com/worklife/article/20151214-how-muslim-headscarves-became-a-huge-fashion-empire. Accessed 18 Aug 2021.

MBSC. 2020. *2020 MBSC Impact Report Creating Sustainable Social & Economic Value*. MBSC. https://www.mbsc.edu.sa/impact/#General_statistics.

McElwee, Gerard, and Rahma Al-Riyami. 2003. Women Entrepreneurs in Oman: Some Barriers to Success. *Career Development International* 8 (7): 339–346. https://doi.org/10.1108/13620430310505296.

Mehtap, Salime, Leyla Ozmenekse, and Andrea Caputo 2019. "I'm a Stay at Home Businesswoman": An Insight into Informal Entrepreneurship in Jordan. *Journal of Entrepreneurship in Emerging Economies* 11 (1). https://doi.org/10.1108/JEEE-10-2017-0080.

Mellor, Noha, and Khalil Rinnawi. 2016. *Political Islam and Global Media: The Boundaries of Religious Identity*. New York: Routledge.

Meuleman, Johan. 2011. Dakwah, Competition for Authority, and Development. *Bijdragen Tot De Taal-, Land-En Volkenkunde/journal of the Humanities and Social Sciences of Southeast Asia* 167 (2–3): 236–269.

Michaelson, Ruth. 2019. An 'Oasis' for Women? Inside Saudi Arabia's Vast New Female-Only Workspaces. *The Guardian*, 20 July. Retrieved from https://www.theguardian.com/cities/2019/jul/20/an-oasis-for-women-inside-saudi-arabias-vast-new-female-only-workspaces.

Ming-Yen, Teoh Wendy, and Chong Siong-Choy. 2007. Theorising a Framework of Factors Influencing Performance of Women Entrepreneurs in Malaysia. *Journal of Asia Entrepreneurship and Sustainability* 3 (2): 1.

Mohsina, Nazneen, and Amit Ranjan. 2019. *The Radicalisation of Bangladeshi Migrant Workers in Singapore*. Institute of South Asian Studies (ISAS). https://www.isas.nus.edu.sg/papers/the-radicalisation-of-bangladeshi-migrant-workers-in-singapore/. Accessed 22 Aug 2019.

MomentMag. 2013. [Video] *Why Amina Wadud Led a Mixed-Gender Muslim Prayer*. YouTube. Available at https://www.youtube.com/watch?v=E_flQbtI1U4.

Montgomery, Richard, Debapriya Bhattacharya, and David Hulme. 1996. Credit for the Poor in Bangladesh. The Brac Rural Development Programme and the Government Thana Resource Development and Employment Programme. In *Finance against Poverty*, eds. David Hulme and Paul Mosley, 94–176. London: Routledge. https://doi.org/10.4324/9780203978924.

Moser, Sarah. 2012. Circulating Visions of 'High Islam': The Adoption of Fantasy Middle Eastern Architecture in Constructing Malaysian National Identity. *Urban Studies* 49 (13): 2913–2935.

Mridha, Limana Solaiman. 2015. Rural Entrepreneurs: Women Step up to Lift Their Families out of Poverty. *The Independent*. https://www.theindependentbd.com/arcprint/details/22791/2015-11-13. Accessed 18 Aug 2021.

Mubarok, M Zaki, and Ahmad Fauzi Abdul Hamid. 2018. The Rise of Radicalism and Terrorism in Indonesia and Malaysia. *Review of Islam in Southeast Asia* 1 (1): 29–43.

Murray, Alison J. 1991. *No Money No Honey: A Study of Street Traders and Prostitutes in Jakarta*. Singapore: Oxford University Press.

Nagata, Judith. 1980. Religious Ideology and Social Change: The Islamic Revival in Malaysia. *Pacific Affairs* 53 (3): 405–439.

Nahar, Papreen, and Annemiek Richters. 2011. Suffering of Childless Women in Bangladesh: The Intersection of Social Identities of Gender and Class. *Anthropology & Medicine* 18 (3): 327–338.

Olivier, Bob. 2016. The Malaysian Islamization Phenomenon: The Underlying Dynamics and Their Impact on Muslim Women. *Islam and Christian-Muslim Relations* 27 (3): 267–282.

Papanek, Hanna, and Laurel Schwede. 1988. Women Are Good with Money: Earning and Managing in an Indonesian City. *Economic and Political Weekly*: WS73–WS84.

Pikkat, Krista, and Jasmina Šopova. 2018. Bibi Russell: Finding Magic in Fingers. *The UNESCO Courier*. April–June. UNESCO. Available at https://unesdoc.unesco.org/ark:/48223/pf0000261912.

Rafiki, Ahmad, and Fahmi Natigor Nasution. 2019. Business Success Factors of Muslim Women Entrepreneurs in Indonesia. *Journal of Enterprising Communities: People and Places in the Global Economy* 13 (5): 584–604. https://doi.org/10.1108/jec-04-2019-0034.

Rahman, Aminur. 1999. *Women and Microcredit in Rural Bangladesh: Anthropological Study of the Rhetoric and Realities of Grameen Bank Lending*. USA: Westview Press.

Raihan, Selim, and Sayema Haque Bidisha. 2018. Female Employment Stagnation in Bangladesh' *A Research Paper on Economic Dialogue on Inclusive Growth in Bangladesh*. South Asian Network on Economic Modeling (SANEM), The Asia Foundation, DFID, UKaid.

Ram, Sadho. 2016. *8 Malaysian Female Entrepreneurs You Should Know Who Have Made It Big in Their Fields*. SAYS. https://says.com/my/lifestyle/women-entrepreneurs-in-malaysia-who-broke-the-glass-ceiling. Accessed 18 Aug 2021.

Redvers, Louise. 2016. *The High-End, Designer Fashion Hidden Beneath the Abaya*. BBC. https://www.bbc.com/worklife/article/20160623-the-high-end-designer-fashion-hidden-beneath-the-abaya. Accessed 10 Aug 2021.

Robinson, Kathryn. 2009. *Gender, Islam, and Democracy in Indonesia*. Oxon and New York: Routledge.

Ross, Michael L. 2008. Oil, Islam, and Women. *American Political Science Review* 102 (1): 107–123. https://doi.org/10.1017/s0003055408080040.

Rudnyckyj, Daromir. 2013. From Wall Street to Halal Street: Malaysia and the Globalization of Islamic Finance. *The Journal of Asian Studies* 72 (4): 831–848.

Sadi, Muhammad A., and Basheer M. Al-Ghazali. 2012. The Dynamics of Entrepreneurial Motivation Among Women: A Comparative Study of Businesswomen in Saudi Arabia and Bahrain. *Asian Academy of Management Journal* 17 (1): 97–113.

Sakai, Minako, and Bhirawa Anoraga. 2020. Education, Digital Enterprise and Islam in the Indonesian Modern Embedded Economy. In *Muslim Women in the Economy: Development, Faith and Globalisation*, eds. Shamim Samani and Dora Marinova, 214–228. Oxon and New York: Routledge. https://doi.org/10.4324/9780429263194.

Sakai, Minako, and Amelia Fauzia. 2016. Performing Muslim Womanhood: Muslim Business Women Moderating Islamic Practices in Contemporary Indonesia. *Islam and Christian-Muslim Relations* 27 (3): 229–249. https://doi.org/10.1080/09596410.2015.1114243.

Salehin, Mohammad Musfequs. 2016. Piety, Gender Relations and Muslim Women's Empowerment: The Case of Islamic Ngos in Bangladesh. In *Islam and Development: Exploring the Invisible Aid Economy*, eds. Matthew Clarke and David Tittensor, 183–206. London: Routledge. https://doi.org/10.4324/9781315589893.

Schröter, Susanne. 2013. Gender and Islam in Southeast Asia: An Overview. In *Gender and Islam in Southeast Asia: Women's Rights Movements, Religious Resurgence and Local Traditions*, ed. Susanne Schröter, 7–52. Leiden: Brill.

Shah, Saeeda. 2018. 'We Are Equals'; Datum or Delusion: Perceptions of Muslim Women Academics in Three Malaysian Universities. *British Journal of Sociology of Education* 39 (3): 299–315.

Shamsul, Amri Baharuddin. 1997. Identity Construction, Nation Formation, and Islamic Revivalism in Malaysia. In *Islam in an Era of Nation-States*, ed. Robert W. Hefiner, 207–228. Honolulu: University of Hawaii Press.

Sharma, Karina, and Khulood Ahmed. 2020. Meet the Saudi Arabian Designer Ready to Make a Statement with Her Latest Collection. *Vogue*. https://en.vogue.me/fashion/video-razan-alazzouni/. Accessed 18 Aug 2021.

Sharma, Mihir S. 2021. Bangladesh Rises to Be South Asia's Standout Star as India, Pak Fall Behind. *Business Standard*. https://www.business-standard.com/article/economy-policy/bangladesh-rises-to-be-south-asia-s-standout-star-as-india-pak-fall-behind-121060100237_1.html. Accessed 18 Aug 2021.

Shiraishi, Saya. 1995. Children's Stories and the State in New Order Indonesia. In *Children and the Politics of Culture*, ed. Sharon Stephens, 169–183. Princeton, NJ: Princeton University Press.

Sidani, Yusuf. 2018. *Muslim Women at Work: Religious Discourses in Arab Society*. New York: Springer.

Silvey, Rachel. 2006. Consuming the Transnational Family: Indonesian Migrant Domestic Workers to Saudi Arabia. *Global Networks* 6 (1): 23–40.

Sirry, Mun'im. 2013. Fatwas and Their Controversy: The Case of the Council of Indonesian Ulama (Mui). *Journal of Southeast Asian Studies* 44 (1): 100–117. https://doi.org/10.1017/S0022463412000641.

Sloane-White, Patricia. 2017. *Corporate Islam: Sharia and the Modern Workplace*. Cambridge: Cambridge University Press.

Sloane-White, Patricia. 2018a. Company Rules: Sharia and Its Transgressions in the Malay-Muslim Corporate Workplace. *Journal of Current Southeast Asian Affairs* 37 (1): 89–116. https://doi.org/10.1177/186810341803700104.

Sloane-White, Patricia. 2018b. Working in the Islamic Economy: Sharia-Ization and the Malaysian Workplace. *Sojourn* 33 (S): S264–S295. https://doi.org/10.1355/sj33-Sj.

Solati, Fariba. 2017. *Women, Work, and Patriarchy in the Middle East and North Africa*. New York: Springer.

Sullivan, Norma. 1994. *Masters and Managers: A Study of Gender Relations in Urban Java*. Crows Nest, NSW: Allen & Unwin.

Sultan, Mohammad Tipu, and Farzana Sharmin. 2020. An Exploratory Investigation of Facebook Live Marketing by Women Entrepreneurs in Bangladesh. In *Social Computing and Social Media. Participation, User Experience, Consumer Experience, and Applications of Social Computing*, ed. Gabriele Meiselwitz, 415–430. Cham: Springer International Publishing. https://doi.org/10.1007/978-3-030-49576-3_30.

Sundaram, Jomo Kwame. 1989. Malaysia's New Economic Policy and National Unity. *Third World Quarterly* 11 (4): 36–53.

Syed, Jawad, Faiza Ali, and Sophie Hennekam. 2018. Gender Equality in Employment in Saudi Arabia: A Relational Perspective. *Career Development International* 23 (2): 163–177. https://doi.org/10.1108/cdi-07-2017-0126.

Tambunan, Tulus. 2008. SME Development in Indonesia: Do Economic Growth and Government Supports Matter? https://papers.ssrn.com/sol3/papers.cfm?abstract_id=1218922. Accessed 9 Sept 2021.

Tambunan, Tulus. 2009. Women Entrepreneurs in Indonesia: Their Main Constraints and Reasons. *Journal of Asia Entrepreneurship and Sustainability* V(3): 37–51.

Tambunan, Tulus. 2015. Development of Women Entrepreneurs in Indonesia: Are They Being Pushed or Pulled? *Journal of Social Economics* 2 (3): 131–149.

Tambunan, Tulus. 2016. Barriers to Women's Entrepreneurship. In *Routledge Handbook of Entrepreneurship in Developing Economies*, eds. Colin C. Williams and Anjula Gurtoo, 260–277. London: Routledge. https://doi.org/10.4324/9781315725826.ch21.

Tambunan, Tulus. 2017. Women Entrepreneurs in Mses in Indonesia: Their Motivations and Main Constraints. *Journal of Women's Entrepreneurship and Education* 1–2: 56–86.

Vogel, Frank E. 2011. Saudi Arabia: Public, Civil, and Individual Shari'a in Law and Politics. In *Shari'a Politics: Islamic Law and Society in the Modern World*, ed. Robert W. Hefner, 55–93. Bloomington: Indiana University Press.

White, Sarah C. 2012. Beyond the Paradox: Religion, Family and Modernity in Contemporary Bangladesh. *Modern Asian Studies* 46 (5): 1429–1458. https://doi.org/10.1017/s0026749x12000133.

Wie, Thee Kian. 2002. The Soeharto Era and After: Stability, Development and Crisis, 1966–2000. In *The Emergence of a National Economy: An Economic History of Indonesia, 1800–2000*, eds. Howard Dick, Vincent J.H. Houben, J. Thomas Lindblad, and Thee Kian Wie, 194–243. Australia and Honolulu: Allen & Unwin, University of Hawai'i Press.

Williams, Colin C. 2018. *Entrepreneurship in the Informal Sector: An Institutional Perspective*. London: Routledge.

Williams, Colin, and Anjula Gurtoo. 2011. Evaluating Competing Explanations for Street Entrepreneurship: Some Evidence from India. *Journal of Global Entrepreneurship Research* 1 (2): 3–19.

Williams, Colin C., and Sara Nadin. 2010. Entrepreneurship and the Informal Economy: An Overview. *Journal of Developmental Entrepreneurship* 15 (4): 361–378.

World Bank. 2019. *The Little Data Book on Gender*. World Bank Group. https://openknowledge.worldbank.org/handle/10986/31689. Accessed 7 Apr 2021.

World Bank. 2020. *Women, Business and the Law*. World Bank. https://wbl.worldbank.org/en/wbl. Accessed 18 Aug 2021.

World Bank. 2021. *Beyond Unicorns: Harnessing Digital Technologies for Inclusion in Indonesia*. World Bank. https://elibrary.worldbank.org/doi/abs/10.1596/36018. Accessed 10 Aug 2021.

World Economic Forum. 2019. *The Global Gender Gap Report 2020*. World Economic Forum. https://www.weforum.org/reports/gender-gap-2020-report-100-years-pay-equality/digest. Accessed 10 Apr 2021.

World Economic Forum. n.d.-a. Bibi Russell Fashion Designer: Bibi Productions Fashion for Development. https://www.weforum.org/people/bibi-russell. Accessed 7 Apr 2021.

World Economic Forum. n.d.-b. Maliha m. Quadir, Founding Director of Shohoj Limited. https://www.weforum.org/people/maliha-m-quadir. Accessed 7 Apr 2021.

Ying, Lim Li. 2019. What Is the Story Behind Neelofa, One of Malaysia's Hottest Instagram Influencers? *South China Morning Post*. https://www.scmp.com/magazines/style/celebrity/article/3030645/why-do-brands-chanel-and-dior-adore-neelofa-one-malaysias. Accessed 7 Apr 2021.

Yulianti, F. 2011. Suapan Nasi Kunyit, Tanda Cinta Ibu Pada Ibas-Aliya Okezone Lifestyle. https://lifestyle.okezone.com/read/2011/11/24/29/533688/suapan-nasi-kunyit-tanda-cinta-ibu-pada-ibas-aliya. Accessed 18 Aug 2021.

Yusof, Vivy. 2011. '[Youtube Channel] Vivy Yusof' Yusof, Vivy. YouTube. Available at https://www.youtube.com/channel/UCHY0v1pMghChYoUAOkqHkhQ.

Yusof, Vivy. 2019. [Video] *My Everyday Hijab Tutorial (3 Simple Styles)*. Yusof, Vivy. 19 July. YouTube. Available at https://www.youtube.com/watch?v=l2olF77y0iU.

Zamberi Ahmad, Syed. 2011. Evidence of the Characteristics of Women Entrepreneurs in the Kingdom of Saudi Arabia. *International Journal of Gender and Entrepreneurship* 3 (2): 123–143. https://doi.org/10.1108/17566261111140206.

CHAPTER 3

Conditions for the Rise of Muslim Mompreneurs in Indonesia

Amelia Fauzia

Abstract This chapter investigates the conditions and enablers of success for women's small businesses based on the study of the Indonesian context. It argues that the concept of a people's economy employed by the government and appropriate interpretations of Islam by Muslim women's organisations together have facilitated the growth of female entrepreneurship. This chapter provides a historical overview of the government's policies, the context of an Islamic economy, and responses of Muslim organisations to women being involved in small businesses. All of these factors have created suitable conditions that assisted women, especially those of the middle class, in becoming Muslim mompreneurs.

Keywords Empowerment · Government policies · Indonesia · Islam · Mompreneurs · SMEs · Women

M. Sakai and A. Fauzia, *Women Entrepreneurs and Business Empowerment in Muslim Countries*,
Gender, Development and Social Change,
https://doi.org/10.1007/978-3-031-05954-4_3

Introduction

This chapter brings our analysis to Indonesia to examine the conditions and enablers that support Muslim women in becoming entrepreneurs. In 2019, there were 65.4 million enterprises in Indonesia of which 99.99% were micro, small and medium-sized businesses (Kementerian Koperasi dan UKM 2021). The Indonesian government has endeavoured to develop entrepreneurship by allocating a diverse range of resources despite the change of governments. These policies have not specifically targeted female entrepreneurship per se; however, the operation of small businesses has generally been dominated by women and consequently, the Indonesian government's policies and programs as explained in this chapter have benefited Muslim mompreneurs. Most micro and small enterprises are operated at the household level (Hastuti et al. 2003a, b; SMERU 2004; Tambunan 2009) and in sectors closely associated with women (World Bank 2016). This chapter argues that government policy and Muslim organisations have supported the growth of Muslim businesswomen by endorsing gender roles: that men are the household head while women should attend to domestic responsibilities as well as aiding their household economy through small businesses. This chapter analyses government policies, Islamic economies and the responses of women's organisations that foster female entrepreneurship.

Government Policies on Small Businesses

Indonesian government policies relating to small business have been based on the concept of people's economy (ekonomi kerakyatan), introduced under Suharto's government or the New Order Era (1966–1998). The policy focuses on unleashing the potential of a large population with lower income to operate cooperatives and small businesses, creating a people's economy. It encouraged the establishment of cooperatives, including the formation of the village unit cooperative (***koperasi unit desa*** [KUD]) and women's cooperatives (***koperasi wanita***). These organisations support entrepreneurial activities at a grassroots level and enhance the development of micro, small and medium entrepreneurial businesses.

The idea of the people's economy was originally promoted by Muhammad Hatta, the first Vice President of Indonesia (Hatta 2019; Lindblad 2002). During Hatta's term in office (1945–1956) along with President Sukarno, this economic concept did not develop well.

During the Suharto era (1966–1998) it gained importance and benefited those on lower and middle incomes, including those in remote areas of Indonesia. The work of the Suharto government was continued by subsequent Indonesian governments, and efforts were made to encourage the growth of cooperatives by strengthening two essential elements. One element is cooperatives, namely microfinance institutions, to support businesses, and the other is the capacity for business development through human resources to operate small and medium enterprises (Ministry of Cooperatives and Small and Medium Enterprises 2001; SMERU 2004).

The idea of the people's economy resulted in the government's inclusion of micro enterprises in the existing term of SMEs. In its policy, this term has become Micro, Small and Medium Enterprises—MSMEs, or UMKM when abbreviated in Indonesian. The inclusion of micro enterprises allows a greater opportunity for women to contribute to the national economy. Women are mainly found operating micro-scale enterprises (with assets below Rp. 50 million or USD 3,571) and small enterprises (with assets between Rp. 50 million and Rp. 500 million or USD 3,571 to USD 35,714). Few women operate medium-sized enterprises (with assets between Rp. 500 million to Rp. 10 billion or USD 34,714 to USD 714,286)[1] or large enterprises. The approximate number of women running enterprises of each of these sizes is 38,760,811 (micro), 479,207 (small), 39,278 (medium) and 3,382 (large) (Kementerian Koperasi dan UKM 2021). In the gender-neutral policy for MSMEs, the focus of the people's economy campaign ensured small businesses run by women became much more commonplace among households. Though these policies, institutions and programs were not deliberately intended for this, they have supported Muslim mompreneurs.

Policies in Strengthening Small Businesses

The Indonesian government introduced a series of programs that are gender neutral. Policies promoting small enterprises started in the 1970s in the Suharto era with a standard program that provided capital loans to small entrepreneurs. The policy was called Kredit Investasi Kecil or KIK. Only near the end of Suharto's term did the government develop more vigorous moves to assist small enterprises, for example through the issuance of the Law on Small Enterprises (No. 9/1995) that empowered entrepreneurship. These policies created an economic environment suitable for conducting small businesses by providing better financing opportunities, providing guarantees for loans and coaching in business operations. The post-Suharto period brought further enhancement of the people's economy policy with a number of new laws and institutional changes that focused on strengthening cooperatives and small enterprises. These did not particularly emphasise offering support to women entrepreneurs (Kementerian Koperasi dan UKM 2021). This policy direction continued in the reformation period with the issuance of the Law on Banking (No. 7/1999), which includes articles supporting microfinance institutions and the government's establishment of state-owned enterprises called Madani National Capital (Permodalan Nasional Madani [PNM]) to provide microfinance. The Law on Decentralisation (No. 22/1999) spread the initiatives of entrepreneurial programs that were previously centralised to all districts and cities across Indonesia. Building on this law, President Susilo Bambang Yudhoyono (2004–2014) issued presidential instructions to create an investment climate and a new policy titled, Speeding the Development of Real Sectors and Empowerment of Micro, Small and Medium Enterprises. His cabinet issued Law on Micro, Small and Medium Enterprises (No. 20/2008) by adding the term 'micro enterprises', which affirmed the government's inclination towards promoting small businesses.

The government's policy towards entrepreneurship was also enhanced through a national education campaign ordered by Presidential Instruction (No. 4/1995) concerning the National Campaign to Promote and Cultivate Entrepreneurship. Based on this instruction, all levels of education were required to implement the policy, including primary and secondary schools, through to higher education institutions.[2] The Ministry of Education and Culture[3] of Suharto's cabinet began to update the national curriculum to include entrepreneurship in every educational unit from primary school to higher education curriculum. The government also included entrepreneurship courses in vocational high schools and in the economics and technology faculties.[4] In colleges and universities, entrepreneurship education has been in place since 1997 (Badan Penelitian dan Pengembangan Pusat Kurikulum 2010). As a result of this inclusion in their education, younger Indonesians mostly have a better understanding of entrepreneurship. The policies outlined above provide a significant path to entrepreneurship for both males and females in Indonesia (Susilaningsih 2015). This has paved a way for middle-class Indonesians to take up entrepreneurship.

Enhancing Government Institutions for Supporting Entrepreneurial Activities

The focus on the people's economy has also manifested in the institutionalisation of the government ministries and agencies working on small business and entrepreneurship. The government has focused to varying degrees on promoting this sector of the economy since the colonial era (Azhari et al. 2017; Lindblad 2002). The Department or Ministry of Cooperatives and Small and Medium Enterprises (also known as the Ministry of Cooperatives)[5] has been charged with the responsibility for the implementation of government policies related to small businesses at the national, provincial, district and city levels. It has developed two interrelated entities, one for cooperative institutions and the other for the quality and activities of micro and small enterprises.

Before 1983, the institutional position of the portfolio of cooperatives varied across different governments. At times it operated as an independent department, but at other times it was integrated with other ministries such as trade, transmigration and village development. Since 1983 the cooperative affairs have gained importance, ultimately becoming a single ministry. In 1993, the ministry became the Department of Cooperatives and Small Business Development (Departemen Koperasi dan Pembinaan Pengusaha Kecil). This department increased its focus on small and medium entrepreneurs, and so in 2000 it became the Ministry of Cooperatives, Small and Medium Enterprises.

Since the Yudhoyono government (2004–2014), promotion and assistance to small businesses and entrepreneurial activities have been supported by other government ministries and agencies such as the Ministry of Trade, the Ministry of Industry, the Bank of Indonesia, State-owned Enterprises, Creative Economy Agency (Badan Ekonomi Kreatif or [BEKRAF]) and the Ministry of Women's Empowerment and Child Protection. Giving special attention to female entrepreneurs and enterprises run by women was endorsed by the Ministry of Women's Empowerment and Child Protection (previously, the Ministry of Women's Empowerment)[6] through the Gender Mainstreaming policy issued by President Abdurrahman Wahid (Presidential Decree No. 9/2000). This ministry and the Gender Mainstreaming policy provided an important basis for the existing awareness of and support given to female entrepreneurship. The Ministry conducts an evaluation of progress towards the achievement of gender mainstreaming and female entrepreneurship is included as one of the top five priorities for this assessment (Ministry of Cooperatives and Small and Medium Enterprises 2001; Ministry of Women's Empowerment and Child Protection 2019).[7] In 2019, for example, the Ministry of Cooperatives reported that more than 50% of its grantees and program participants were women. It allocated 2,603 grants to start-ups, each with Rp. 30 million in capital to scale up their business. Of the 2,603 start-ups, 62% were owned by women (Sekretariat TIM PUG Kementerian Koperasi dan UKM 2019: 15) as they were deemed to be disadvantaged and in need of assistance. The Ministry of Women's Empowerment and Child Protection also offered specific programs targeting female entrepreneurship. These programs offer a range of assistance from providing seed funding to training, as well as endorsing collaboration between agencies that support women entrepreneurs (Hastuti et al. 2003a; Kementerian Pemberdayaan Perempuan dan Perlindungan Anak 2018, 2019).

To develop global and digital entrepreneurship trends that can foster small businesses in Indonesia, in 2014 President Joko Widodo established the Creative Economy Agency based on the Presidential Decree No. 6/2015. Even though their mandate is to grow entrepreneurship in the community through both male and female citizens, the government's initiatives in developing the 'creative economy' has indirectly increased opportunities for Muslim mompreneurs. The creative economy refers to the economy revolving around various emerging secondary and tertiary industries that range from software development to fashion design, tourism, arts and research. A survey of the creative economy published in 2017 shows that women make up 53.6% of the Indonesian creative economy's labour force (Badan Ekonomi Kreatif [BEKRAF] 2017: 8). This can be compared to the percentage of the national workforce that is female, which is 38.40%. Women are the dominant workforce in the creative economy, and by 2019 the percentage of women in that workforce had grown to 55.7% (Badan Ekonomi Kreatif [BEKRAF] 2018). This high percentage is due to the proximity of 16 creative economy sub-sectors with some traditional women's areas of business, such as crafts, fashion and culinary goods. These are enterprises in which women in Indonesia can combine with completing their domestic activities as wives and mothers. Government support for the creative economy is part of the broader program supporting small businesses in feminised industries and promoting a model for ideal womanhood. The Creative Economy Agency has delivered a number of new programs, such as

Coding Mum, to foster women entrepreneurs. Coding Mum, a pilot program, was initiated to teach housewives or stay-home mothers how to code computer programs so they could work from home as programmers and increase their household income. In 2017, the program trained 239 new 'coding mums' and expanded to female overseas migrant workers in Singapore, Hong Kong and Malaysia so that they could return to work from home (Badan Ekonomi Kreatif [BEKRAF] 2018). This initiative was followed by other institutions who share concerns over the migrant workers (Kominfo 2021).

Programs Supporting Women Entrepreneurs

With the policies implemented by governmental ministries and agencies, women entrepreneurs received significant unintended benefits as they were, and are, the majority of owners of micro and small enterprises. In addition to that, the Ministry of Cooperatives has developed programs designed specifically for women beneficiaries. These include programs such as the provision of grants and the development of various types of training to improve the capability of women in entrepreneurial activities. Two programs worth mentioning are the Women's Program for a Healthy and Prosperous Family (PERKASSA) and the National Program for Independent Community Empowerment (PNPM). The PERKASSA program started in 2006 and targeted the establishment of thousands of female cooperatives and businesses (Ernita 2014; Situmorang 2010). With a total of 149,667 cooperatives in 2007, the number of female cooperatives was 2,481 or 1.7%. PERKASSA could provide block grants to 10% of the female cooperatives (Situmorang 2010: 4). The PNPM program started in 2007 during the Yudhoyono presidency and was also a program promoting women's cooperatives (Azarbaijani-Moghaddam 2014; Mellina and Ghozali 2019; Syukri et al. 2013). Those programs focused on the establishment of female cooperatives and MSMEs were later subsumed by the program of the Enhancement of Women's Role towards a Healthy and Prosperous Family (Peningkatan Peran Wanita menuju Keluarga Sehat dan Sejahtera or P2WKSS), which enhances the government endorsed patriarchy. It is important to note that women's involvement in cooperatives is not only seen in female-only cooperatives, but also in other cooperatives (Situmorang 2010; SMERU 2004).

Though the specific programs for women entrepreneurs are limited, female participation in the gender-neutral government program is generally higher than male participation rates (Hastuti et al. 2003b; Sekretariat TIM PUG Kementerian Koperasi dan UKM 2018, 2019; SMERU 2004). For example, grants, training and technical assistance for new entrepreneurs provided by the government in 2015, 2017, 2018 and 2019 were spread across 34 provinces and given to as many as 7,288 (52%) females and 6,656 (48%) males (Kementerian Koperasi dan UKM 2019). The involvement of women is not achieved by policy design, but it is more a result of the nature of most micro and small-scale enterprises that happen to be dominated by women. The domination by women of the existing micro and small enterprises is not distinctive to Indonesia, but can be found in other developing countries in Asia (Tambunan 2009: 31). While Indonesian government support is mainly gender neutral, support and various assistance offered by NGOs (local and international) are often targeted to increase female participation. For example, of the 64 institutions working to support MSMEs in 2003, 1,044 programs had been implemented with 11% specific to or prioritising women. The rest (89%) were gender neutral (Hastuti et al. 2003a; SMERU 2004). Our recent survey of government training offered for micro and small entrepreneurs in three provinces of Indonesia found that women made up about 80% of the participants. Offices of cooperatives and SMEs at the district level found about 80% of training participants were women who owned micro businesses supplying food and beverage, fashion, handicrafts, beauty products and services and the like (Fauzia et al. 2021).[8] The World Bank's Indonesia research also found that the most common business sectors for women entrepreneurs were grocery stalls, manufacturing of food, beverages and textiles and social services (World Bank 2016). These business sectors are relatively closely associated with the traditional daily activities of women as wives and mothers. Women have made use of this opportunity, hence their strong involvement in state-run programs.

The government's People's Economy campaign combined with grass-root movements for Islamic microfinance, namely Islamic law compliance cooperatives (Kopsyah-Koperasi Syariah) and Baitul Maal wat Tamwil (BMT) (Sakai 2008, 2014, 2018) that later engaged Muslim institutions to facilitate the programs. These Islamic microfinance institutions are cooperative business entities that run business according to sharia or Islamic law principles. In the early 2000s, the government provided financial capital loans to various types of cooperatives and BMT under programs such as the Micro Business Loan Scheme (Kredit Usaha Mikro [KUM]). Engagement of Muslim communities in the People's Economy campaign has been a driver of support for the inclusion of Muslim women in the cooperatives and in micro entrepreneurship.

One of the politicians to advocate the people's economy and BMT was middle-class Indonesian Muslim Adi Sasono. He was the chair of the Indonesian Association of Muslim Intellectuals (Ikatan Cendekiawan Muslim Indonesia [ICMI]), which in 1991 established the first Islamic bank, Bank Muamalat (Hefner 2003), and subsequently supported Islamic cooperatives and microfinance companies. BMT quickly spread to various provinces in Indonesia after the Suharto era and continued as one of the grassroots financial institution supporters of small businesses (Sakai 2010, 2014). BMT offered financial services, entrepreneurial training and social empowerment activities. Their clients are small businesses, often owned by women. A number of women's cooperatives established and endorsed by either the central government or local governments provided women with business opportunities including empowerment through training and other support.

Small Business Training for Women

Studies of women in Indonesia during the Suharto era find evidence of state-sponsored patriarchy demonstrated by what Julia Suryakusuma (1996) called 'State Ibuism' or state endorsement of the concept that a woman's role is to be a wife and mother. What has become apparent since the 2000s is that through state-sponsored women's institutions, middle-class wives of civil servants and those in rural areas have been encouraged to start microbusinesses with reference to the state-endorsed ideal of womanhood. This ideal is based on the constructed nature of womanhood or *kodrat wanita*, that is a fluid but strong perception established by the women themselves, by the government and in public discourse that 'hinders women's participation but [does] not totally [prevent it]' (Kusmana 2017: 267). The concept of *kodrat*, or destiny, provides a basis to construct both female and male social roles so that women are placed in more difficult positions than men (Blackburn 2004; Robinson 2009). While this *kodrat* has positioned women as the ones who deal with household management—taking care of the children and the husband, with men as the breadwinners (and this is also stipulated in the Marriage

Law [No. 1/1974])—the government has also endorsed women to contribute to the family's welfare. This indirectly encourages women to seek employment in feminised job roles to support the family with additional income, especially when the husband's income is not sufficient to meet household's needs.[9]

State policy that defines women's role as facilitating family harmony and welfare has been targeted at the middle-class civil servants' wives and provides the framework for strengthening state ideology (Blackburn 2004; Robinson 2000, 2009; Sullivan 1994; Suryakusuma 1996). These wives are expected to work to foster their children's development and overall family wellbeing, while supporting the husband's duties as civil servants. Recently, to maintain their family's middle-class lifestyle, women have been assuming a role to contribute to the welfare of the family. In this vein, becoming a mompreneur appears to be an attractive choice for the middle-class woman.

Let us now explore how the main women's organisations established during the Suharto period provided training opportunities for the growth of women's entrepreneurship. Our intention is to show that Indonesia has provided formal and informal training for middle-class women, which has created a pool of capable women who have taken up entrepreneurship as new business opportunities expanded since the 2000s.

Dharma Wanita

Entrepreneurial training has been embedded in the organisation of Dharma Wanita. Dharma Wanita is an association for wives of civil servants, and literally means Duty for Women. Dharma Wanita was incorporated into every government office, led by the wives of those (men) who occupied all levels of government office positions, from Indonesian president to the lowest level of bureaucracy (Robinson 2009; Suryakusuma 1996: 73). Established in 1974, Dharma Wanita's work has included expanding women's role in the economy to embrace the development agenda while strengthening the state ideology by controlling the wives of government officials (Suryakusuma 1996: 100). Following government directives to women's organisations, Dharma Wanita promoted five roles for women (Panca Dharma Wanita) namely, a wife and faithful companion, an educator and provider of family guidance, a household manager, a worker who supplements family income and a member of community (Rahman et al. 2005: 4). Sullivan's study on Dharma Wanita in the early 1980s (1983: 148) did not emphasise women's economic role in the household.

Dharma Wanita organised various activities, including running training courses in sewing, cooking and fashion as well as organising rotary savings association (*arisan*). The wife's position was determined by the rank of her husband as a public servant. During Suharto's government, Suharto's wife was the head of the organisation as the ideal mother and wife of the nation. When the Suharto regime fell in 1998, Dharma Wanita continued to flourish by adapting to the policies of different governments, from the Habibie Presidency in 1998 to Joko Widodo (2014–). The organisation has had some transformation in its membership and its governance and it strengthened its focus on education about the economy skills. Delivering informal training courses remains its main activity. Cooking training has been one of the organisation's routine annual programs and continues to date, as exemplified by Dharma Wanita of Jakarta province (Lusianawati 2015).

Not all Dharma Wanita units have conducted successful entrepreneurial activities and training; however, a number of Dharma Wanita units have succeeded in running their own entrepreneurial programs and developing cooperatives. One well-known example is Patra Dharma Wanita in East Kalimantan, which has a cooperative that owns a number of businesses, including a supermarket and food catering services (Jabbar 2018). These entrepreneurial activities have indirectly endorsed the feminised gendered economy of the middle-class civil servant's wives.

PKK as an Avenue to Learning About Micro Business

For rural areas the government provided a program called Guidance for Family Welfare (Pembinaan Kesejahteraan Keluarga [PKK]). This institution was originally called the program of Education for Family Welfare (with the same abbreviation). It was intended to promote children's education and was inserted into school curriculum (Robinson 2009; Sakai 2019; Sullivan 1994). In 1972, the Suharto government reformed it to become Guidance for Family Welfare, and it acknowledged that mothers had an important responsibility for educating and fostering the welfare of their family, as part of the state ideology on gender (Suryakusuma 1996). Also in 1972, the Ministry of Home Affairs established PKK units at all the administrative levels of villages, districts, cities and provinces.

The wives of male officials often served as the head of the PKK branch in their respective area (Robinson 2009: 74; Sullivan 1983).

Since its establishment in 1972, PKK has conducted a number of successful campaigns about vaccination, family planning, nutrition, study groups and business training that was targeted at increasing the welfare of families (Adzmy and Disyacitta 2018; Marcoes 2002; Sullivan 1983, 1994). It has benefited children's development, but has sacrificed women's time to voluntary works (Newberry 2012). PKK has provided opportunities for rural women to learn how to start small-scale household businesses. The organisation has implemented ten main programs covering Pancasila, mutual cooperation, food, clothing, housing and household management, education and skills, health, promoting cooperatives, preserving the environment and promoting healthy living (Ro'fah 2016; Sullivan 1983). PKK has organised various programs that have enhanced the state's concept of the ideal woman and has facilitated the upgrading of mothers' skills in cooking, sewing and handicraft, all of which are useful to manage their household. Cooperatives have provided training for mothers to develop their business skills. PKK has indirectly promoted small-scale entrepreneurial skills for non-elite household mothers in villages throughout the country under the guise of family welfare, which has later made two-income families commonplace (Robinson 2009: 74).

IWAPI: Coaching and Training of Middle-Class Businesswomen

Compared to the two organisations previously mentioned, which are the state's top-down approach to the betterment of civil servants and rural communities, the Indonesian Business Women Association (Ikatan Wanita Pengusaha Indonesia [IWAPI]) was developed by businesswomen with the aim of enhancing female entrepreneurship. IWAPI was established in 1975 by businesswomen Dewi Motik Pramono and Kemala Motik. Both were successful businesswomen and well-known writers, lecturers and motivational speakers (Sukarno et al. 2019). In 1976, this organisation became a member of the Indonesian Chamber of Commerce and Industry (Kamar Dagang dan Industri Indonesia [KADIN]) and the only registered female entrepreneur organisation. With support from the government, in two decades IWAPI had established branches in most provinces in Indonesia. The establishment of IWAPI demonstrates the government's commitment to supporting the female development agenda.[10] Members of IWAPI are businesswomen who mainly trade in feminised areas such as food and beverages, fashion and beauty, and handicrafts: industries that continue to be dominated by women entrepreneurs in contemporary Indonesia (Sakai 2019).

IWAPI's members were initially drawn from upper middle-class women from wealthy families but later included women with medium and small-sized enterprises, in a bid to grow its membership. In 2015 its mission was 'to empower and strengthen women in SMEs, to improve the ability of its members gaining access to businesses, and to gain access to new technologies, marketing, and finance' (IWAPI 2015; Sakai 2019). This organisation provided networks, coaching and training. The organisation remains the largest and most well-established female business association in Indonesia. In 2015 it claimed to have about 40,000 members across 256 branches and 30 provinces in Indonesia, and it collaborated closely with government ministries and agencies as well as a number of international organisations (IWAPI 2015).

Although IWAPI membership is not entirely Muslim, it has recently undergone a certain level of Islamisation among its members and activities, as members are trying to adapt to an ideal womanhood amidst increases of the Muslim middle-class. There has been some community expectation that IWAPI members follow the business ethics and example set by Khadijah, the first wife of the Prophet (Ryandono et al. 2019). As more middle-class women have embraced Islam as a guiding principle in their life, so have monthly Islamic prayer gatherings become commonplace at IWAPI activities (IWAPI 2021).

After the political democratisation of 1998, these three organisations (Dharma Wanita, PKK and IWAPI) continued to play an important role amidst the growing Islamisation in Indonesia. State control was reduced in 2000, the PKK was renamed the Empowerment for Family Welfare (Pemberdayaan Kesejahteraan Keluarga) and Dharma Wanita changed its charter so membership was not obligatory for wives of civil servants (Chin and Mohd Daud 2018; Robinson 2009; Robinson and Bessell 2002). The three organisations adjusted to focus more on entrepreneurial activities facilitated by the government, such as National Family Planning Coordination Body (BKKBN) and the Ministry of Cooperatives. We argue that these recent changes reflect that the government has embraced the idea of mompreneur who help their husbands safeguard the welfare of their families (KPPPA 2019).

Emerging Islamic Business Opportunities

Islamic businesses have indirectly provided opportunities for Muslim women to establish their own enterprises. The accelerated Islamisation in Indonesia triggered a rise in the consumption of goods labelled *halal*, the consumption and production of fashion products with Islamic nuances and the rapid development of Islamic charities (Ab Rahman 2018; Fischer 2011). Islamic businesses that have appeared in recent years have been driving entrepreneurship in Indonesia and other Southeast Asian countries (Sakai and Anoraga 2020; Sloane 1999; Tambunan 2009).

Commodities associated with Islamic economies are mainly related to the food and beverages, clothing, accommodation, tourism and services sectors. They have provided opportunities for Muslim women to participate in business activities, such as producing headscarves, prayer clothing, café and *halal* food. Sharia economy regional development policies and thriving online marketplaces have indirectly become opportunities as well as resources for mompreneurs. The two developments are supported by Muslim communities, including Islamist groups,[11] who see these developments as parts of Islamic propagation (Nisa 2019).

The Impact of Decentralisation and Sharia Economy Policies on Mompreneurs

The government policy on the sharia economy and decentralisation have cleared the way for bringing Islamic businesses into provinces, districts and cities. With the Law on Decentralisation (No. 22/1999), local governments can declare their region as a halal business destination in competition with other districts/provinces for tourists and the growing *halal* business sector. This is seen as a promising way to develop their economy, and it utilises people's connection with their Islamic identity.

Indonesian consumption of Muslim fashion and other *halal* commodities has been growing. Due to the expanding consumption of halal food, Muslim-friendly travel and Muslim fashion, in 2020 Indonesia was ranked the fourth biggest contributor to the Islamic business sector in the world (DinarStandard 2020: 17). It is in the global top ten countries for the number of Islamic businesses in 2020/2021. Since 2014 Joko Widodo's government has embraced Islamic business and halal industries for developing the national economy. It established the

National Committee for Syariah Finance (Komite Nasional Keuangan Syariah) (Presidential decree No. 91/2016)[12] and launched Master Plan of Syariah Economy (BAPPENAS 2018). Following the decree, the government has designated 10 provinces out of 34 as Muslim-friendly tourist destination provinces (KNEKS 2020), namely Lombok, Aceh, West Sumatra, Riau, Jakarta, West Java, Central Java, Yogyakarta, East Java and South Sulawesi. The government has used both decentralisation and sharia economy policies in ways that direct the provinces to grow their economies with increasing conservative Islam.

Regional autonomy has also created opportunities in boosting economies by promoting regional identities, products and regional business networks (Holtzappel and Ramstedt 2009). One important effect of this is the creation of greater entrepreneurial activity in the Islamic economy framework. A leading province for this phenomenon is West Java. The *Halal* Tourism policy has been implemented in provincial planning to empower local businesses trading in food, accommodation, transportation, travel, cultural attractions, souvenirs, crafts and entertainment (Taufik 2019). Various districts that have potential for tourism, such as the city of Bogor and the district of Bandung of West Java, follow this policy. This has created new business opportunities, mainly for Muslim women surrounding networks and communities of fellow entrepreneurs to expand their business and educate others.[13] Another example is the province of West Nusa Tenggara. In 2015, the government of West Nusa Tenggara issued two regulations, No. 51/2015 on *Halal* Tourism and No. 2/2016 on Muslim-Friendly Tourism. The implementation of a *halal* tourism policy in both West Java and West Nusa Tenggara provinces has not given any special attention to women entrepreneurs. However, we have seen an increase in micro and small entrepreneurial activities run by women because they are affected by the increasing number of tourists arriving following the introduction of the halal tourism policy (Asmara 2021).

The increase in Islamic businesses, ranging from food, tourism, fashion, media, recreation, cosmetics and drugs has been seen across Indonesia, including in import and export industries (BAPPENAS 2018; KNEKS 2020; Sumedi 2020), and following the development pattern of other nations, including neighbouring countries such as Malaysia, Thailand, the Philippines and Singapore (Bergeaud-Blackler et al. 2016).

One of the enablers of female entrepreneurship is the Muslim fashion business, to which women contribute not only as producers of modest

Muslim clothes, but also as small traders. There have been growing markets and customers for Islamic clothing, especially in traditional markets such as the well-known Tanah Abang market in Jakarta. An example is the *hijab* market, which sells more fashionable types of veils than conservative ones with dark colours. The Muslim clothing market is huge, and around 80% of its products are made for local consumption (Global Business Guide Indonesia 2016c). In 2015, the value of the export of Muslim-wear reached USD 4.57 billion or around Rp. 58.5 trillion. There are 1,107,955 companies engaged in making and selling these products, of which 70% are small enterprises (Global Business Guide Indonesia 2016b). Of the 750,000 SMEs engaged in the clothing sector in Indonesia, around 30% of them are Muslim-wear producers, with large companies having 40% of the market share, and small and medium-sized enterprises each having a 30% share of the market (Global Business Guide Indonesia 2016a). These Muslim fashion needs support modest clothing designers and halal cosmetics as essential parts of the middle-class Muslim lifestyle consumption, as we explain in Chapters 5 and 6.

Digital Market Places

The aforementioned growth of Islamic businesses has brought opportunities for Muslim women to be actively involved in the use of the internet and other digital technologies, either as consumers, traders, manufacturers or service providers. The growth of *halal* industries has led to online sharia-compliant marketplaces that support the development of Islamic businesses in Indonesia. Two types of digital marketplace are emerging; the first focuses on *halal*-related businesses, and the second sells products that comply with Islamic sharia to attract Muslim traders and consumers.

An example of the first type is a platform known as duniahalal.com launched in 2017 as the first *halal* marketplace (https://duniahalal.com/). Dunia Halal has marketed about 30,000 products with a sales turnover of about Rp. 80 to 90 billion from Rp. 100 billion of investment (Darandono 2017). This marketplace has facilitated retail and trade of goods and merchandise that are produced and sold by small business entrepreneurs, including women. An example of the second type of marketplace is Tokopedia. Being one of the largest digital marketplaces in the country, in 2019, Tokopedia launched a sharia-compliant marketplace called Tokopedia Salam (n.d.) to allow its users to shop for a variety of products and services in the emerging Muslim *halal* market. It claims to market about 21 million Muslim-friendly products and to have more than 700,000 sellers. Tokopedia indicates that 80% of its consumers purchase *halal* food and beverages and 85% seek Muslim fashion (Mulia 2019).

Digital marketplaces have benefited from the growing *halal* industries, which endorse middle-class Muslim businesses and lifestyles in Indonesia and beyond (Fischer 2017; Jurriëns and Tapsell 2017). These digital marketplaces provide facilities for Muslims to pay almsgiving (*zakat*), Islamic endowment (*waqf*) and other donations, which has become an important element of being a middle-class Muslim. Bukalapak, another popular marketplace, whose founders have close ties with the Islamist circle, is among the first marketplaces to provide a program to facilitate Muslim almsgiving in partnership with Islamic charitable organisations. Gojek, a digital start-up specialising in transport service, has transformed into a multi-service tech platform, and facilitates *halal* business and online payment for *zakat* in its menu 'Gogive'.

These businesses support Islamic consumption and Islamic lifestyle online (Hasan 2011; Nisa 2013, 2018a, b). These platforms cater to the needs of the Muslim middle class, as shown in their advertisements. For example, a Tokopedia Salam advertisement commonly uses an image of a Muslim woman who stays at home and undertakes devotional activities while being active and modern yet is also a mompreneur (Tokopedia, n.d.). Online business combined with *dakwah* is a phenomenon that is frequently found among Salafi and Islamist women's circles. Another online business example, @ummualila, is run by the wife of well-known Muslim preacher Felix Siauw, an activist of the recently banned Hizbut Tahrir Indonesia. Ummu Alila owns a number of businesses, including in fashion, halal food, hijab and halal travel. Her businesses are marketed using Instagram and online marketplaces.

Digital technology has not only helped women in dealing with daily activities but has also expanded opportunities for women to engage in entrepreneurship. Muslim mompreneurs take advantage of social media, such as Instagram, and digital marketplaces. In view of the growing Islamisation in the public sphere (Hasan 2009), Islamic industries have provided opportunities for Muslim women to run businesses without compromising their ideal Muslim womanhood of being a good wife and mother.

Responses of Muslim Women's Organisations to Small Business Development

Muslim women's organisations became enablers of the growth of female entrepreneurs by their concepts of the ideal family and their empowerment programs. This section discusses three organisations of different socio-religious backgrounds, Aisyiyah, Muslimat and the Muslim Women Entrepreneurs Association (Ikatan Pengusaha Muslimah Indonesia [IPEMI]).

Both Aisyiyah and Muslimat developed within established Islamic organisations, Muhammadiyah and Nahdlatul Ulama, while IPEMI, Association of Indonesian Women Entrepreneurs, was established in 2015. In this context, small business development has been a part of educational, social and economic programs within Aisyiyah and Muslimat. All activities are related to the roles of women—such as managing kindergartens, orphanages and elderly support programs—as well as small-scale economic programs that are mainly related to improving family welfare. By 2013, Aisyiyah owned about 4560 educational institutions ranging from kindergartens through to Islamic universities and maternity schools, as well as 280 health institutions and 459 social institutions (PP Aisyiyah 2020). Muslimat also manages 232 health institutions, 16,376 educational institutions and 666 small business and microfinance institutions (Muslimat NU 2020). IPEMI focuses on entrepreneurship as part of booming MSMEs in Indonesia and its creation should reflect the growing Islamisation and increase in Islamic sharia businesses.

Three organisations have emphasised the role modelling of Muslim women in disseminating their messages. Aisyiyah is named after Aishah (with the same pronunciation but different transliteration), the youngest wife of the Prophet Muhammad (Syamsiyatun 2016, 2020). Aisyiyah members look up to Aishah—as a wife and a 'mother of believers'—who contributed to society and to the education of the community. Aisyiyah members live by the words of Ahmad Dahlan, the founder of Muhammadiyah, who said that the domestic matters should not become a barrier to undertaking community matters (Setiawati 2010). Contrary to Aisyiyah, IPEMI members look up to Khadijah, the first wife of Muhammad, as an important role model, with Khadijah representing a successful businesswoman, wife and mother. The name Muslimat, an NU-affiliated women's organisation, derives from an Arabic word meaning Muslim women. It does not directly refer to both early Muslim women figures but generally accepts women, especially local Muslim women based in *pesantren*, who follow the theology of Ahlu Sunnah wal Jamaah.[14] Both Aisyiyah and IPEMI are mainly based in urban areas and generally attract educated, middle-class women (Fuad 2002; Ro'fah 2016; Sakai 2019).

Support for each organisation reflects such social stratification. IPEMI's stronghold is the capital of Indonesia, Jakarta, while Aisyiyah is strong in Yogyakarta where Muhammadiyah was established. Muslimat draws support from rural areas, particularly East Java, attracting members with lower incomes. They are predominantly educated by traditional Islamic boarding schools and the organisation has built an extensive network of Islamic learning groups, *majelis taklim* (Mulyani 2007; van Doorn-Harder 2006).

Aisyiyah and Muslimat: Creating Harmonious and Healthy Families

Both Aisyiyah and Muslimat have established and promoted an ideal concept of womanhood with their own interpretations of Islamic teachings. Their versions of ideal Islamic womanhood promote women's role in ensuring the family's welfare and support women's economic role. In general, the entrepreneurial activities of Muslim women have been endorsed to support their family's welfare and to ensure a harmonious family life. They refer to Aishah and Khadijah as their role models to foster a happy and healthy family.

Aisyiyah has launched the concept of *keluarga sakinah* (harmonious family) and Muslimat has developed the concept of *keluarga maslahah* (healthy family). These concepts partly respond to the Suharto government's family planning program (Menchik 2014). They fit with the idea of women being responsible for the welfare of the family including justification for them working and doing business as mompreneurs. *Sakinah* and *maslahah* are both Arabic words and are mentioned in the Quran. *Sakinah* literally means serenity or peace of mind and *maslahah* means benefit and public interest. In the context of the family, both refer to a happy family, which should be interpreted in individual contexts. The program or principle of *keluarga sakinah* was created in 1985 by Aisyiyah (van Doorn-Harder 2006). In 2016, the Central Board of Aisyiyah and the Religious Reform Council of Muhammadiyah reinforced and promoted this idea again. The meaning of a harmonious family is 'a family that is formed on the basis of a legal marriage and is registered with the

Office of Religious Affairs. It is based on mutual love and respect with a full sense of responsibility in bringing an atmosphere of peace, tranquility, and happiness to life in the world and hereafter that is blessed by God' (Pimpinan Pusat Aisyiyah and Majelis Tarjih dan Tajdid Muhammadiyah 2021: 25).

Aisyiyah's guidance on having a harmonious family includes socio-cultural principles and economic activities:

> In order to meet the needs of the family, basically the husband functions as a person in charge of the establishment of the family by providing a living for the family, namely maintenance for his wife and children [An-Nisa 4:34]. Besides the husband as a breadwinner, a wife can also work to earn according to her profession or expertise (examples include public or private employment, working in a factory, running a small business such as a beauty salon, tailoring, running food stalls, and so on). Islam allows women to work and receive the same rewards as men. Al-Qur'an verse An-Nisa 4:32 indicates this. (Pimpinan Pusat Aisyiyah and Majelis Tarjih dan Tajdid Muhammadiyah 2021: 191 translation by the author)

Further, the definition of a harmonious family, Aisyiyah includes seven principles:

1. Develop a commitment to building a happy and lasting family based on a belief in God, the Most Gracious and Most Merciful.
2. Marry based on the principle of autonomy, maturity (taking into account mature age), noble agreement, family eternity, marriage registration, having a solid foundation and monogamy.
3. Establish relationships between members in the family with the principle of *mu'asyarah bil ma'ruf*, namely loving each other, respecting each other, empowering each other and without domestic violence.
4. Carry out rights and obligations based on love and full responsibility.
5. Involve male family members in domestic tasks and maintenance of reproductive health.
6. Carry out family education to produce family members who are useful for the advancement of religion, family, society, the nation and the state.
7. Foster a happy family on the spiritual, education, economic, health and environmental pillars as well as on socio-political and legal affairs.

The concept of *keluarga sakinah*, developed formally since the 1980s, has such support in public that the term is used widely beyond the circles of Muhammadiyah and Aisyiyah. *Keluarga sakinah* can be interpreted to suit the needs of leaders and members of Aisyiyah. For example, Fig. 3.1 depicts a religious family with two children who are wearing simple clothes; it shares much with Salafi interpretations, a phenomenon that is gaining support among Muhammadiyah members (Burhani 2013; Fuad 2002). The importance of family has also been voiced by Nasyiatul Aisyiyah, the younger women's wing of Muhammadiyah. It developed a program called the Movement for Strong Young Families or Gerakan Keluarga Muda Tangguh (PPNA 2020). This program includes ten pillars that should be implemented in each family (Nasyiatul Aisyiyah 2019).[15]

Muslimat also supports the idea that a family is the basis of a woman's duty. The concept of *keluarga maslahah* has become the core of all activities of women in the NU circle. The concept has been endorsed in various NU publications and at its events, and it was created as a response to the state's campaign on family planning (Menchik 2014; van Doorn-Harder 2006, 2013). The NU's website promotes that 'the *maslahah* family is a concept for a happy, prosperous, and obedient family following the religious teachings within NU. A *maslahah* family is a family that can meet and maintain its primary (principal) needs, both physically and mentally. The fulfilment or maintenance of physical needs means that the family is free from the bondage of poverty and physical illness' (NU online 2012). Further, the NU published guidance on a *maslahah* family:

The characteristics of the *maslahah* family (*mashalihul usrah*) is family that has the following elements:

1. A pious husband and wife, namely those who can bring benefits for themselves, their children and their environment, so that their behaviours and actions are reflected accordingly and [they] can be role models (*uswatun hasanah*) for their children and others.
2. Children who are good (*abrar*), with noble characters, and good spiritual and physical health. And that they are productive and creative so that in time they can live independently and not be a burden to others or society.
3. Each is good in their social relations among members of family and with others. Family members who know their environment and have good relationships with neighbours without sacrificing their principles and beliefs.

4. Adequate sustenance (clothing, food, and housing). That is, a family does not have to be rich or abundant in wealth, the important thing is to be able to support life and family life, from the needs of clothing, food and housing, education costs, and worship (NU online 2012, translated by the author).

Fig. 3.1 A pamphlet on the concept of a harmonious family by Aisyiyah in 2019 (*Source* Keluarga Sakinah [Basri 2019])

This concept has been developed and implemented by an institution called the Nahdlatul Ulama Institute for Family Welfare (Lembaga Kemaslahatan Keluarga NU [LKKNU]) (Menchik 2014; van Doorn-Harder 2006: 230). LKKNU is a not-for-profit institution under the umbrella of Nahdlatul Ulama that operates within the Department of Population, Family Planning and Environment of NU. The adoption of family planning by Muslimat and NU in its board structure is a result of interaction with the government during the Suharto era. This institution was created in response to the government program of family planning and to date it works closely with the BKKBN office for promoting the family planning program.

Fostering Businesses of Aisyiyah Members

With the principle of *keluarga sakinah*, Aisyiyah has taken a lead in assisting members to develop their business skills, either in collaboration with its existing traditional social business institutions called *amal usaha* (such as orphanages, hospitals and schools) or separate activities organised under the framework of entrepreneurship. Aisyiyah's entrepreneurship programs have led to the creation of microfinance institutions, enterprises, mompreneurs and its networking and training institutions.

For example, in 2010, Aisyiyah reported to have run 12 Islamic microfinance institutions 49 shops, four life-skill programs, 87 home industries, 157 family-based enterprises, 1,578 micro and small enterprises run by women, as well as 639 revolving capital loans groups or KUBE (Setiawati 2010). In 2020, it reported having 568 cooperatives and 1,426 Aisyiyah Economic Business Development entities or Bina Usaha Ekonomi Aisyiyah (BUEKA) (PP Aisyiyah 2020). Designed to assist mompreneurs, the activities of Aisyiyah outlined above are interrelated. In addition to activating government-driven programs such as cooperatives and KUBE, Aisyiyah created BUEKA, the Aisyiyah Entrepreneurship School (Sekolah Wirausaha Aisyiyah [SWA]) and the Aisyiyah Entrepreneurs Association (Ikatan Pengusaha Aisyiyah [IPAS]). These three organisations have been developed as entrepreneurial incubator programs to facilitate Aisyiyah's members to enhance their entrepreneurial skills and to increase their access and capital. This has become an opportunity where mompreneurs can earn an income for their families without neglecting their household duties (Afsiah et al. 2018; Djohantini et al. 2016).

All three programs target types of businesses that are considered to be an extension of women's domestic work. Aisyiyah's Council for Economics and Employment endorses its members becoming Muslim mompreneurs to support their family's welfare (Aisyiyah Jawa Tengah, n.d.). Aisyiyah encourages business activities that align with women's daily activities, and so have unintentionally encouraged members to work in feminised jobs, such as beauty and make-up, and to open traditional shops, beauty salons and the like (AFN 2019; Aisyiyah 2016).

The idea of womenpreneurs or mompreneurs is well accepted among the Aisyiyah members as part of *keluarga sakinah*. At a training session in 2019, the chief of Aisyiyah, Siti Noordjannah Djohantini, stated that one of the organisation's missions was 'advancing the economy and entrepreneurship towards improving quality of life' (Sakinah 2019). Entrepreneurship is one of their programs and is designed to empower women. Aisyiyah's mompreneurship supports the state-endorsed gender role that maintains that the role of women is to be a wife and a mother, and to care for the family's welfare.

Muslimat: Incorporating Traditional Business with Entrepreneurship

Muslimat encourages entrepreneurship through traditional businesses embedded in *pesantrens* with a focus on the idea of *keluarga maslahah*. In this way, Muslimat operates cooperatives, micro economy businesses, small loans programs and other small businesses (van Doorn-Harder 2006: 209). In 2015, Muslimat reported having 131 registered cooperatives and 10 job training centres (Parawansa 2015: 195). In 2020, it reported operating 154 cooperatives, 11 job training centres and 355 service outlets for members of cooperatives (Muslimat NU 2020).

Muslimat locates entrepreneurship under the Department of the Economy, Cooperatives and Agribusiness in the framework of developing the economic needs of rural communities. The leadership of the Muslimat organisation consists of wives of Nahdlatul Ulama elites and public figures. Its members are mainly married Muslim women aged 40 or older and who were raised within the culture of *pesantren*. Even though *pesantren* are 'patriarchal institutions that offer little space for women in public context' they have gendered aspects where women play an important role in the reproduction of the culture, but women do not get directly involved in business activities (Smith and Woodward 2013: 3). Business and entrepreneurial activities among members of Muslimat (and Nahdlatul Ulama) are mainly limited to supporting the needs of Islamic boarding schools. Women are expected to support their husband and family members in managing *pesantren* to propagate Islam (Mulyani 2007; Smith and Woodward 2013; van Doorn-Harder 2006). For example, NU did not support women to assume leadership positions except for in emergencies. In 1999, it withdrew support for Megawati Sukarnoputri to become the elected president (Robinson 2004), but supported Abdurrahman Wahid, NU chairman, to become President of Indonesia along with Vice President Megawati Sukarnoputri. In Islamic businesses, an NU-affiliated Muslim woman who took up the position of managing BMT said she was undertaking her role because of the lack of suitable male managers (Sakai and Fauzia 2016).

Reflecting NU's support for male leadership has prevailed in Islamic boarding schools and their businesses; women do not appear to be at the forefront of running businesses. Instead, some women affiliated with NU have made a presence in politics and NGO sectors. For example, both Yenny and Alissa Wahid, daughters of the former President Abdurrahman Wahid, have a high profile, running established NGOs in Indonesia related to civil society and politics. The Wahid Institute (2021) run by Yenny Wahid as Director collaborates with international organisations for research and advocacy. Khofifah Indar Parawansa, the Chairperson of Muslimat since 1999 and continuing in 2021, served a number of times as a government minister, and now as the Governor of East Java. Whether rural NU members and Muslimat women see Parawansa's prominent political role significantly affecting the existing patriarchal gender norms remains to be seen.

Our discussions in December 2016 in Surabaya, located in the heartland of NU members, with leaders of Muslim women's organisations and female entrepreneurs, uncovered important enablers for Muslimat mompreneurs. Women's entrepreneurship is supported in a specific context where the business is a part of *kyai* family and the economy of *pesantren* is mainly based on sharing work and community welfare (Isbah 2012, 2016; Sakai and Marijan 2008). Muslimat's engagement with government programs has been increasing since the Abdurrahman Wahid presidency in 1999. Government support for women's economic empowerment comes from various ministries and agencies, such as the BKKBN, the Ministry of Cooperatives, the Ministry of Women's Empowerment and many others.[16] Collaboration with private corporations is also designed to improve mompreneurs' digital literacy. An example of these collaborations has seen the development of a training program with Gojek in 2019 (Catriana 2019). These collaborations assist Muslim women in developing small businesses and literacy in digital technology for mompreneurs, predominantly in feminised sectors such as fashion and cookery.

Pesantren used to run businesses through a business unit called *kopontren* to support the financial costs to run their education and this has led to some *pesantren* developing microfinancing institutions. Recently they have moved to making use of digital markets and applications (DISKUK Jabar—Dinas Koperasi dan Usaha Kecil Jawa Barat 2020). Wives of the *pesantren* leaders who have digital literacy could potentially support their husbands, although women are not usually encouraged to be directly involved in *kopontren* businesses (Isbah 2012).

In comparison to other Muslim countries, such as Saudi Arabia, the way Muslimat and other Indonesian Muslim women's organisations conduct their entrepreneurial activities is relatively unhindered by social and religious barriers.[17] Training activities organised by Muslimat are conducted in the mixed gender public space (Wulandari 2019). Diverse religious authorities, including some from Nahdlatul Ulama, allow Muslim women to study and work together with male counterparts and this became an important factor for cultivating a conducive climate for entrepreneurship. Various digital business platforms have seen women as a potential agency in their business and have offered literacy and opportunities for women. For example, Gojek provides training for women in collaboration with Aisyiyah and Muslimat (Eviyanti 2019; Wulandari 2019).

IPEMI: Aspiring to Become a Muslimah Mompreneur

The Indonesian Muslim Women Entrepreneurs Association (Ikatan Pengusaha Muslimah Indonesia [IPEMI]) espoused the idea that successful Muslim mompreneurs need to be engaged in devotional acts, such as through Islamic study groups and have spousal approval for and blessings on their activities. This organisation was established in 2015 to assist Muslim women entrepreneurs to develop their businesses. Growing within the era of strong government support for the people's economy and the Islamic economy, IPEMI has a strong inclination towards implementing the Islamic economy and promoting Islamic-only businesses, supporting halal industries, practising devotional acts, following Islamic teachings and engaging in Islamic charity. Accordingly, its members and the targets of its assistance are also strictly Muslim.

However, IPEMI's articulation of religious narratives and practices operates within the framework of supporting Indonesian nationalism. The objective of IPEMI is to contribute to the creation of a stronger Indonesian economy through encouraging small and micro enterprises (PP IPEMI 2021). In a number of publications and activities, its stated long-term target is 'to be the largest organisation for Muslim women entrepreneurs in Indonesia which is beneficial for the prosperity of Muslim women and the Indonesian people in general. Female entrepreneurship should aim to achieve economic independence with an Indonesian character and noble morality' (PP IPEMI 2021). IPEMI's effort to develop Muslim mompreneurs has been an inspiration to support a new role model for Muslim business women (Sakai 2019).

IPEMI's founders, M. Lutfi Handayani, Nur Wahidah Saleh and Ingrid Kansil came from three societal groups, intellectual Muslims who are members of ICMI, Muslim women activists who own and lead Islamic study groups (*majelis taklim*), and Muslim businesspersons and public figures. *Majelis taklim,* an Islamic study group network, provided a strong basis for the establishment of IPEMI, as the founders thought it could support the economic empowerment of Muslim women. 'After attending study [*majelis taklim*] at homes and at mosques, we saw many mothers opened stalls, selling products such as *hijabs* and various culinary delights. From there, we thought that there should be a platform to help them increase the productivity of their businesses' (Farah 2018). Tuti Alawiyah, whom they consulted, supported the idea that *majelis taklim* could be utilised for supporting female business development. Nurhayati Subakat, a well-known Muslim businesswoman and the CEO of the nation-wide *halal* cosmetics brand Wardah, also joined the organisation as the Chair of the Board of IPEMI.[18] With a high-profile celebrity wife—Ingrid Kansil—as the chair, IPEMI grew to attract public support and members within a short period of time. Ingrid is a former model and well-known figure in Indonesia. She is married to Syarief Hasan, a politician and member of parliament from the Democrat Party, who served as Minister of Cooperatives between 2009 and 2014. With the involvement of high-profile figures and the informal engagement with the Ministry of Cooperatives, IPEMI aims to promote both Indonesian nationalism and Islamic values through their support for female entrepreneurship.

The aims of IPEMI's programs range from recruiting Muslim women members who are involved in entrepreneurship activities, and assisting their businesses, to a more global aspiration of enhancing the Muslim community and contribution of Muslim women entrepreneurs to national development (IPEMI 2015; Sakai 2019).

IPEMI promotes a vision of womanhood that turns Muslim women's domestic role into economic activities to demonstrate that she is a good Indonesian citizen adhering to Islamic faith. This vision has been influenced by the recent increase in the propagation of Islam that supports *halal* industries. IPEMI intends to attract three types of Muslim women: successful Muslim businesswomen, aspiring Muslim businesswomen and Muslim women who want to earn an additional income for their family. In 2021, IPEMI claimed to have 3 million members, scattered across all 34 provinces of Indonesia, in 340 districts and cities, and it has overseas members from 16 countries, including Saudi Arabia, the USA, Australia and Russia.

IPEMI has worked in collaboration with government, corporations and NGOs to achieve its aims by encouraging more Muslim women to be entrepreneurs. IPEMI has supported entrepreneurship in feminised sectors, and they promote sharia-compliant businesses. For example, it initiated the development of 1000 units of *halal* kiosks and women-only Muslim beauty salons for its members (JPPN 2017). Their focus to promote feminised sectors is similar to that of the Aisyiyah and Muslimat organisations, where the majority of mompreneurs businesses are in fashion, catering and trades.

IPEMI is a new form of a women's business association that is based on Islamic values. According to IPEMI, the main difference from IWAPI is their approaches to business. IPEMI advocates that meetings and business networking activities should not conflict with a woman's primary duties as a mother and wife. They follow Tuti Alawiyah as a role model of a wife and mother who succeeded in becoming a nation-wide preacher and used her Islamic study groups as a way to empower other women (Interview, Nur Wahidah 2 December 2017). They also organised regular study group meetings in each IPEMI branches (Rahman 2017).[19] IPEMI advocates that Muslim women should not compromise their primary duties, as dictated by their gender, in favour of conducting their business activities.

Islamic teachings, according to IPEMI, will become important values for guiding business activities and development, as there is a balance between life in the world and in the afterlife (*dunia dan akhirat*). Islamic study group activities have been crucial to IPEMI's development. Kansil argues that religious teachings could protect businesspersons from negative competition and the Islamic brotherhood creates a network of mutual aid among members (Farah 2018). To strengthen Islamic devotional acts (*ibadah*), as well as to facilitate communication among members who are spread across Indonesia, IPEMI publishes a monthly magazine called *ibadah*, which promotes 'The Islamic Way of Life, Sharia Economy and Community'. This magazine is a means to strengthen and promote a role modelling of IPEMI leaders as ideal Muslim mompreneurs who are religious, modern and working for family care. For example, edition of April–May 2016 depicts Ingrid Kansil and the chief of both the Jakarta branch of IPEMI and of Nusantara SMEs (UKM/IKM Nusantara), Candra Manggih Rahayu, as inspiration for other Muslim mompreneurs (Fig. 3.2).

IPEMI, in the words of Lutfi, supports the idea that women should have the opportunity to engage in entrepreneurship, even to work outside the home and in the public arena, but ultimately that they must remain adherent to Islamic teachings, namely that they fall under the supremacy of men, who are leaders of the household (interview, 2 December 2017). IPEMI advocates that spousal permission is essential for women to be able to work and this practice is strictly implemented at IPEMI. 'Permission from one's husband' for working and going outside home, has been an important subject of discussion in religious circles and has become a key indicator to the level of women's participation in the public sphere, although divorce is common and, in reality, women have to support themselves financially.[20] In our interview with Ibu Nur Wahidah, she often highlighted the examples of Ingrid Kansil in handling the demands of her family and her role as the chair of the organisation. Wahidah explained, 'Mrs Ingrid always said "Our meetings should take place after I have discharged my obligations at home. My husband is still here, sorry." She does not wish to run any meetings when her husband is around not to disturb him' (Interview, 2 December 2017). Our research on BMT female managers finds that spousal permission has been one of the significant strategies for women in their negotiation for the right to work, and in practice is being used as a formality (Sakai and Fauzia 2016). Religiosity and family are two important aspects for Muslim mompreneurs. When asked about tips for other mompreneurs on how to be successful, Kansil mentioned three. The first is to declare the work as *ibadah*, secondly,

Fig. 3.2 *Ibadah* magazine cover titled Muslim mompreneurs as inspirators for change (*Source* IPEMI *Ibadah* magazine [2016])

one should get permission from their husband, and the third is to keep a network (Farah 2018).

IPEMI and other Muslim women's organisations construct images and discourses about ideal Muslim womanhood. They represent a role model of Muslim women who are pious (*sholihah*) yet modern, loyal and respectable wives, responsible mothers working for the welfare of family and community. They share traits with the wives of the prophet.

With support from these Muslim women's organisations, ample business opportunities are emerging for Indonesian Muslim women to become mompreneurs, using online or offline platforms. Becoming a mompreneur is seen to be following Islamic teachings and a part of devotional acts (*ibadah*) and Islamic propagation (*dakwah*). Their discourses on ideal womanhood pose no contestations upon an accepted ideal endorsed by the government and in line with the concepts of family harmony and wellbeing. These organisations, especially Aisyiyah and Muslimat, have used the concept of family welfare to negotiate womanhood since their early establishment, such as through voluntary work in the areas of early childhood, women's education, health and orphanages. Muslimat, Aisyiyah and IPEMI are examples of how Muslim women's organisations are actively responding to the idea of mompreneurs and are developing programs to support entrepreneurship.

Women's business organisations such as IWAPI have also responded to the increasing popularity of entrepreneurships, which accommodates growing trends of Islamic Syariah. Cultural and structural support for Muslim women in becoming mompreneurs is exemplified in Chapters 5 and 6 of this book. As illustrated in this chapter, women's organisations and government support are two important enablers for the growth of Muslim mompreneurs in Indonesia.

Conclusion

This chapter has shown that in comparison to other Muslim countries, Indonesia presents a unique case of supporting Muslim mompreneurs. A combination of support from government policies, informal training provided by the state-endorsed patriarchy that encouraged mothers to learn how to start a business, resource opportunities from grassroots networking and incubators created through specifically Islamic business opportunities, as well as active Muslim women's organisations have all made significant contributions to setting the conditions for the increase in Muslim mompreneurs. The state's policy has been gender neutral, intending to support entrepreneurship for both males and females, and it is indiscriminate in terms of religion. Yet the extensive organisational networks that exist for women have provided resources for Muslim women to take agency in developing entrepreneurship.

The entrepreneurial sector in Indonesia is growing in feminised sectors, due to the large involvement of Muslim women as owners of micro, small and medium enterprises. In addition to the government, Muslim organisations offer significant support to female entrepreneurship. These organisations offer training programs that align with the government's concept of state-sponsored patriarchy, which conforms with mainstream interpretations of Islamic teachings that allow women to work to support their family with permission from their husbands. Muslim women's organisations have actively engaged in and become supporters of women's economic activities. This particular expectation places demands on women to balance their career aspirations and family life, and so entrepreneurship has been identified as one of the viable solutions to the problem of balancing these competing life choices. While motherhood could become an agency for mompreneurs, societal expectation of ideal womanhood brings challenges to unmarried Muslim women. The next chapter will discuss how Muslim women, including unmarried career women, negotiate the gender expectation.

Notes

1. USD 1 = Rp 14,000 (April 2021).
2. See Chapter 6 for youth entrepreneurship training at the university level.
3. From the Suharto to Joko Widodo periods, the name of this ministry has changed a number of times that in principle has modified descriptors of national education, culture and research. When referring to this ministry, this chapter will use the Ministry of Education, unless referring to it in the context of a specific period.
4. See more on this issue in Chapter 6.
5. The name of this ministry has changed over time. For consistency and simplicity, this chapter will use the Ministry of Cooperatives, unless referring to it in the context of a specific period.
6. The Suharto administration created the Ministry of Women in 1983 which slightly changed its name to the Ministry of Women's Affairs in 1998. But President Abdurrahman Wahid renamed it the Ministry of Women's Empowerment in 1999. It has a strong value of reforming society for

the benefit of women who are powerless under state-sponsored *ibuism* (using the phrase *urusan wanita*) and empowering women (using the word *pemberdayaan perempuan*). In 2009, President Susilo Bambang Yudhoyono renamed this the Ministry of Women's Empowerment and Child Protection, showing the government emphasises gender development. This is the current name of the ministry at the time of writing in 2021.

7. The other four priorities are; violence against women and girls, political participation, gender responsive social protection and gender responsive budgeting.
8. This research was conducted in three provinces of West Java, South Sulawesi and West Nusa Tenggara from 2018 to 2021 in collaboration with Home Affairs and offices of cooperatives in provinces and districts.
9. A husband's low income provides one reason for women to work. This phenomenon is found in developing Asian countries (Tambunan 2009). Civil servants during the New Order period had relatively low incomes, which often resulted in corruption (Gray 1979).
10. An international agenda in the 1960s including women's issues in development projects was seen as a way to engage women in growing economies. The Indonesian government adopted this agenda (later gender and development).
11. Islamist groups such as the Welfare and Justice Party (PKS) and the banned Hizbut Tahrir Indonesia (HTI) tend to follow the Salafi understanding and way of living that created communities such as *hijabers*.
12. In February 2020, the committee was renamed Komite Nasional Ekonomi dan Keuangan Syariah (KNEKS). The revision shows the emphasis on the economy of Syariah. The KNEKS developed its Master Plan for a Syariah Economy and was led by the president and nine head of ministries and agencies related to the economy and finance.
13. See the case of Bogor City in Chapter 6.
14. Ahlu Sunnah Wal Jamaah is a group committed to following the Sunnah of the Prophet Muhammad and mainly follow the Sunni Islam.
15. They are (1) Sturdy Akidah and Akhlakul Karimah; (2) Physical, Spiritual, and Environmental Health; (3) Independence; (4) Justice with the Spirit of Al-Ma'un; (5) Peace Mission; (6) Democracy; (7) Anti-Violence; (8) Equality of Access; (9) Eco-Friendly/Ecofamily; and (10) Disaster Response. Each of these pillars will become a spiritual value in the family and also in the Nasyiatul Aisyiyah program of activities during this period (Nasyiatul Aisyiyah 2019).
16. My interview with the Chair of Muslimat in West Nusa Tenggara in 2019 found that Muslimat has been actively collaborating with government offices at the provincial and district/city levels. They received a grant from the Ministry of Marines for developing business and entrepreneurial

skills of the wives of fishermen in a number of fishing villages, and from the Ministry of Manpower to strengthen women's literacy and economy within immigrant worker villages.

17. See Chapter 2.
18. See Chapter 5 for the case study of Nurhayati Subakat.
19. For women's Islamic study groups see Chapter 5.
20. See Chapter 2.

References

Ab Rahman, Asmak. 2018. *New Developments in Islamic Economics: Examples from Southeast Asia*. Bingley: Emerald Publishing Limited.

Adzmy, Fadzryl Muhammad, and Fikri Disyacitta. 2018. The Indonesian Family Welfare Guidance Programme (PKK) and the Revitalisation of Corporatist State Organisations: A Case Study of the Mobilisation of Support for Dewanti Rumpoko in the 2017 Batu Municipal Election. *Power Conflict Democracy* 6 (1): 1–30. https://doi.org/10.22146/pcd.31291.

AFN. 2019. Geliat Ekonomi Umat PCA Aisyiyah Bina Usaha Ekonomi Keluarga. *Yogya Pos*. Retrieved from https://www.yogyapos.com/berita-geliat-ekonomi-umat-pca-aisyiyah-bina-usaha-ekonomi-keluarga-307.

Afsiah, Nurul, Muslich Anshori, and Imron Mawardi. 2018. Analysis of Women Social Entrepreneurship on Micro and Small Enterprises. *Journal of Innovation in Business and Economy* 2 (1): 1–12. https://doi.org/10.22219/jibe.v2i01.5736.

Aisyiyah Jawa Tengah. n.d. Kegiatan-Kegiatan Majelis Ekonomi Aisyiyah. http://jateng.aisyiyah.or.id/id/page/majelis-ekonomi-dan-ketenagakerjaan.html. Accessed 17 Oct 2020.

Aisyiyah, Majelis Ekonomi dan Ketenagakerjaan. 2016. Kegiatan Pelatihan Delfit. http://ekonomi.aisyiyah.or.id/id/galeri/foto/kegiatan-pelatihan-delfit/824.html. Accessed 28 Oct 2021.

Asmara, Galang. 2021. Implementation of Concept 'Halal Tourism' in Nusa Tenggara Barat and Their Effect in Increasing Number of Tourists. *Advances in Social Science, Education and Humanities Research, Atlantis Press* 605: 108–113.

Azarbaijani-Moghaddam, Sippi. 2014. *Gender Inclusion Strategies in PNPM*. World Bank. https://openknowledge.worldbank.org/handle/10986/22128. Accessed 10 Aug 2021.

Azhari, G., M.N. Syechalad, and MS Abd Majid. 2017. The Role of Cooperative in the Indonesian Economy. *International Journal of Humanities and Social Science Invention* 6 (10): 43–46.

Badan Ekonomi Kreatif (BEKRAF). 2017. Data Statistik dan Hasil Survei Ekonomi Kreatif, Kerjasama Badan Ekonomi Kreatif dan Badan Pusat

Statistik. Badan Ekonomi Kreatif. https://www.kemenparekraf.go.id/asset_admin/assets/uploads/media/pdf/media_1589840584_Data_Statistik_dan_Hasil_Survey_Ekraf_2015.pdf. Accessed 20 Nov 2021.

Badan Ekonomi Kreatif (BEKRAF). 2018. Opus, Ekonomi Kreatif Outlook 2019. Badan Ekonomi Kreatif (BEKRAF). https://www.kemenparekraf.go.id/asset_admin/assets/uploads/media/pdf/media_1589839384_OPUS_-_Creative_Economy_Outlook_2019_(Indonesia_Version).pdf. Accessed 10 Aug 2021.

Badan Penelitian dan Pengembangan Pusat Kurikulum. 2010. *Bahan Pelatihan Penguatan Metodologi Pembelajaran Berdasarkan Nilai-Nilai Budaya Untuk Membentuk Daya Saing dan Karakter Bangsa: Pengembangan Pendidikan Budaya dan Karakter Bangsa*. Jakarta: Kementerian Pendidikan Nasional, Badan Penelitian dan Pengembangan, Republik Indonesia.

BAPPENAS. 2018. *Indonesia Islamic Economic Masterplan 2019–2024*. Jakarta: Kementerian Perencanaan Pembangunan Nasional/Badan Perencanaan Pembangunan Nasional. Available at: https://knks.go.id/storage/upload/1560308022-Indonesia%20Islamic%20Economic%20Masterplan%202019-2024.pdf.

Basri, Muhammad Ridha. 2019. Keluarga Sakinah. Suara Muhammadiyah. https://suaramuhammadiyah.id/2019/12/02/keluarga-sakinah-2/. Accessed 1 May 2021.

Bergeaud-Blackler, Florence, Johan Fischer, and John Lever. 2016. *Halal Matters: Islam, Politics and Markets in Global Perspective*. Abingdon, NY: Routledge.

Blackburn, Susan. 2004. *Women and the State in Modern Indonesia*. New York: Cambridge University Press.

Burhani, Ahmad Najib. 2013. Liberal and Conservative Discourses in the Muhammadiyah: The Struggle for the Face of Reformist Islam in Indonesia. In *Contemporary Developments in Indonesian Islam Explaining the "Conservative Turn"*, ed. Martin van Bruinessen, 105–144. Singapore: ISEAS Publishing.

Catriana, Elsa. 2019. Ikut Pelatihan Gojek Wirausaha Ribuan Muslimat NU Siap Go Digital. https://money.kompas.com/read/2019/12/12/160547526/ikut-pelatihan-gojek-wirausaha-ribuan-muslimat-nu-siap-go-digital. Accessed 10 Sept 2021.

Chin, Grace V.S., and Kathrina Mohd Daud. 2018. *The Southeast Asian Woman Writes Back: Gender, Identity and Nation in the Literatures of Brunei Darussalam, Malaysia, Singapore, Indonesia and the Philippines*. Singapore: Springer.

Darandono. 2017. Pertaruhan Ndang Sutisna Kembang Duniahalal.Com. SWA. https://swa.co.id/swa/trends/pertaruhan-ndang-sutisna-kembang-duniahalal-com. Accessed 1 May 2021.

DinarStandard. 2020. *2020/21 State of the Global Islamic Economy Report Thriving in Uncertainty*. Dubai Islamic Economy Development Center. Available at: https://www.salaamgateway.com/reports/state-of-the-global-islamic-economy-202021-report-2.

DISKUK Jabar—Dinas Koperasi dan Usaha Kecil Jawa Barat. 2020. Koperasi Pondok Pesantren (Kopontren) Al Muhajirin Kembangkan Inovasi Berbasis Digital. http://diskuk.jabarprov.go.id/2020/03/11/koperasi-pondok-pesantren-kopontren-al-muhajirin-kembangkan-inovasi-berbasis-digital/. Accessed 10 Aug 2021.

Djohantini, Siti Noordjannah, Zainudin Fanani, Sri Endarwati, Laras Wiendyawati, Nurul Ngaini, and Ni'mah Afidati. 2016. *Buku Panduan Bueka (Bina Usaha Ekonomi Keluarga Aisyiyah)*. Yogyakarta: Majelis Ekonomi Pimpinan Pusat Aisyiyah.

Ernita, Ernita. 2014. Partisipasi Perempuan dalam Pengembangan Koperasi dan UMKM di Indonesia. *Jurnal Al Ulum* 2 (1): 19–24.

Eviyanti, Ade. 2019. Sekolah Wirausaha Aisyiyah Sidoarjo Gelar Kuliah Umum 'Belajar Marketing Bersama Gojek'. https://pwmu.co/111180/09/27/sekolah-wirausaha-aisyiyah-sidoarjo-gelar-kuliah-umum-belajar-marketing-bersama-gojek/. Accessed 27 Sept 2019.

Farah. 2018. Ingrid Kansil: Menyelaraskan Entrepreneurship Dengan Peningkatan Akidah. *Farah Magazine*. https://www.farah.id/read/2018/10/08/191/menyelaraskan-enterpreneurship-dengan-peningkatan-aqidah?page=1. Accessed 8 Oct 2021.

Fauzia, Amelia, Minako Sakai, Felix Tan, Sri Hidayati, Elvi Fetrina, and Haula Noor. 2021. *Pemberdayaan Ekonomi Perempuan Muslim Berbasis Teknologi Digital dan Nilai Toleransi*. Jakarta: Social Trust Fund UIN Jakarta.

Fischer, Johan. 2011. *The Halal Frontier: Muslim Consumers in a Globalized Market*. New York: Palgrave Macmillan.

Fischer, Johan. 2017. Middle-Class Projects in Modern Malaysia. *Asian Anthropology* 16 (1): 54–69. https://doi.org/10.1080/1683478X.2016.1270030.

Fuad, Muhammad. 2002. Civil Society in Indonesia: The Potential and Limits of Muhammadiyah. *SOJOURN: Journal of Social Issues in Southeast Asia* 17 (2): 133–163.

Global Business Guide Indonesia. 2016a. Indonesia Aiming to Be the Islamic Fashion Capital by 2020. http://www.gbgindonesia.com/en/manufacturing/article/2016/indonesia_aiming_to_be_the_islamic_fashion_capital_by_2020_11646.php. Accessed 28 Oct 2021.

Global Business Guide Indonesia. 2016b. Indonesia SMEs: Increased Government Support to Overcome Challenges. http://www.gbgindonesia.com/en/main/why_indonesia/2016/indonesia_smes_increased_government_support_to_overcome_challenges_11603.php. Accessed 28 Oct 2021.

Global Business Guide Indonesia. 2016c. Indonesia's Garment and Textile; Short Term Woes. GBGI. http://www.gbgindonesia.com/en/manufacturing/article/2016c/indonesia_s_garment_and_textile_sector_short_term_woes_11512.php. Accessed 28 Oct 2021.

Gray, Clive. 1979. Civil Service Compensation in Indonesia. *Bulletin of Indonesian Economic Studies* 15 (1): 85–113.

Hasan, Noorhaidi. 2009. The Making of Public Islam: Piety, Agency, and Commodification on the Landscape of the Indonesian Public Sphere. *Contemporary Islam* 3 (3): 229–250. https://doi.org/10.1007/s11562-009-0096-9.

Hasan, Noorhaidi. 2011. Islam in Provincial Indonesia: Middle Class, Lifestyle, and Democracy. *Al-Jami'ah* 49 (1): 119–158.

Hastuti, Filaili, Priambada Rizki, Akhmadi Rizki, Bambang Soelaksono, Hariyanti Sdaly, et al. 2003a. *Buku I: Peta Upaya Penguatan Usaha Mikro/Kecil di Tingkat Pusat Tahun 1997–2003*, December 2003. Jakarta: Lembaga Penelitian SMERU. Available at: https://smeru.or.id/id/content/buku-i-peta-upaya-penguatan-usaha-mikrokecil-di-tingkat-pusat-tahun-1997-2003.

Hastuti, Sulaksono, Febriany Bambang, Perwira Vita, Akhmadi Daniel, Wawan Munawar, et al. 2003b. *Buku Ii: Upaya Penguatan Usaha Mikro Dalam Rangka Peningkatan Ekonomi Perempuan (Sukabumi, Bantul, Kebumen, Padang, Surabaya, Makassar)*. Jakarta: Lembaga Penelitian SMERU. Available at: https://smeru.or.id/id/content/buku-ii-upaya-penguatan-usaha-mikro-dalam-rangka-peningkatan-ekonomi-perempuan-sukabumi.

Hatta, Mohammad. 2019. *The Co-Operative Movement in Indonesia*, 1957. Ithaca, NY: Cornell University Press.

Hefner, Robert W. 2003. Islamizing Capitalism: On the Founding of Indonesia's First Islamic Bank. In *Shari'a and Politics in Modern Indonesia*, eds. Azyumardi Azra and Arskal Salim, 148–167. Singapore: ISEAS Publishing.

Holtzappel, Coen J. G., and Martin Ramstedt. 2009. *Decentralization and Regional Autonomy in Indonesia: Implementation and Challenges*. Singapore: ISEAS Publishing.

IPEMI. 2015. *Program Kerja IPEMI Periode 2015–2020*. Ikatan Pengusaha Wanita Muslimah Indonesia. https://www.facebook.com/ipemi.muslimah/posts/program-kerja-ipemiperiode-2015-2020a-program-jangka-pendek-1-2-tahun1-pembentuk/104696396533639/. Accessed 7 Apr 2021.

Isbah, M. Falikul. 2012. Religiously Committed and Prosperously Develop: The Survival of Pesantren Salaf in Modern Indonesian Islamic Education. *Review of Indonesian and Malaysian Affairs* 46 (1): 83–104.

Isbah, M. Falikul. 2016. Examining the Socio-Economic Role of Islamic Boarding Schools (*Pesantren*) in Indonesia. PhD Thesis, School of Humanities and Social Sciences Canberra, UNSW.

IWAPI, DPP. 2015. Sejarah & Tokoh Pendiri Ikatan Wanita Pengusaha Indonesia (IWAPI). http://iwapi.id/profile-mission/. Accessed 1 June 2020.

IWAPI, Humas DPP. 2021. Pengajian Online Doa Bersama untuk Indonesia. Facebook.com. https://web.facebook.com/1609508689343669/photos/a.1623308954630309/2622159724745222/. Accessed 12 Oct 2021.

Jabbar, Abi Abdul. 2018. Koperasi Wanita Patra Bukti Perempuan Bisa Berdikari. https://www.madaninews.id/2332/koperasi-wanita-patra-bukti-perempuan-bisa-berdikari.html. Accessed 30 Nov 2020.

JPPN. 2017. 30 Warung dan Salon Muslimah IPEMI di Bekasi Diresmikan. *JPPN*, August 30. Retrieved from https://www.jpnn.com/news/30-warung-dan-salon-muslimah-ipemi-di-bekasi-diresmikan.

Jurriëns, Edwin, and Ross Tapsell. 2017. *Digital Indonesia: Connectivity and Divergence*. Singapore: ISEAS-Yusof Ishak Institute.

Kementerian Koperasi dan UKM. 2019 'Rekapitulasi Bantuan Pemerintah bagi Wirausaha Pemula per Propinsi 2015–2019' Indonesia, Kementerian Koperasi dan UKM Republik. Jakarta: Kementerian Koperasi dan UKM, Republik Indonesia. Available at: https://kemenkopukm.go.id/uploads/laporan/1602752668_Wirausaha%20Pemula%20(2015-2019).pdf.

Kementerian Koperasi dan UKM. 2021. Data Usaha Mikro, Kecil, Menengah (UMKM) dan Usaha Besar (UB) Tahun 2018–2019. https://www.kemenkopukm.go.id/data-umkm. Accessed 20 Oct 2021.

Kementerian Pemberdayaan Perempuan dan Perlindungan Anak. 2018. *Laporan Tahunan Pengarusutamaan Gender (PUG)*. Jakarta: Kementerian Pemberdayaan Perempuan dan Perlindungan Anak (KPPA), Republik Indonesia.

Kementerian Pemberdayaan Perempuan dan Perlindungan Anak. 2019. *Laporan Tahunan Pengarusutamaan Gender (PUG)*. Jakarta: Kementerian Pemberdayaan Perempuan dan Perlindungan Anak (KPPA), Republik Indonesia.

KNEKS. 2020. Indonesia Menuju Pusat Halal Dunia. https://knks.go.id/storage/upload/1603506992-Siaran%20Pers%20Webinar%20Strategis%20-%20Indonesia%20Menuju%20Pusat%20Halal%20Dunia%20FINAL.pdf. Accessed 20 Apr 2021.

Kominfo, Deyon. 2021. BPSDMP Kominfo Yogyakarta Gelar Pelatihan IT untuk Eks Pekerja Migran. Dinas Komunikasi dan Informatika Kabupaten Cilacap. https://kominfo.cilacapkab.go.id/bpsdmp-kominfo-yogyakarta-gelar-pelatihan-it-untuk-eks-pekerja-migran/. Accessed 13 Dec 2021.

KPPPA. 2019. Menteri Bintang Ingin Perempuan Jadi Pahlawan Ekonomi Keluarga. Publikasi dan Media Kementerian Pemberdayaan Perempuan dan Perlindungan Anak. https://www.kemenpppa.go.id/index.php/page/read/29/2442/menteri-bintang-ingin-perempuan-jadi-pahlawan-ekonomi-keluarga. Accessed 7 July 2021.

Kusmana. 2017. Contemporary Interpretation of Kodrat Perempuan: Local Discourse of Muslim Women's Leadership in Indonesia. PhD Thesis, Erasmus University.

Lindblad, Thomas J. 2002. The Later Colonial State and Economic Expansion, 1900–1930s. In *The Emergence of a National Economy, an Economic History of Indonesia, 1800–2000*, eds. Howard Dick, Vincent Houben, Thomas Linblad, and Thee Kian Wie, 111–152. Crows Nest and Honolulu: Allen & Unwin and University of Hawai'i Press.

Lusianawati, Devi. 2015. Dharma Wanita Held Cooking Training. https://m.beritajakarta.id/en/read/9110/dharma-wanita-held-cooking-training. Accessed 2 Apr 2021.

Majalah Ibadah. 2016. Majalah Ibadah: The Islamic Way of Life. *Majalah Ibadah: The Islamic Way of Life* VII (45).

Marcoes, Lies. 2002. Women's Grassroots Movements in Indonesia: A Case Study of the Pkk and Islamic Women's Organisations. In *Women in Indonesia: Gender, Equity and Development*, eds. Kathryn Robinson and Sharon Bessell, 187–197. Singapore: ISEAS Publishing. https://doi.org/10.1355/9789812305152.

Mellina, Tesa, and Mohammad Ghozali. 2019. The Effectiveness of PNPM-SPP Program on Society Welfare: Islamic Economic Perspective. *Jurnal Ilmiah Al-Syir'ah* 17 (1): 77–90.

Menchik, Jeremy. 2014. The Co-Evolution of Sacred and Secular: Islamic Law and Family Planning in Indonesia. *South East Asia Research* 22 (3): 359–378.

Ministry of Cooperatives and Small and Medium Enterprises. 2001. Co-Operative and Small/Medium Enterprises Development in Indonesia. *Journal of Economic Cooperation and Development* 22 (3): 1–26. https://jecd.sesric.org/pdf.php?file=ART01040101-2.pdf.

Ministry of Women's Empowerment and Child Protection. 2019. National Report Beijing Platform for Action (Bpfa) +25 Indonesia (2014–2019). Ministry of Women's Empowerment and Child Protection, Republic of Indonesia.

Mulia, Khamila. 2019. Tokopedia Launches Sharia-Compliant Service with More than 21 Million Muslim Friendly Products. *KrAsia*. Retrieved from https://kr-asia.com/tokopedia-launches-sharia-compliant-service-with-more-than-21-million-muslim-friendly-products.

Mulyani, Eka Sri. 2007. Muslim Women and Education in Indonesia: The Pondok Pesantren Experience. *Asia Pacific Journal of Education* 27 (1): 85–99.

Muslimat NU. 2020. Sejarah Singkat Muslimat NU. http://muslimatnu.or.id/sejarah-singkat/. Accessed 1 May 2021.

Nasyiatul Aisyiyah. 2019. *'Tanfidz Keputuan Tanwir 2 Nasyiatul Aisyiyah. Gerakan Keluarga Muda Tangguh untuk Kesejahteraan Bangsa' Aisyiyah, Pimpinan Pusat Nasyiatul*. Yogyakarta: Pimpinan Pusat Nasyiatul Aisyiyah.

Newberry, Jan. 2012. Empowering Children, Disempowering Women. *Ethics and Social Welfare* 6 (3): 247–259. https://doi.org/10.1080/17496535.2012.704057.

Nisa, Eva F. 2013. The Internet Subculture of Indonesian Face-Veiled Women. *International Journal of Cultural Studies* 16 (3): 241–255.

Nisa, Eva F. 2018a. Creative and Lucrative Daʿwa: The Visual Culture of Instagram Amongst Female Muslim Youth in Indonesia. *Asiascape: Digital Asia* 5 (1–2): 68–99.

Nisa, Eva F. 2018b. Social Media and the Birth of an Islamic Social Movement: ODOJ (One Day One Juz) in Contemporary Indonesia. *Indonesia and the Malay World* 46 (134): 24–43.

Nisa, Eva F. 2019. Muslim Women in Contemporary Indonesia: Online Conflicting Narratives behind the Women Ulama Congress. *Asian Studies Review* 43 (3): 434–454. https://doi.org/10.1080/10357823.2019.1632796.

NU online. 2012. Keluarga Maslahah. NU. https://www.nu.or.id/post/read/40414/keluarga-maslahah. Accessed 10 Sept 2021.

Parawansa, Khofifah Indar. 2015. *NU, Perempuan Indonesia: Sudut Pandang Islam Tradisional*. Bandung: Nuansa Cendikia.

Pimpinan Pusat Aisyiyah, and Majelis Tarjih dan Tajdid Muhammadiyah. 2021. *Tuntunan Menuju Keluarga Sakinah*. Yogyakarta: Suara Muhammadiyah.

PP Aisyiyah. 2020. Data Amal Usaha Aisyiyah. http://www.pp.aisyiyah.or.id/id/page/amal-usaha.html. Accessed 10 May 2021.

PP IPEMI. 2021. About IPEMI. https://ipemipp.or.id/about. Accessed 10 May 2021.

PPNA. 2020. Risalah Keluarga Muda Tangguh Nasyiatul Aisyiyah. http://nasyiah.or.id/Berita/baca/285/Risalah-Keluarga-Muda-Tangguh-Nasyiatul-Aisyiyah-1.html. Accessed 1 May 2021.

Rahman. 2017. IPEMI Balikpapan Gelar Pengajian Rutin Bulanan. http://www.kabarkaltim.co.id/2017/12/ipemi-balikpapan-gelar-pengajian-rutin.html. Accessed 10 Oct 2021.

Rahman, Lisabona, Edriana Noerdin, Sita Aripurnama, and Ratna Laelasari Yuningsih. 2005. *Representasi Perempuan dalam Kebijakan Publik di Era Otonomi Daerah*. Jakarta: Women Research Institute.

Ro'fah. 2016. *Posisi dan Jatidiri 'Aisyiyah: Perubahan dan Perkembangan*. Yogyakarta: Suara Muhammadiyah.

Robinson, Kathryn. 2000. Indonesian Women: From Orde Baru to Reformasi. In *Women in Asia: Tradition, Modernity and Globalisation*, eds. Louise Edwards and Mina Roces, 139–169. London: Routledge. https://doi.org/10.4324/9781003118411.

Robinson, Kathryn. 2004. Islam, Gender and Politics in Indonesia. In *Islamic Perspectives on the New Millennium*, eds. Virginia Hooker and Amin Saikal, 183–196. Singapore: Institute of Southeast Asian Studies. https://doi.org/10.1355/9789812305367.

Robinson, Kathryn. 2009. *Gender, Islam, and Democracy in Indonesia*. Oxon and New York: Routledge.

Robinson, Kathryn, and Sharon Bessell. 2002. *Women in Indonesia: Gender, Equity and Development*. Singapore: Institute of Southeast Asian Studies.

Ryandono, Muhammad Nafik Hadi, Sesha Ayu Permatasari, and Ida Wijayanti. 2019. Business Behavior in an Islamic Perspective: Case Study of Muslim Woman Entrepreneurs in Ikatan Wanita Pengusaha Indonesia (IWAPI). In *12th International Conference on Business and Management Research (ICBMR 2018)*. Atlantis-Press. Available at: https://www.atlantis-press.com/proceedings/icbmr-18/55914317. Accessed 20 Nov.

Sakai, Minako. 2008. Community Development Through Islamic Microfinance: Serving the Financial Needs of the Poor in a Viable Way. In *Expressing Islam: Religious Life and Politics in Indonesia*, eds. Greg Fealy and Sally White, 267–286. Singapore: ISEAS Publishing. https://doi.org/10.1355/9789812308528.

Sakai, Minako. 2010. Growing Together in Partnership: Women's Views of the Business Practices of an Islamic Savings and Credit Cooperative (Baitul Maal Wat Tamwil) in Central Java, Indonesia. *Women's Studies International Forum* 33 (4): 412–421. https://doi.org/10.1016/j.wsif.2010.02.015.

Sakai, Minako. 2014. Establishing Social Justice Through Financial Inclusivity: Islamic Propagation by Islamic Savings and Credit Cooperatives in Indonesia. *TRaNS: Trans-Regional and-National Studies of Southeast Asia* 2 (2): 201–222.

Sakai, Minako. 2018. *Penggiat Bisnis Syariah: Muslimah, Kewirausahaan dan Pemberdayaan Masyarakat*. Jakarta: Dompet Dhuafa.

Sakai, Minako. 2019. Embracing Islam, Work and Family: Women's Economic Empowerment in Islamising Indonesia. *Intersections: Gender and Sexuality in Asia and the Pacific* 43 (July). http://intersections.anu.edu.au/issue43/sakai2.html#n18.

Sakai, Minako, and Amelia Fauzia. 2016. Performing Muslim Womanhood: Muslim Business Women Moderating Islamic Practices in Contemporary Indonesia. *Islam and Christian-Muslim Relations* 27 (3): 229–249. https://doi.org/10.1080/09596410.2015.1114243.

Sakai, Minako, and Bhirawa Anoraga. 2020. Education, Digital Enterprise and Islam in the Indonesian Modern Embedded Economy. In *Muslim Women in the Economy: Development, Faith and Globalisation*, eds. Shamim Samani and

Dora Marinova, 214–228. Oxon and New York: Routledge. https://doi.org/10.4324/9780429263194.

Sakai, Minako, and Kacung Marijan. 2008. Harnessing Islamic Microfinance. *Policy Briefs, Crawford School of Economics and Government* (9).

Sakinah, Kiki. 2019. PP Aisyiyah Dorong Muslimah Berwirausaha. https://republika.co.id/berita/dunia-islam/islam-nusantara/19/03/28/pp2j4w458-pp-aisyiyah-dorong-muslimah-berwirausaha. Accessed 20 Oct 2020.

Sekretariat TIM PUG Kementerian Koperasi dan UKM. 2018. *Laporan Pengarusutamaan Gender (PUG) Kementerian Koperasi dan UKM Tahun 2018*. Jakarta: Kementerian Koperasi dan UKM, Republik Indonesia. Available at: https://kemenkopukm.go.id/uploads/laporan/1602752744_LAPORAN%20PUG%202018.pdf.

Sekretariat TIM PUG Kementerian Koperasi dan UKM. 2019. *Laporan Pengarusutamaan Gender (PUG) Kementerian Koperasi dan UKM Tahun 2019*. Jakarta: Kementerian Koperasi dan UKM, Republik Indonesia. Available at: https://kemenkopukm.go.id/uploads/laporan/1602752769_LAPORAN%20PUG%202019.pdf.

Setiawati, Trias. 2010. The Way to Sakinah Family: National Program of 'Aisyiyah Muhammadiyah in Indonesia. https://iais.org.my/attach/ppts/14DEC2010/Trias%20Setiawati.pdf. Accessed 10 Dec 2021.

Situmorang, Johnny W. 2010. Analisis Tipologi dan Posisi Koperasi Penerima Program PERKASSA: Studi Kasus di Sumatera Selatan. *Jurnal Pengkajian Koperasi dan UKM* 5 (1): 1–29.

Sloane, Patricia. 1999. *Islam, Modernity, and Entrepreneurship Among the Malays*. New York and Basingstoke: Palgrave Macmillan.

SMERU. 2004. 'Assistance Programs to Strengthen Microbusinesses: Upaya-Upaya Penguatan Usaha Mikro' Akhmadi, Nuning. Jakarta: The SMERU Research Institute. Available at: https://smeru.or.id/en/content/assistance-programs-strengthen-microbusinesses.

Smith, Bianca J., and Mark Woodward. 2013. *Gender and Power in Indonesian Islam: Leaders, Feminists, Sufis and Pesantren Selves*. Abingdon, Oxon, New York: Routledge.

Sukarno, Muhammad Bagus, and Ratna Endang Widuatie. 2019. Peran Ikatan Wanita Pengusaha Indonesia di Kabupaten Jember Tahun 1993–2016. *Istoria, Jurnal Pendidikan dan Sejarah* 15 (1): 111–118.

Sullivan, Norma. 1983. Indonesian Women in Development: State Theory and Urban Kampung Practice. In *Women's Work and Women's Roles Economics and Everyday Life in Indonesia, Malaysia and Singapore*, ed. Lenomer Manderson. Australia: Australian National University (ANU).

Sullivan, Norma. 1994. *Masters and Managers: A Study of Gender Relations in Urban Java*. Crows Nest, NSW: Allen & Unwin.

Sumedi, Didi. 2020. Potensi Produk Halal Indonesia di Pasar Global. https://kneks.go.id/storage/upload/1603523489-Paparan%20Dirjen%20Daglu%20-%20Webinar%20KNEKS.pdf. Accessed 7 Aug 2021.

Suryakusuma, Julia I. 1996. The State and Sexuality in New Order Indonesia. In *Fantasizing the Feminine in Indonesia*, ed. Laurie J. Sears, 92–119. New York: Duke University Press.

Susilaningsih. 2015. Pendidikan Kewirausahaan di Perguruan Tinggi: Pentingkah untuk Semua Profesi? *Jurnal Economia* 11 (1): 1–9. https://doi.org/10.21831/economia.v11i1.7748.

Syamsiyatun, Siti. 2016. *Pergolakan Putri Islam: Perkembangan Wacana Gender Dalam Nasyiatul 'Aisyiyah*. Yogyakarta: Suara Muhammadiyah.

Syamsiyatun, Siti. 2020. Conflicts and Islah Strategy of Muslim Women Organization: Case Study of 'Aisyiyah in Intra and Inter-Organizational Divergence. *Al-Jamiah* 58 (2): 355–390.

Syukri, Muhammad, Sulton Mawardi, and A. Akhmadi. 2013. *A Qualitative Study on the Impact of the PNPM-Rural in East Java, West Sumatra, and Southeast Sulawesi*. SMERU Research Institute. https://smeru.or.id/en/content/qualitative-study-impact-pnpm-rural-east-java-west-sumatra-and-southeast-sulawesi. Accessed 7 Aug 2021.

Tambunan, Tulus. 2009. Women Entrepreneurship in Asian Developing Countries: Their Development and Main Constraints. *Journal of Development and Agricultural Economics* 1 (2): 27–40.

Taufik, Dedi. 2019. *Pedoman Pariwisata Halal Jawa Barat*. Bandung: Kantor Propinsi Jawa Barat.

The Wahid Institute. 2021. The Wahid Institute. http://www.wahidinstitute.org/wi-id/. Accessed 10 Dec 2021.

Tokopedia. n.d. Tokopedia Salam. https://www.tokopedia.com/salam. Accessed 20 July 2021.

van Doorn-Harder, Nelly. 2006. *Women Shaping Islam: Indonesian Women Reading the Qur'an*. Urbana: University of Illinois Press.

van Doorn-Harder, Nelly. 2013. Polygamy and Harmonious Families: Indonesian Debates on Gender and Marriage. In *Gender and Islam in Southeast Asia: Women's Rights Movements, Religious Resurgence and Local Traditions*, ed. Susanne Schröter, 55–71. Leiden: Brill.

World Bank. 2016. Women Entrepreneurs in Indonesia: A Pathway to Increasing Shared Prosperity. World Bank. https://openknowledge.worldbank.org/handle/10986/24751. Accessed 7 Apr 2021.

Wulandari, Retno. 2019. Gojek Gelar Pelatihan Wirausaha untuk Muslimat NU. https://republika.co.id/berita/dunia-islam/islam-nusantara/19/08/14/pw7h6u320-gojek-gelar-pelatihan-wirausaha-untuk-muslimat-nu. Accessed 10 Oct 2021.

CHAPTER 4

Predicaments of Unmarried Career Women

Minako Sakai

Abstract This chapter focuses on unmarried Muslim career women in Indonesia and other Muslim-dominant countries. Some are turning to Muslim match-making or are lured into considering polygamy. It highlights that a professional career path for Muslim women based on education and work opportunities alone has not altered the necessity to become a wife and mother to fulfil the expectations around gender roles in Islam. Being married and raising a family remain a higher priority than establishing a professional career. This chapter draws on media studies and narratives of Muslim women, showing that unmarried women are struggling to be socially and religiously accepted in society. Individualistic career choices do not guarantee the subjective wellbeing of educated Muslim women.

Keywords Career women · Indonesia · Islam · Marriage · Polygamy · Popular culture · Single women

M. Sakai and A. Fauzia, *Women Entrepreneurs and Business Empowerment in Muslim Countries*,
Gender, Development and Social Change,
https://doi.org/10.1007/978-3-031-05954-4_4

Introduction

This chapter will focus on marriage as a significant social institution that affects conditions for women to work. As the primary role of Muslim women is to be wife and mother, and following the role models of Khadijah and Aishah, the expectations of a woman being married remain strong in Muslim societies.

This chapter examines changes surrounding Muslim marriage practice in recent times. Enhanced access to education for women, coupled with increasing opportunities to be employed in paid work has raised the average marriage age significantly and increased the number of men and women in Muslim-dominant countries who do not marry. As a result, a so-called spinster crisis (Mohammed 2012) has emerged in Muslim-dominant countries, which has triggered various responses encouraging women to marry. Some of these efforts are contradictory to state and international policies made to bolster access to education for women, including the Sustainable Development Goals (SDGs). Therefore, highly educated Muslim women face conflicting views about the importance of Muslim marriage and family, and education and work (Cameron and Contreras Suarez 2017). As middle-class Muslims embrace Islamic values in their everyday life, popular culture in these societies also shames women who have never married by labelling them as sinful. Although singleness for both men and women is generally perceived as a social failure and incompetence (Himawan et al. 2018a: 491), marriage and bearing children are among the core values of the virtue and womanhood of Muslim women. Consequently, this chapter highlights the predicaments of educated childless career women who are prone to stigmatisation and a sense of failure as a Muslim. Consequently, we argue that the idea of becoming a mompreneur is a positive way to address the conundrum, as we explore in Chapters 5 and 6.

In this chapter, the first section will provide an overview of the changes associated with marriage patterns in Arab and Muslim-dominant countries, which will include the spinster crisis. The second section analyses responses from Islamic organisations and governments to encourage marriage. The third section will explore popular culture focusing on Muslim spinsters in Indonesia and the predicament of educated Muslim women's empowerment. The fourth section will analyse narratives of single Muslim women and their views on their status of singlehood, drawing from case studies from contemporary Indonesia.

Delaying Marriage and the Spinster Crisis

Spinster is a derogatory word in English which refers to a woman who has never married. Spinster was used to describe single women who spun yarn to earn an income in the 1300s and subsequently became a legal term to refer to a single woman. An equivalent word in Arabic is *anis* or *unusa*, which means a branch that withers or becomes useless (Traboulsi 2019). Both words have connotations that something must be wrong with unmarried women.

Marriage in the Arab world, as exemplified by Aishah's marriage to the Prophet Muhammad, was common but it is becoming less so (Abbott 1942; Ahmed 1986; Shehada 2008). In Egypt, educated Muslim women are delaying marriage until after they have developed their career (El-Halawany 2009). Table 2.1 shows that as Arab societies moved away from agrarian economies to industrialisation, and children remained in education for longer, early marriage declined significantly. The practice of young marriages remains relatively unchanged in countries such as Palestine, Syria, Yemen, Egypt, and Iraq, while in Lebanon, Bahrain, Kuwait, Libya, Tunisia and Algeria there is a higher number of spinsters. Saudi Arabia and Morocco remain somewhere between these two groups. However, recent research on Palestinian women in Israel (Sabbah-Karkaby and Stier 2017) highlights that educated Palestinian women also delay marriage, confirming the same global trajectory of the decline of early marriage in favour of increased education as indicated in Fig. 4.1.

The Saudi Youth Development Survey in 2019 (2020) shows that the majority of the youth aged 15–34 are unmarried, with the percentage of never-married Saudi youth aged 15–34 is 66.23%. While the main two reasons for delaying marriage for both genders include the high cost of living and marriage, women responded that they are keen to finish their education (15.7%) and that they have difficulty in finding the right partner (11.7%). The gender gap in this respect is strongest, with only 1.9% of men citing that difficulty in finding the right partner is for them delaying marriage.

Similar trends of decline in early marriage are reported in Southeast Asia (Himawan et al. 2018b; Jones and Yeung 2014), indicating the preference of marrying later in these societies. In Indonesia, the percentage of never-married women aged 35–39 grew to 3.8% from 1.4%

Fig. 4.1 The percentage of ever-married women in selected Muslim-dominant countries (*Source* United Nations, Department of Economic and Social Affairs, Population Division [2019])

in 1970. 6.83% of the population was single in 2000 and the single population of this age group increased to 7.18% in 2010 (Himawan et al. 2018a). Furthermore, increasingly, married women possess a higher level of education than their husband, as shown in Fig. 4.2 (Rashad et al. 2005). With the increased enrolment rates of women in higher education, as discussed in Chapter 2, it suffices to state that women are staying longer in education before they are married, resulting in later marriage. These data highlight the fact that it is difficult for educated women to fulfil their preference for a marriage partner who has at least an equivalent level of education, thus contributing to the trend of delayed marriage (Nurmila 2016; Utomo 2014). In addition, the preference of men for younger women with a lower level of education results in a reduced pool of eligible men for educated women to marry. This is because it is perceived easier to assert male authority over younger women with a lower level of education (Retnaningsih 2013).

Over the course of time, the pattern of older marriage has also meant that there has been an increase in the number of women in Muslim-dominant countries who have never married. There is no official consensus about an age that defines a woman as a spinster, yet, for

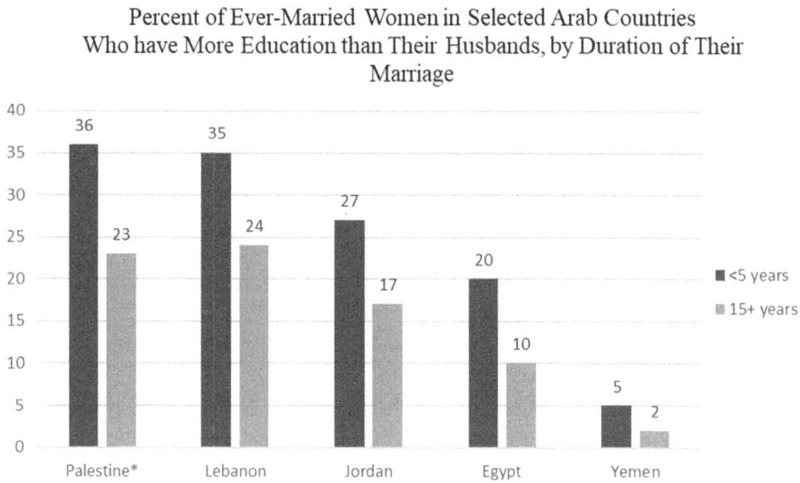

* Includes Palestinians living in Gaza and the West Bank (including East Jerusalem)

Fig. 4.2 The percentage of ever-married women in selected Arab countries (*Source* Rashad et al. [2005: 5])

example, Saudi Arabia defines a spinster as a woman of 32 years old or over who has never been married (Kingdom of Saudi Arabia, General Authority for Statistics 2020). In 2016, as many as 10% of women were classified as spinsters. The Saudi Youth Development report in 2019 shows that 13.4% of women aged 25–34 are unmarried. Negative perceptions are felt by women working outside the home and can contribute to preventing them from marriage (Alkhteeb and Sultan 2014).

The increase in the number of women who have never married is not limited to Muslim countries. For example, in China, after the implementation of the one child policy between 1979 and 2015, parents invested equally in the education of their daughters as well-educated daughters secured high-income professional jobs, resulting in a shift away from marriage. Concerned, the government has launched a scare campaign to shame older single women as 'leftover' women. Parents are actively involved in securing a partner for their daughters to avoid this scenario, but women are generally not keen to settle for just any marriage proposal (To 2015). Even in Western countries a couple-centred culture prevails, and there is stigmatisation of single women who cannot belong to that couple-centred culture, despite the fact that the legal framework is supportive of personal choices (Budgeon 2016).

What distinguishes Muslim women who never marry from the 'left-over' women in the Western world or China is the religious sanction that accompanies marriage in the Muslim world; unmarried women have failed to comply with the expected gender role as a wife and mother through marriage and have not received the blessings of marriage. Marriage is considered to be a gate to enter heaven, making unmarried women fearful that they will be denied entry to heaven. Furthermore, being sexually active before or outside marriage is generally a disgrace on the reputation of the individual as well as the family in Muslim-dominant countries (Imtoual and Hussein 2009).

One of the relevant Qur'an surah An-Nur (24:32), often used to endorse marriage is translated as

> And marry the unmarried among you and the righteous among your male slaves and female slaves. If they should be poor, Allah will enrich them from His bounty, and Allah is all-encompassing and knowing.

In addition to the Qur'anic verses, other Islamic sources such as *hadith* state the importance of marriage for Muslims as below:

A *hadith* from *Sunan Ibn Majah* compilation (Majah 2015, hadith no 1846)

> It was narrated from Aishah that: The Messenger of Allah said: 'Marriage is part of my sunnah, and whoever does not follow my sunnah has nothing to do with me. Get married, for I will boast of your great numbers before the nations. Whoever has the means, let him get married, and whoever does not, then he should fast for it will diminish his desire.'

As the study of Islam, including the recitation of the Qur'an, gains popularity among middle-class Muslims in Indonesia, books and internet sites are disseminating the main idea that marriage is a way to receive a livelihood from God (*rezeki*) and marriage is a way to follow Islam.

The increased interest and popularity of Islamism among middle-class Muslims (Sakai and Fauzia 2014) has also contributed to the heightened the present sense of importance of marriage for Muslims. For example, the founder of the Muslim Brotherhood in Egypt demarcated specific roles for men and women, emphasising women's primary role as mother and wife, to nurture the family at home (Freer 2018). In Indonesia, the Muslim Brotherhood-inspired Islamism has been advocated by the Prosperous Justice Party, an Islamist party commonly known as PKS (Partai Keadilan Sejahtera), which promotes the segregation of men and women in public, and emphasises a domestic role as the appropriate one for Muslim women (Rinaldo 2013). As such, Islamic interpretations of gender roles are disseminated through school-affiliated Islamic study groups, and educated middle-class Muslims tend to reiterate the view that marriage is a part of Islamic propagation. Cahyadi Takariawan, popularly known as Pak Cah or Mr. Cah, is a well-known Muslim author who has published a series of educational books on family and marriage. He is a graduate of Gajah Mada University, a leading Indonesian state university, with a degree in pharmacy and was a founding member of PKS. His key ideas are expressed in the title of his book *Di Jalan Dakwah Aku Menikah or I Will Marry in the Path of Islamic Propagation* (Takariawan 2005). His Islamist ideas are packaged in the Wonder Family series, which use English titles, as shown below. This series disseminates Islamic discourses that marriage implements Islamic teaching and raising a pious family is righteous behaviour for Muslims as they face the challenge of making appropriate choices in a modern world. Becoming a secular individual may result in losing one's identity as a Muslim.

Other books also emphasise the importance of marriage as a way to enter the heaven. For example, El Salman Ayashi. Rz, a popular Islamic novelist, published a book *Ternyata Orang yang Menikah itu Lebih Mudah Masuk Surga* or *The Married Couple Will Enter Heaven Easily* (Ayashi Rz 2012).

The importance of marriage for Muslim women seems to remain unchallenged even outside Muslim-dominant countries. The emphasis on marriage seems slow to change for second-generation migrant Muslims who adhere more strongly to Muslim traditions in Western countries (Ali et al. 2017: 1170). However, though marriage is emphasised as an important obligation for a practising Muslim, a Muslim migrant woman who has grown up in a Western country can find it difficult to find a suitable Muslim husband. The eligible pool of Muslim men in Western countries is relatively small and it is further limited by a preference for a partner sharing the same ethnic origins, such as being Pakistani (Mohammed 2012). Migrant Muslim men, on the other hand, tend to turn to their parents' home country to look for a young virgin girl over a well-educated older migrant Muslim woman (Ahmad 2019). It seems that the higher the level of education a woman has, the smaller the matching eligible spouse pool is. The BBC TV series, aired in 2012 titled *Strictly Soulmates: Muslim* (britishdocs 2012) documented how difficult it was for 31-year-old Dimpy Malik—a Muslim general practitioner of Pakistani descent living in Hertfordshire, UK, just outside London—to find a suitable husband who was also a doctor. She said she had a very strong faith in Allah but was not a strong practising Muslim. Her family and brothers are actively involved in assisting her in her pursuit of a marriage partner, but she was not able to find an ideal man who, for her, was also a medical doctor living in the UK. Her view of an ideal marriage denotes what is deemed socio-culturally appropriate for Muslim migrant women. In the program she says, 'I always wanted to marry a doctor. Doctors in the Pakistani community are at the top of the food chain. So, if I was going to marry someone,·who is not a doctor, I would not be comfortable with that'. The narrator reports that she had turned down 60 proposals by then as she did not find any man measuring up to her ideal.

As the Qur'an states that men are guardians of their wife, a man is generally expected to be better educated and financially stronger than the woman he marries. The ideal for women is to marry someone who meets this social gender norm. If a Muslim woman has reached the top of the social hierarchy and aims to fulfil the existing gender norms, the pool of eligible men becomes extremely small. As established Muslim men can have access to a wider pool of eligible women, including in their home countries, these established women face an extremely difficult situation when they become professionals in countries like the UK, as the pool of marriageable men is extremely small.

This social situation has created what Mohammed (2012) calls a spinster crisis in the UK. Highly educated single Muslim women are turning to matchmaking events to find a suitable spouse. The number of Muslim women of South Asian origins studying at the university level has been increasing since the 1990s. These women are motivated by their desire to increase their eligibility and also to have a safety net should a marriage break down (Ahmad 2001). The older women become, the harder they find it to be matched with a spouse. As a result, they are afraid of remaining single for a long period of time. This is explored in the next section. As Islam emphasises marriage as a being duty and a precondition for entrance to heaven, remaining single is believed to be disobedient to God.

Seeking Polygamy Over Spinsterhood

As the issue of gender equality has come to the fore, the practice of polygamy has been strongly condemned by activists for women's rights because it is seen as oppression of women to have to accept their husband's desire to marry another woman. The Qur'an states that men can have up to four wives so long as they are fair to all the wives. Jurists have added that they must have permission from the first wife.

Qur'an surah An-Nisa (4:3),

> And if you fear that you will not deal justly with the orphan girls, then marry those that please you of [other] women, two or three or four. But if you fear that you will not be just, then [marry only] one or those your right hand possesses. That is more suitable that you may not incline [to injustice].

Thus, some news reports are exposing that educated professional Muslim women in the UK are choosing to become part-time wives, sharing an appropriate Muslim man of good standing to be able to obey the teaching that they should marry. Media coverage of this phenomenon emerged in 2011, around the same time as the spinster crisis was identified. One of the first articles was titled The British Muslim Men who love 'both their wives' (Khatkar 2011). This BBC article analysed the reality of second or third-generation Muslims who are creatively coping with their reality based on the Islamic practice of polygamy. At a young age, British second-generation Muslim men usually accept a wife from their motherland chosen by their parents. However, these men may fall in love with someone other than their first wife. Muslim women, on the other hand, may have experienced divorce and are not keen to cause the pain of this for another woman if their lover wants to leave their first wife. In the UK, second marriages are neither recognised nor sanctioned and are not deemed legal. In the eyes of Muslim migrant communities, however, religiously sanctioned second marriage is considered more appropriate than a man engaging in illicit relations or turning to prostitution to fulfil his desires.[1] As the number of professional Muslim women pursuing their careers and delaying marriage increases, they are increasingly faced with the harsh reality that marriage does not come easily. They do not want to sleep around with multiple non-Muslim partners, as such behaviour is deemed inappropriate for Muslim woman. They want their companion, yet perhaps not on a full-time basis. They may be happy with being a part-time co-wife of an established professional Muslim man, who often will have married a cousin chosen by their parents and sent from South Asian mother countries (Dettmer 2013). These professional women have come to grips with the reality that they will not meet a professional Muslim man through dating events who would make a suitable monogamous husband.

As a solution and using internet-based Muslim dating sites, they actively seek married Muslim men who are looking for a second wife. The demand for this kind of relationship is so high that in 2017, Azad Chaiwala, a British Muslim entrepreneur and YouTuber who was seeking a second wife, launched a dedicated website for those also seeking a second wife (https://www.secondwife.com/). The BBC's article published on 23 October 2017 (BBC News 2017) reports that over 100,000 men registered their interest in the website, while the registration of Muslim women is one quarter of that number. This article features a British Muslim doctor named Tarek who married an older British Muslim woman, Tracy, as his second wife. He believes he is capable of looking after more than one wife. The second wife, Tracy, wanted both to maintain her independence and to have a companion and saw polygamous marriage was to her advantage. However, she confessed that it is hard for her to accept this reality, 'I've found myself being more insecure . . . it's really affecting me', she said, 'As much as I love Tarek, I wouldn't do it again, because it's not easy emotionally, it really isn't'. Tarek says it is the husband's role to be wise, fair and kind but adds, 'The woman has the choice. She can walk away from the "marriage" at any point' (BBC News 2017).

As polygamous marriage is not recognised by the UK legal system, women do not receive any legal protection from such a marriage. The relationship is, however, deemed compliant with Islamic jurisprudence and this generally offsets the feeling of guilt for practising Muslims. Women also use Islamic interpretations to justify their intimate relationship and emotional needs to avoid religious condemnation. In reality, a lot of co-wives who are also successful business or professional women remain quiet about sharing a husband but see this arrangement as a practical solution to their problems. A tabloid article, published in 2013 in the *Daily Beast* (Dettmer 2013), explained the views of a co-wife named Aishah, stating that it was her choice to become a co-wife of a successful Muslim businessman and as she passed her mid-30 s as a single woman she had wanted to be married. She keeps it secret that she shares her husband but is apparently satisfied, as she remarked, '"I didn't want to remain single and I wanted my relationship to be endorsed by my religion, so sleeping around or living with a non-Muslim wasn't an option," she says. "This works for me"' (Dettmer 2013).

Her immediate family members are aware that she is a co-wife. They are reassured that she is not breaching Islamic teaching because her intimate relations are endorsed by Islam (Dettmer 2013). In 2021, Azad Chaiwala, now established as an entrepreneur and YouTuber, launched another website called polygamy.com, offering his polygamous matchmaking site to people of any faith. He stated that 30% of the subscribers are women seeking commitment in relationships rather than a temporary romance (Zuberi 2021).

Fauzia Ahmad (2014), a British Muslim sociologist who grew up in the UK, confirms a rise of polygamous marriage among British Muslims is becoming a necessity for highly educated British Muslim women and British Muslim men who are trapped in an unhappy arranged marriage. The British Shariah Council has received an increased number of enquiries from Muslim women who cannot find a suitable spouse seeking advice about becoming a co-wife (Ahmad 2014). These women are not willing to give up their well-paid jobs to look after their husbands full-time but are keen to find a companion. Muslim men predominantly prefer a wife who is homemaker (Ahmad 2018) and do not know how to treat a professional, educated, high-income earning wife, who may seem threatening to the Islamic norm of the husband as provider (5Pillars 2013).

The practice of becoming a co-wife appears to be the only option for older professional Muslim women in the UK if they do not want to remain single or be accused of sinful behaviour. The presence of a specialised website for seeking a co-wife in the UK highlights the challenges for Muslim women in finding an intimate relationship; they need to be in a relationship sanctioned by Islam, irrespective of their professional success or financial independence. The expectation that they should also be a wife and a mother seems to weigh more heavily on the minds of professional Muslim women.

Uncontrolled Sexual Desire of Women

In Muslim-dominant Southeast Asia, the underlying problem of the increasing number of unmarried women is the prevalence of perceptions that women's sexual attraction will cause men to lose their self-control.

Anthropologists such as Peletz (1996) and Siegel (2000) have shown that in the Malay world, Islam is used to control desires by the teaching of *akal* (rationality) (Peletz 1996; Siegel 2000). A society driven by desires will challenge Islamic norms of order. Furthermore, pre-existing Hindu influence upon women's sexuality also underpins the view that women need to be controlled by men because unmarried women in society pose a risk as shown by the Gerwani (Gerakan Wanita Indonesia or Indonesian Women's Movement) movement in Indonesia (Wieringa 2003). The perception that attractive single women who have passed a certain marriable age in the community are a threat to that community leads to these individual women being the subject of neighbourhood gossip in Indonesia.[2]

The perception that women should not pursue their sexual desire drives the practice of Female Genital Mutilation (FGM) in the Muslim world. In Indonesia, the state tried to ban the practice of FGM in 2006, but because of resistance from Muslim communities, the state issued regulations on the practice in 2010 to ensure they must be conducted by a medical practitioner. Traditionally, the practice of FGM in Indonesia was symbolic, often a mere act of rubbing or scraping of the genitalia but the government's regulation in 2014 that the practice be undertaken by medical practitioners has led to the practice more commonly involving cutting of the skin. Currently, it is estimated that about 50% of women have experienced some form of FGM (Budiharsana 2016). The continuing practice supports the widely held perception in Malaysia and Indonesia that sexual desires will drive Muslim women wild and lead to illicit sexual encounters and that FGM is needed to mitigate this outcome (Renaldi 2018).

The number of single or unmarried women participating in the workforce is also on the rise in Muslim-dominant Southeast Asian countries. Between 2006 and 2012, about 47% of unmarried Malaysian women were active in the workforce (Azmawati et al. 2015). The high number of female workers has led to the perception that workspaces have become dangerous for married men because of the presence of so many single women who may try to seduce them. The use of veiling is increasingly preferred, as Muslim women are conscious that they are in a public space, and they want to remain pious within these challenging modern social contexts.

Promoting Muslim Marriage Through *Ta'aruf*

Promoting polygamy or bigamy (two wives) as a solution to being both a successful career woman and a successful Muslim, is not limited to the UK. In Saudi Arabia, the state publishes the number of single women every year, commenting on the ever-increasing number. As a result, Hawazin Mirza, a lecturer at King 'Abd Al-'Aziz University in Jeddah, sparked a debate on TV in 2017 when she stated her idea that a polygamy academy should be established in Saudi Arabia to train single women for polygamy (MEMRI 2017).

Also in 2017, Saudi Arabian media reported that WhatsApp groups were being created to facilitate polygamous marriages and to reduce the number of divorcees, widows and spinsters in Saudi Arabia. Reportedly 900 women signed up for the group (Young 2017).

In Indonesia, polygamy is generally frowned upon (van Doorn-Harder 2013), but the practice is not banned because it is permissible under Islamic law. As explained in Chapter 2, Indonesian Islamic authority is becoming increasingly diffused, and Muslims tend to follow the teachings of multiple preachers. In 2006, Abdullah Gymnastiar, a modern Muslim preacher popularly known as Aa Gym, rose to fame particularly among middle-class women because of his teachings on the application of Islamic faith to everyday life (Hoesterey 2008). His popularity was drastically reduced when he took a second wife. Despite his efforts, he was unable to regain his celebrity status. Recently, with the rise of conservative interpretations of Islam, however, polygamy advocators have begun to emerge. For example, Fadil Muzakki Syah, a member of parliament and a lawmaker from the National Awakening Party, or PKB (Partai Kebangkitan Bangsa), boasts about living harmoniously with his three co-wives. Despite sensational media coverage, polygamy is not gaining strong support as an appropriate solution for the rising number of single women in Indonesia (Chew 2019).

One alternative solution backed by educated middle-class Muslims is the increasing practice of arranged courtship, known as *ta'aruf* (Smith-Hefner 2018). Since the 1980s, it has not been uncommon for university students who have been dating without parental supervision to be found cohabiting (Anwar 2012). At the same time, strongly Islamic ideas inspired by the Muslim Brotherhood, Indonesian Islamic Propagation Council (Dewan Dakwah Islam Indonesia [DDII]) were penetrating university campuses and led to the formation of Islamic study groups, such as Campus Dakwah Institute (Lembaga Dakwah Kampus [LDK]) (Muhsin et al. 2019). The rise of university campus-based Islamic study groups led to the establishment of PKS, a national political party, after the political democratisation of Indonesia in the 2000s. As a result of these developments, Islamist preachers—such as Muhammad Fauzil Adhim, chair of University Students' Propagation Institute of Indonesia or Lembaga Dakwah Kampus Nusantara and academic at the Islamic University of Indonesia (Universitas Islam Indonesia or UII) in Yogyakarta—emerged as popular advocates of the importance of not postponing marriage, as marriage is a religious requirement and it also assists in avoiding sinful sexual behaviour (Smith-Hefner 2005). In fact youth sexual behaviour, including among middle-class Indonesian students, has become more common, and the Islamic moral standard surrounding sexual behaviour varies across the youth (Smith-Hefner 2019).

Over the last two decades, Fauzil Adhim, a popular Islamic preacher, has published a series of books regaling the benefits of marriage and of raising a harmonious Muslim family (Nurjamal 2016). One of his key messages is that it is not appropriate to delay marriage for the sake of a career and education, because in the meantime, young people have to fend off their sexual desires. As a result, the view that marriage and raising a family is becoming increasingly important has made educated single people reconsider their life choices, because in making their educational goals and career aspirations a priority they are deemed to have neglected a religious requirement, as is illustrated below.

Muslim Matchmaking

Recently, *ta'aruf* has been facilitated by professional Muslim marriage institutions or marriage counselling service providers. They are catering to the needs and expectations of educated middle-class Indonesian Muslims who are used to pre-marriage counselling and training being undertaken to prepare for marriage. Finding a suitable life partner is a challenging task for middle-class Muslims living in Jakarta. Because they work long hours, with exhausting commutes in Jakarta, they find it difficult to meet people for social occasions outside of work. As the majority of these businesspeople attended secular education and universities, they have few social ties with local Islamic figures, who often run Islamic boarding schools and are also matchmakers. To date, mainstream Muslim women's organisations have not addressed the increased number of spinsters in Indonesia.

As discussed in Chapter 3, these organisations advocate the importance of a harmonious and healthy family.

In provincial Indonesia, these Muslim figures are expected to act as matchmakers because of their extensive networks enabling them to identify suitable couples (Arsal 2014; Fauzi 2019). Urban middle-class Muslims often lack such connections. Internet-based matchmaking sites are generally seen as risky and inappropriate, as safeguarding of personal information online in Indonesia remains difficult. Younger generations of Indonesians are comfortable using apps for business and commercial purposes, as demonstrated by digital start-up success stories like Gojek and Bukalapak, but find looking for love online more challenging. The pressure to find a suitable partner is also gradually affecting men as well as women. The word *jomblo* (singlehood, or a single person without a steady partner) began to emerge as an everyday term referring to a single person who is actively looking for a spouse. Originally referring to *gadis tua* (older women), the term *jomblo* began to include men and women. In short, being *jomblo* represents *nasib* (a fate) of not being able to find a partner, while being labelled single represents a life choice to stay single.

Young, educated Muslims are increasingly turning to the practice of *ta'aruf*, or a courtship arranged in line with Islamic teaching and often mediated by Islamic institutions that provide matchmaking services to Muslims.

In Jakarta, the AQL (Ar-Rahman Quranic Learning Center) offers pre-marriage counselling to Muslims looking for a prospective life partner. AQL, located in central Jakarta, offers Qur'anic education services along with social welfare programs including Islamic *waqf*.[3] The centre was established in 2008 by Bachtiar Nasir who was educated at Pondok Modern Darussalam Gontor, East Java and also the Islamic University of Medina in Saudi Arabia. AQL introduced the Ar-Rahman Pre-Wedding Academy (APWA), which is a pre-marriage educational institution offering preparation for those who are willing to undertake *ta'aruf* matchmaking in line with Islamic principles. On their website https://apwa.wordpress.com/about/, APWA cites a Qur'anic verse Surah Ar-Rum (30:21) and on the importance of marriage education says, 'We do not permit a person without a degree in civil engineering to construct a building. But we allow anyone to get married [even those] without adequate knowledge of how to live a married life. A successful society is an outcome of a successful marriage' (own translation).

This statement epitomises the importance of preparedness for marriage. In support of professionals, in Jakarta, APWA offers training over the weekends, allowing participants to undertake a pre-marriage module offered on Sundays. On the completion of their course, they are invited to leave their personal details for prospective marriage partners. APWA management explores the compatibility and suitability of the candidates who have completed their training course. We visited the centre in 2013 and, at the time, approximately 50 participants were present, sitting apart based on their gender. The instructors explained interpretations of the Qur'an related to raising a family. All the women were dressed in long Muslim clothing with a headscarf, which is a condition of participating in this event. The management's view on the increasing interest in their activities was that middle-class Muslims in Jakarta were struggling to meet suitable spouses and were thus becoming more anxious as they become older. The completion of their pre-marriage training program provides a certain level of expectation that they will be able to meet a Muslim who shares their views and outlook. Interaction between participants is strictly limited and participants do not mingle except when they are sitting in the same lecture theatre. The Islamic interpretations used are those common in Saudi Arabia, reflecting the Islamic education of the leader, Bachtiar Nasir, who has been actively involved in Indonesian politics and issues of Islam.

A similar development for *ta'aruf* matchmaking is Rumah Ta'aruf, established in Yogyakarta, Central Java in 2001 and labelled as Introduction and Matching. In 2014, after a series of changes, the organisation adopted a new name, Rumah Ta'aruf MyQuran (2021).

How does the system of *ta'aruf* matchmaking work? This organisation takes the details of all the applicants, and male applicants who have expressed interest in potential matches can have a meeting with a woman in a public place. In-person meetings with an intermediator are allowed up to three times to determine if the man is ready to propose. There are recent reports that this matchmaking institution has successfully assisted in marrying 70 couples across Indonesia (Henry 2019). The organisation posts some basic information about the candidates on their website to seek interest from the wider public and the applicants come from all across Indonesia. The data about applicants disclosed on the website indicate that 788 male applicants were listed between 2010 and 2017, while 1994 female applicants were listed during the same period. The overtly strong interest among female Muslim applicants illustrates the anxiety that exists surrounding becoming a spinster, despite the fact that the phenomenon of *jomblo* affects both genders (Livia 2019). Furthermore, with only a few exceptions the applicants' ages range between 20 and 30. The clear absence of older singles on the website indicates that people experience a stigma and perhaps a loss of hope in the possibility of marriage as they mature into their 40s and beyond.

The Holy Love of Zahrana

Since the mid-2000s, Indonesian popular culture has absorbed Islamic values and celebrities, and so there is now a booming Islamic popular culture (Hoesterey and Clark 2012). As the Indonesian middle-class embraces Islam, popular culture serves as a medium to disseminate Islamic messages (Heryanto 2011; Weintraub 2011).

Until the mid-2000s, with few exceptions, Indonesian popular culture was not focused on Islamic themes. The majority of TV shows aired in Indonesia in the 1990s were imported from India and Latin America, and focused on themes of love, money and wealthy families (Heryanto 2008). In the mid-2000s, however, *Ayat-Ayat Cinta* or *Verses of Love* (El Shirazy 2004) was published as a series in the Islamic Daily Newspaper, *Republika*, and it received so much attention that a popular film was also produced. The author of *Ayat-Ayat Cinta*, Habiburrahman El Shirazy, is an Indonesian Muslim graduate from an Islamic High School in Central Java. He completed his university education in Islamic theology in Al-Azhar University in Cairo, Egypt. Upon his return to Indonesia, he wrote his first novel, *Ayat-Ayat Cinta*, to convey Islamic teaching to young Muslim Indonesian readers who are not yet trained to read Islamic texts or study Islamic theology. His books to date focus on themes of love and youth, the desire for a spouse and family, and Indonesia. He believes that love is an important and universal theme connecting young people. *Ayat-Ayat Cinta* has many Qur'anic verses that have easy interpretations and applications in everyday life (Sakai 2012).

The works of Habiburrahman El Shirazy have been widely read by university students because of their timely insertion of Qur'anic verses and interpretations, which depict the life stories and struggles of university-educated youth. As previous research by Jones and Gubhaju (2009) demonstrated, education and labour-force participation opportunities have led increasingly to women's decisions to delay marriage (Jones and Gubhaju 2009). As a result, it is not uncommon to find unmarried

Indonesian women academics in higher education. As later marriage has become a concern to society, Habiburrahman has chosen to focus his literature on the dilemma faced by bright Muslim women who succeed in education and pursue their career as international researchers, but also struggle to find a suitable husband, which in turn causes their parents to worry about their spinster daughters. He published a novel titled *Cinta Suci Zahrana* or *The Holy Love of Zahrana* (El Shirazy 2011), which was later made into a film in partnership with him (Fig. 4.3).

I met Habiburrahman in Canberra in the Indonesian Embassy, Australia in 2006 when we were both invited to a cultural event. Since then, I have communicated with Habiburrahman through a series of meetings, mainly in Indonesia but also in Australia. In our conversations he has remarked that after the success of the movie *Ayat-Ayat Cinta*, he saw the positive effects of using novels and films to engage with Indonesian university students who are eager to learn about Islam. He also wanted to re-categorise the Indonesian film industry as a means for Islamic propagation. For this reason, he was keen to direct the film and conducted a series of roadshows to recruit exemplary Muslims as role models from the community to star in his films, with the aim that they would become ambassadors of Indonesian Islam. His recruiting of the

Fig. 4.3 The Roadshow of *Cinta Suci Zahrana* with Habiburrahman (middle) and Minako Sakai (left) in 2011 (*Source* Photo by the author)

cast for a film based on a double novel called *Ketika Cinta Bertasbih (When Love is Exalting)* (El Shirazy 2007) was a national success and the subsequent episodes of this film were broadcast on Indonesian TV due to popular demand. His intention in recruiting the cast was to choose, not so much by onscreen acting abilities, but rather, he wanted to find a group of young Muslims keen to act as role models for Indonesian Muslim youth (Sakai 2012). The recruitment of new film stars successfully led to the discovery of a new Muslim actress, Oki Setiana Dewi, who later became a national Muslim celebrity, a graduate of the University of Indonesia, and a female Islamic preacher who commenced her Ph.D. study in the Islamic State University in Jakarta (Sakai 2019). As a young intelligent Muslim woman who has completed higher education at a prestigious Indonesian university and can successfully raise a harmonious family while working to contribute to society, Oki represents a new role model.

I was invited to participate in the roadshow of book launches of *Cinta Suci Zahrana* and casting recruitment sessions held in 2011 in more than 20 universities in Indonesia. University student bodies at secular universities were eager to host events on campus. I attended seven events in June 2011 in Central Java, discussing the content of the book with Habiburrahman and participants exchanged ideas and responses during the roadshows and other ongoing events that were held up until 2020.

In university seminar presentations, Habiburrahman told the audience that he wrote *Cinta Suci Zahrana* to highlight one of the current problems faced by Indonesian Muslim youth: their priority of a career over raising a family. Many Indonesians in their mid-20s delay marriage because they are too busy studying higher education and pursuing their careers. Without much thought or notice they reach their 30s, by which time most other potential partners are already married. If they are not married, young people are forced to manage their sexual and emotional desires, which can result in unethical behaviour. Educated women face difficulties in finding a suitable spouse as men in Indonesia usually prefer to marry 'down' (Smith-Hefner 2018). The phenomenon of the rising number of single women in academia is not limited to Indonesia but has also been identified in Malaysia. Highly educated and financially well-off Muslim women find themselves surrounded by men who do not live up to their expectations of an ideal partner (Vignato 2012).

Cinta Suci Zahrana explores the complexity surrounding the dilemma of gender roles, which Zahrana, a young academic-oriented Muslim woman, is facing in contemporary Indonesia, where modern individual career aspirations and patriarchal Islamic values conflict. Three important aspects of modern Muslim life are explored in the story.

The first is that many people prefer secular and professional education over Islamic education in Indonesia because of the apparent relevance to professional jobs and social status (Azra et al. 2010; Hefner 2008). Zahrana's father had limited education and did not avail himself of career development opportunities as a clerk in a local government agency. Although her parents would have preferred her to go to an Islamic boarding school and State Education University to become a teacher, Zahrana chose to study in the best state high school and graduated as the best student. She also left her hometown to study at Gadjah Mada University (UGM), Yogyakarta, one of the most prestigious state research-intensive universities in Indonesia, where she majored in architecture. Her choice of a modern professional career as a lecturer would be perfect if she were a man who is expected to be the family breadwinner.

Secondly, Indonesian parents like their children to live nearby to provide a social security safety net for their old age (Abikusno 2018). There is an expectation that children will look after their ageing parents while they raise their own family. Zahrana, an aspiring junior female academic, graduated as the best student from the university but being the only child in the family, she refused a junior faculty position and a scholarship to study for her master's degree in the Netherlands. Instead, she returned to her hometown of Semarang where she took up a lecturing position while pursuing her master's in Bandung, West Java. This was a compromise she made for her parents. As part of her research, she was invited to higher education institutions for research collaboration and frequently travelled alone overseas. The story in the novel highlights the dilemma with which Muslim women are faced. Zahrana is expected to marry and have children, yet she had declined multiple seemingly suitable marriage proposals because she was solely focused on her academic career.

Thirdly, the societal expectations and perceptions of a single woman, despite her excellent professional achievements, remain negative and hostile. As Zahrana reached 34 years of age, her parents felt worried and even embarrassed about her choice to follow a self-oriented academic career and pursuit of a Ph.D. overseas as opposed to finding a husband and marrying. Her family's neighbours started to question whether she had any problems that could explain why she remained single. Furthermore, she was proposed to by her boss to become his second wife, but he had been known to have sexually harassed other women. These incidents echo the prevalent perception that women over 30 years old are not wanted or sought after because their reproductive fertility had declined. Thus, they have to accept what could be deemed an unfair and unfavourable marriage despite the fact that they have become successful in their professions.

The author does not discourage women from pursuing their academic career or higher education. Habiburrahman's wife has completed a master's degree in early child education from Muhammadiyah University in Solo, and she runs an Islamic early education centre in Salatiga, Central Java where they live. Habiburrahman's novel depicts Zahrana's childhood friend, Lina, who married young and ran a business with her husband, and who is also preparing for her master's. This book also features female figures who excelled in studying Islamic theology (El Shirazy 2011: 166), and the presence of such figures motivates Zahrana's married friend, Lina not to give up her pursuit of a master's and a Ph.D. The conclusion of this book depicts Zahrana marrying a younger man, a former university student she supervised, and planning to take up a Ph.D. scholarship to study in China with her husband. When she decides to accept his marriage proposal, despite her seniority in her academic standing, she demands that her husband should take over relational seniority by asking him to stop calling her the honorific mother, *ibu*, used to address teachers and female professionals in Indonesia, but instead to call a younger sister, a customary form of address used by a husband as an elder man to address his wife. This illustrates a symbolic change indicating that the man leads the household in their marriage as expected in patriarchy, endorsed by the state and in line with the interpretations of Islam.

In summary, the key message conveyed in this book is that marriage should not be postponed, despite the apparent focus on modern professional career pursuits and higher education. In marriage men are the head of the family irrespective of a woman's professional standing.

Narratives of Single Muslim Women

The last section of this chapter explores narratives of single professional Muslim women in Indonesia. It uses a range of data derived from seven cases I had close contact with in Indonesian higher education, supplemented by published internet blogs. The women were willing to share their experiences of being unmarried as they thought it would give some insight for other women sharing the same fate, yet their names were changed to protect their privacy.

Spinsterhood is not an entirely new topic in the current academic literature; however, existing studies of the narratives of women's singlehood are analysed from the perspectives of psychology and women's studies (Ibrahim 2018; Imtoual and Hussein 2009; Retnaningsih 2013; Septiana and Syafiq 2013; Zainal 2018) without specific reference to the Islamic values of becoming an ideal woman. Vignato (2012) has analysed how Muslim women in Aceh and Malaysia negotiated the expectations of marriage as an interplay between local societies and Islamic marriage practice. Our focus differs from the existing studies on single women (Himawan et al. 2018b; Retnaningsih 2013) as we explore the interplay between Islam and womanhood: how these women have actively used interpretations of Islam, aligning themselves with the role models of ideal Muslim women. The following two key elements were highlighted in their narratives:

Takdir: Leaving It to God

The single women I spoke to often wondered why God did not send them a husband. Quite consistently, women made remarks about their singlehood being a message from God. All of them wore headscarves as part of their daily clothing as they thought deepening their devotional activities would assist them in becoming a more pious Muslim and they would receive greater assistance from God. Accepting God's provision in life is expressed in the Indonesian word of *takdir*, meaning destiny determined by God. Key themes from their narratives were that they found solace in becoming a figurative mother for their extended family members or stepchildren and in undertaking devotional acts to become better Muslims. Although none mentioned Khadijah or Aishah specifically as a role model, becoming an adopted or figurative mother, or becoming a stepmother was identified as an important action for them to belong to a family, even if they were not biologically connected.

For these women, delaying marriage was and still is perceived as an unintended outcome rather than their own choice. Looking after the needs of their extended family was among the reasons they could not marry when they met a suitable partner. The content of the blog posting titled *Usia 36 Tahun Belum Nikah Baca Kisahku Ini Sebelum Menyebutku Perawan Tua*, (*36 Years Old, Unmarried, Read My Story Before Calling*

Me a Spinster) (Fimela 2018), encapsulates the challenges of these women who have taken a family carer's role early, as is expected of a Muslim woman. Fimela is a 36-year-old woman who has never married. She is from Pekanbaru, Riau, a provincial town located in Northern Sumatra of Indonesia. Her father died when she was four years old, and she had four brothers to look after. In Malay culture domestic chores such as cooking, washing and cleaning belong to women. Her mother, as a single parent to five children, and Fimela, from a young age and as the sole daughter, took on the task of looking after her brothers. Her brothers all married and left home, leaving her and her mother. She worked at a local radio station to support herself and her mother. She had met two possible suitors, but she did not want to leave her mother alone, and so those relationships ended. By this time, she was in her mid-30s and remained single, and her extended relatives and neighbours always asked her why, as if it were her choice. She did not disclose to anyone the reason, which was that she could not leave her mother alone. Her ageing mother became sick and told her that she would like to see her marry and have children before she died. Fimela's narrative reflects her belief that destiny and provision of life is in God's hands (*takdir hidup dan ketentuan dari-Nya*). Her concluding statement elaborates her views:

> Nothing is too late or too early in the undertakings of God. I believe that God has already prepared the right time for me and will arrange my life according to his plans. (Fimela 2018; my translation)

Atika has a similar story. Her parents were too busy with their work and as the eldest daughter of the family she took on the care of her nine siblings, following the Malay tradition in South Sumatra. In fact, her younger siblings saw her more like their little mother as she was the one who bathed them and cooked for them. She was a schoolteacher, and her parents would not allow her to marry a local man who was not a university graduate, as he did not meet their expectations. Her parents needed her to take care of the younger children. She remained single until her early 40s. She also looked after her nephews and nieces because their parents moved to different towns on short-term contracts. To provide a stable environment for her nephews and nieces, they stayed with their grandparents and Atika.

The story of Emi repeats the same pattern. Emi was a university academic in Palembang. She was living with her elderly mother and her nephew. Her father died when she was young, and her mother raised her as a single parent. Her brother was in Jambi and was working hard to make ends meet. Since she was earning a good income, she was able to look after her ailing mother and her nephew while completing his schooling. In her 20s, Emi had met a suitable man who was an academic in another town. Because she was looking after her mother and nephew and wanted to pursue her Ph.D. to advance her career as an academic, leaving her university job to marry him would have been a huge backward step for herself and for her dependents. They discontinued the relationship after many years, and she found herself single in her early 30s.

Takdir is among the Islamic terms frequently used by these Muslim women. For example, Ayudia said her parents have accepted that she has not met a suitable partner and they remain hopeful and are willing to wait until her *jodoh* (suitable marriage partner) comes into her life. She is a university lecturer and Ph.D. student in her early 40s, and she was optimistically waiting for her spouse to arrive. She commented that since she was single at the time, she would rather use her time to advance her career. She is not refusing to get married, because she believes that God surely has a plan for her but she is simply leaving God to reveal it.

Eliana, who is 35 years old, said she and her elder sister were both unmarried. Her sister is a university lecturer. Eliana is a dental specialist undertaking research at a prestigious state university, and her parents understand that marriage only takes place when it is suitable. She believes that marriage is a devotional act. She has accepted marriage proposals before but did not end up marrying, which indicated to her that those marriages were not meant to be. She believes marriage will take place when the right moment comes and that one of the conditions for this to occur is that she needs to be ready and will achieve this readiness through self-improvement as a good Muslim woman. Meeting her future husband will not come from dating but by being ready, she emphasised. She attends a weekly Islamic study group and she subscribes to popular tweets of Indonesian Muslim preachers such as Felix Siauw,[4] Yusuf Mansur,[5] Jamil Azzaini,[6] Komaruddin Hidayat[7] and Ippho Santosa.[8] These are popular Muslim male preachers who advocate that Islam guides a Muslim's way of life. Through listening to these preachers, she learnt that she had to cover her body more strictly to become a better Muslim. She also takes public transport as a means of travel with an intension to give *amal* (voluntary offerings) to those who ask for them. For example,

Yusuf Mansur is known to advocate the benefit of voluntary almsgivings as they would in turn increase the benefit to the giver (Kailani 2015). Street beggars are common in Indonesia and Eliana has been giving offerings since she was young. This is her way of becoming a better Muslim and to prepare herself for marriage.

Eliana has a well-respected position in the Indonesian community but the fact that she remains single undermines her confidence and pride as a Muslim woman. 'I am like an old product, which no-one wants to buy. I thought I am not virtuous enough in the eyes of God, so I dressed more conservatively. I am trying to be a good Muslim woman. When is God going to give me a husband?' (Interview, 28 November 2017).

Another informant, Naila, approaching her mid-40s, works in university administration, and supports her family financially, and has been paying the educational costs for her brother for many years. She wanted to marry but she remained single to look after her younger brother. She felt she was pitied at work as she did not have a husband. She thinks that everyone sees her as a failing Muslim woman. She lamented her fate in our conversation. 'What am I lacking? Am I still missing something? Why is God punishing me? I have looked after my family and why is it not enough for me?' (Interview, 23 November 2017).

Another case, that Zemira, resonates with the theme of the unpopularity of spinsters in contemporary Indonesia. Zemira is a highly respected academic and she is quite open that she is a so-called *perawan tua* (spinster) in her university. As an optimist she has accepted that marriage is not the only way to become a better Muslim. She was not disturbed by the fact that everyone at work knows she is single. As she has time to work for the community, she started getting involved in rubbish removal and recycling as a way to contribute to her community. Doing good for the community is widely seen as a devotional act and she was challenging the conservative views circulated by Islamists in contemporary Indonesia that early marriage is the preferred life choice. She stated, 'There are many ways to enter heaven. If not by marriage for me, I will explore other ways' (Interview, 25 November 2017).

All seven women interviewed for this chapter were dressed in loose Islamic clothing. Some even covered their palms to reduce the exposure of flesh in a public space. Some of them met us without wearing a headscarf. It is common for women to wear a headscarf during their activities in public spaces. They were all professional women who travelled away from home on business trips and training sessions. Since they were often mingling with married men, they wanted to create space between themselves and male colleagues and wanted to ease potential tension with the wives of their colleagues. Some of the women I spoke to were clearly physically attractive, and they told me that they started to wear a headscarf because they wanted to appear modest in the company of married men and to increase their social mobility. These comments echoed the findings of a study by Mernissi (1987) on the use of the veil. Modesty is, they understand, part of becoming a better Muslim woman. They expressed their hope that God would reward them as they were making extra effort to become better Muslims. Sometimes they felt disappointed that they remained unmarried despite the fact that they engaged in voluntary fasting twice a week, they covered their body, and were looking after their families.

The predicaments experienced as part of Muslim women's career advancement in this chapter clearly demonstrate that access to education and pursuing a professional career with a high income has not brought happiness to some single Muslim women because in part they have failed to become a wife and a mother following the role models of Khadijah and Aishah, the mothers of the believers.[9]

Becoming a Mother

Scholars have identified that mothering or becoming a mother is closely associated with the natural role of Muslim women. Evidence that scholars point to includes Islamic sources as well as the lived experiences of Muslim mothers. For example, Islamic textual sources are often quoted to highlight the importance of the position of the mother, including the *hadith*, the official collection of accounts of the deeds and sayings of the Prophet Muhammad. 'Paradise lies at the feet of the mother' is often cited to show the importance of Muslim mothers, as illustrated by the works of (Badissy 2016; Oh 2010; Pappano 2016; Wadud 2006). The Prophet is also believed to have indicated that Muslims should all be dutiful to their mothers (Murphy-Geiss 2010). These teachings are widely circulated to perpetuate the view that good mothers and good women are indivisible roles.

In view of this universal depiction of Muslim women's main role, it is not surprising that one aspect these Muslim women had emphasised was their desire to have children once they were married. Eliana, a dental specialist, said to me that it would be good to become a stay-at-home mother after her marriage but at the same time she needs to contribute to society through her profession as a medical expert. She was given this opportunity by God and not giving back to the community is not ideal. Thus, she has refused to marry a man who asked her to stop working just because he would like her to. Therefore, she feels that her *rezeki* (livelihood) is not based on raising a family. Rather, she wants to be able to treat serious health issues through her occupation. She did express, however, that even though she is a successful professional, she feels envious of her friends who have become mothers.

Three of the women in our research married late in their 40s and they did not have children of their own. Gayatri married a widow with two children and became a stepmother. She continued her senior academic position in a prestigious state university but added this new role. The couple felt sorry that they did not have their own children, but they considered this the discretion of God. Atika married one of her old suitors to become a co-wife. After all her single years she decided on this, even though her husband wanted to divorce his first wife. She thought it was better for their children to keep the family together and she does not have to live in the same city. By then in her late 40s, it was her last chance to possibly start a family with a man she had originally wanted to marry. Another interviewee, Emi, married a divorced man with two children, yet the children stayed with his first wife.

Despite their wishes and the fact that they did eventually marry, neither Atika nor Emi became mothers. Both of them went through fertility treatment but without success. Neither gave up their dream of becoming a mother. Although these couples do not have children, in public they called each other mother and father to appear as if they were a family with children. For example, immediately after their marriage, Emi asked her husband to call her *bunda* (mother), as she was hoping to start a family, and she called her husband, *ayah* (father). Atika was called mama, a common English term that is used widely in Indonesia to refer to a mother.

When I asked why they were using these terms for each other, they said, with some hesitance, that it was because they wished that they would become parents and they were showing the world that they are ready for parenthood. In Indonesia, it is customary to address one's husband as a brother and one's wife as a sister but when the couple has a child, these terms of address gradually change to mother and father.

This method of appearing or acting to be a mother is often used by single women who have never married in Indonesia. It resonates with the way Aishah begged her husband to call her mother, even though she had produced no children of her own. It is customary for these women to use *anak* (child) and *cucu* (grandchild) to refer to children of their relatives. The use of figurative kinship is common and in fact these women had raised children of their relatives. Single women tend to voluntarily disclose family matters involving their 'child' or 'grandchild' in public. Talking about family life is common in Indonesia and people would assume that everyone has a child. As the Indonesian middle-class embraces Islam in everyday life, the Arabic terms of *abi* for father and *umi* for mother have begun to be more commonly used. Some people address themselves as *umi* instead of the Indonesian word *ibu*, to show that they are mothers, irrespective of whether they are genuinely mothers or not. *Being a mother* gives much more social status to Indonesian Muslim women than being a single woman who has never married.

A well-known Indonesian transgender singer and an actress Dorce Gamalama, born in a strong Islamic region of West Sumatra, went through gender reassignment. She presents herself as a devout Muslim woman and considers herself to be a mother because she looks after 600 orphans and has adopted four children. The purpose of her gender reassignment was not to use her body to seduce men or flirt with them, but to be a complete human being, including being a mother, as seen in the photos and text featured in Merdekawan (2018). Dorce stated in 2020, 'If you want to throw away children because you are ashamed, give them all to me, I will take care of them with full affection. If the children are not happy with a mother like me, it is easy, I will become a father' (Azizah 2020).

In this humorous message, Dorce makes the important point that an ideal Muslim woman is a mother. As a transgender woman she cannot produce her own children but she is happy to adopt children, presenting the well-circulated image of a good Muslim woman, and an affectionate mother. This is as is expected of any Muslim woman, and echoes the model of Khadijah and Aishah, who are both known as mothers of all believers. She sold a traditional Minangkabau house she inherited to raise funds for orphans in Palestine, Syria and Indonesia in 2020 (Mahartika 2019). She also established a foundation to run an early childhood education centre and a primary school for orphans called Sekolah Islam Kasih

Sayang Ibu or Islamic School of Mother's Care in Bekasi, Jakarta (Seta 2018).

Contrary to Dorce's open-minded happiness, she suffers emotionally because she remains single and childless. She commented that she was often advised by her relatives that to marry, she should not be picky in finding a partner or be concerned about the man's state of wealth. Furthermore, at family gatherings she was asked unsolicited questions regarding her spinsterhood. She commented in her writing, 'Frequently I felt that my spinsterhood is a stigma for them' (Fimela 2018).

In my long engagement with the Indonesian community, I often hear people generally comment on their single relatives. 'Why is she only working? Does she not have time? She has enough money to make a pilgrimage. But marriage is also a devotional act. What's wrong with her? She will not bear any children? Who will look after her when they are old?' These comments indicate social expectations that Muslim women should marry to become a wife and bear and raise children. As a result, spinsters tend to find it difficult to attend family gatherings, particularly wedding receptions of younger relatives, as they are afraid of being interrogated about their spinsterhood. As Badissy (2016) has highlighted, this is precisely because women's main role is determined and presented to be subservient to families and men, and a failure to assume this role is seen as a failure to become a good Muslim woman.

Wuri's account attests to this point. Wuri is a senior academic in Indonesia who was willing to share her views on her experience of living as an unmarried woman. She married for the first time in her early 40s to a widower who had two children. She was aware that she would not be able to bear children at her age. When he proposed marriage, she accepted his proposal because she was able to become a mother for his children. In Indonesia it is not uncommon for middle-class women to use a housemaid to cook food and attend to domestic chores while they pursue their career. The mother's role among middle-class families is not always precisely linked with manual chores per se (Jones 2004; Sakai and Fauzia 2016). In this case, her husband, an active politician in Indonesia, wanted her to adopt a traditional gender role by cooking meals and taking care of her family as much as she could. She continued in her academic role while also looking after the family by going to a local market every morning to buy groceries for her family. Her experience is, thus, unique. She called her husband Papa and he called her Mama after their marriage.

I asked if she was comfortable in undertaking such roles as an established academic middle-class woman. She answered:

> Women's main task is to look after family, and I enjoy walking to the local market every morning. I can also cook for my stepchildren as their mother. It is important to undertake these tasks as a Muslim woman. Now, I have my own family and I am very happy with it. (Interview, 01 December 2017)

Conclusion

This chapter has analysed how women's aspirations to pursue professional careers paradoxically created challenges because of the unchanging patriarchal gender norms prevalent in Muslim-dominant societies. Education and job access have been provided to Muslim women but they have had to negotiate these 'opportunities' with the social and cultural norms of marriage in their daily life. This chapter has shown that marriage and raising children remain crucial for Muslim women in Indonesia. The community shuns Muslim women who pursue careers without getting married, as they are seen as neglecting their priority gender role, as expected in Islamic culture. This is the case irrespective of whether they are Muslim women in the West or in Muslim-dominant countries such as Indonesia. The practice of polygamy in Western countries is thus linked with professional Muslim women's efforts to carve out some balance between their professional work and their Muslim family aspirations. For Muslim women in this era, this is a contestation of modernity and Islam.

This chapter has analysed the experience of single professional women and how they can be perceived—and indeed, perceive themselves—as failed Muslim women despite being successful in their professional fields. The findings of the predicaments surrounding women's choices shed light on the contested modern but Islamic environment that leads to Muslim women increasingly choosing to become *mompreneurs*, because it can give flexibility and leeway to balance work and the opportunity to raise family, as we illustrate in Chapter 5. Role models of Muslim women as imagined among Muslims strongly denote becoming a wife and, crucially, a mother.

Notes

1. The study by Charsley and Liversage (2013) shows that Muslim men may seek polygamous marriage for a transnational migration purpose in Western countries.
2. A popular Indonesian short film from 2008 titled *Tilik* (visit to a sick person) depicts how married village women perceive the love affairs of an attractive spinster.
3. See information and videos at AQL Instagram account @aqlislamiccenter and website https://aql.or.id/.
4. Felix Yanwar Siauw, born in 1984, converted to Islam while he was a student of Bogor Agricultural University (IPB). He is widely known for his affiliation with Hizbut Tahrir Indonesia (HTI). With a focus on the issues of morality he preaches Islam to Muslim youth through social media and books.
5. Yusuf Mansur was born in 1976 in Jakarta. He runs the Islamic boarding school of Daarul Qur'an and has published popular books on Islam. His preaching centres on almsgiving.
6. Jamil Azzaini is a writer and motivator and runs Kubik Leadership Group: a training company popular among Indonesia's middle class.
7. Professor Komaruddin Hidayat was born in 1953. He is an Indonesian Muslim academic who taught at UIN Syarif Hidayatullah Jakarta and was appointed Rector of the same university in 2006–2015.
8. Ippho Santosa, born in 1977, is a best-selling author, and a motivator popular among middle-class Muslims. He advocates building wealth as a Muslim. For more about his profile, visit https://ippho.com/.
9. See Chapter 1.

References

5Pillars. 2013. Shortage of "Suitable" Men Results in Successful Muslim Women Sharing Husbands. https://5pillarsuk.com/2013/11/12/shortage-of-suitable-men-results-in-successful-muslim-women-sharing-husbands/. Accessed 18 Aug 2021.

Abbott, Nabia. 1942. *Aishah, the Beloved of Mohammed: A Biography*. Chicago: University of Chicago Press.

Abikusno, Nugroho. 2018. Evaluation and Implementation of Ageing-Related Policies in Indonesia. In *Older Persons in Southeast Asia*, eds. Evi Nurvidya Arifin and Aris Ananta, 392–414. Singapore: ISEAS Publishing. https://doi.org/10.1355/9789812309457.

Ahmad, Fauzia. 2001. Modern Traditions? British Muslim Women and Academic Achievement. *Gender and Education* 13 (2): 137–152. https://doi.org/10.1080/09540250120051169.

Ahmad, Fauzia. 2014. British Muslims' Relationship Crisis: Marriage, Divorce and the Role of Secular and Religious Support Services. http://www.publicspirit.org.uk/. Accessed 5 Jan 2021.

Ahmad, Fauzia. 2018. Muslim Men Are Looking for Wives and the Women Are Looking for Companions, April 30 2018 Rea, Ernie *Beyond Belief*. BBC Radio. Available at: https://www.bbc.co.uk/programmes/p065dnqn. Accessed 20 Aug 2020.

Ahmad, Fauzia. 2019. [Video] the British Muslim Marriage Crisis. *Islam UK* [Video], March 30. Available at: https://youtu.be/mGnsvEndD3U.

Ahmed, Leila. 1986. Women and the Advent of Islam. *Signs: Journal of Women in Culture and Society* 11 (4): 665–691.

Ali, Faiza, Ashish Malik, Vijay Pereira, and Akram Al Ariss. 2017. A Relational Understanding of Work-Life Balance of Muslim Migrant Women in the West: Future Research Agenda. *The International Journal of Human Resource Management* 28 (8): 1163–1181.

Alkhteeb, TarekTawfik, and Zafar Ahmad Sultan. 2014. Role of Women in Economic Development in Saudi Arabia: A Case Study of Al-Kharj Governorate. *International Journal of Academic Research* 6: 10–18.

Anwar, Akhirul. 2012. Mahasiswa Jogja Ajak Pacar Masuk Kos Sudah Biasa Sejak 1980-An. *Solopos.com*. Retrieved from https://www.solopos.com/mahasiswa-jogja-ajak-pacar-masuk-kos-sudah-tren-sejak-1980-an-345740.

Arsal, Thriwaty. 2014. The Woman's Position and Undocumented Marriage (A Case in a Village at East Java Province, Indonesia). *Journal of Culture, Society and Development* 3: 69–78.

Ayashi Rz, El Salman. 2012. *Ternyata Orang Yang Menikah Itu Lebih Mudah Masuk Surga*. Jakarta: Qultum Media.

Azizah, Kurnia. 2020. Dorce Gamalama Terlahir Pria Bernama Dedi Yuliardi, Foto Ini Bukti Sah Jadi Wanita. *merdeka.com*. Retrieved from https://www.merdeka.com/trending/dorce-gamalama-terlahir-pria-bernama-dedi-yuliardi-foto-ini-bukti-sah-jadi-wanita.html.

Azmawati, Azman Azwan, Hashim Intan Hashimah Mohd, and Noraida Endut. 2015. "Don't Marry, Be Happy!"—How Single Women in Malaysia View Marriage. *SHS Web of Conferences*, 18. https://doi.org/10.1051/shsconf/20151803001.

Azra, Azyumardi, Dina Afrianty, and Robert W. Hefner. 2010. Pesantren and Madrasa: Muslim Schools and National Ideals in Indonesia. In *Schooling Islam: The Culture and Politics of Modern Muslim Education*, eds. Robert W. Hefner and Muhammad Qasim Zaman, 172–198. New Jersey: Princeton University Press.

Badissy, Maha. 2016. Motherhood in the Islamic Tradition Rethinking the Procreative Function of Women in Islam. *Muslim World Journal of Human Rights* 13 (1): 131–156.

BBC News. 2017. Sunderland Businessman's Second Wife Website 'Benefits Women'. *BBC*. https://www.bbc.com/news/uk-england-tyne-41667070. Accessed 10 Aug 2021.

britishdocs. 2012. [Video] Strictly Soulmates—Muslim. *Strictly Soulmates, BBC Documentary*, February 9 2012. YouTube. Available at: https://www.youtube.com/watch?app=desktop&v=xVSlbS5gn00&feature=youtu.be.

Budgeon, Shelley. 2016. The 'Problem'with Single Women: Choice, Accountability and Social Change. *Journal of Social and Personal Relationships* 33 (3): 401–418.

Budiharsana, Meiwita. 2016. Female Genital Cutting Common in Indonesia, Offered as Part of Child Delivery by Birth Clinics. *The Conversation*. https://theconversation.com/female-genital-cutting-common-in-indonesia-offered-as-part-of-child-delivery-by-birth-clinics-54379. Accessed 18 Aug 2021.

Cameron, Lisa, and Diana Contreras Suarez. 2017. Women's Economic Participation in Indonesia: A Study of Gender Inequality in Employment, Entrepreneurship, and Key Enablers for Change, 91. Available at: https://www.monash.edu/business/cdes/research/publications/publications2/Womens-economic-participation-in-Indonesia-June-2017.pdf.

Charsley, Katharine, and Anika Liversage. 2013. Transforming Polygamy: Migration, Transnationalism and Multiple Marriages among Muslim Minorities. *Global Networks* 13 (1): 60–78. https://doi.org/10.1111/j.1471-0374.2012.00369.x.

Chew, Amy. 2019. Indonesian Mp Says His Three Wives Are Proof Polygamy Can Be 'Good and Harmonious.' https://www.scmp.com/week-asia/people/article/3031645/indonesian-mp-says-his-three-wives-are-proof-polygamy-can-be-good. Accessed 18 Aug 2021.

Dettmer, Jamie. 2013. Britain's Muslim Communities See Rise in Part-Time Wives. https://www.thedailybeast.com/britains-muslim-communities-see-rise-in-part-time-wives. Accessed 18 Aug 2021.

El-Halawany, Raghda. 2009. 'Spinsters' by Choice: Egypt's Single Ladies Speak Out. https://dailynewsegypt.com/2009/10/22/spinsters-by-choice-egypts-single-ladies-speak-out/. Accessed 18 Aug 2021.

El Shirazy, Habiburrahman. 2004. *Ayat-Ayat Cinta*. Jakarta: Republika-Basmalah.

El Shirazy, Habiburrahman. 2007. *Ketika Cinta Bertasbih*. Jakarta: Republika-Basmalah.

El Shirazy, Habiburrahman. 2011. *Cinta Suci Zahrana*. Jakarta: Ihwah Publishing House.

Fauzi, Muhammad Latif. 2019. Actors and Norms in an Islamic Marriage: A Study of Madura Community in Rural Eastern East Java. *Journal of Indonesian Islam* 13 (2): 297–325.

Fimela. 2018. Usia 36 Tahun Belum Nikah, Baca Kisahku Ini Sebelum Menyebutku Perawan Tua. *Fimela*. https://www.fimela.com/lifestyle-relationship/read/3808297/usia-36-tahun-belum-nikah-baca-kisahku-ini-sebelum-men yebutku-perawan-tua. Accessed 18 Aug 2021.

Freer, Courtney Jean. 2018. *Rentier Islamism: The Influence of the Muslim Brotherhood in Gulf Monarchies*. England: Oxford University Press.

Hefner, Robert W. 2008. Islamic Schools, Social Movements, and Democracy in Indonesia. In *Making Modern Muslims: The Politics of Islamic Education in Southeast Asia*, ed. Robert W. Hefner, 55–105. Honolulu: University of Hawaii Press. https://doi.org/10.1515/9780824863463.

Henry. 2019. Makin Diminati, Rumah Taaruf Sudah Menjodohkan 70 Pasangan. https://www.liputan6.com/lifestyle/read/4129492/makin-diminati-rumah-taaruf-sudah-menjodohkan-70-pasangan. Accessed 18 Aug 2021.

Heryanto, Ariel. 2008. *Popular Culture in Indonesia: Fluid Identities in Post-Authoritarian Politics*. New York: Routledge.

Heryanto, Ariel. 2011. Upgraded Piety and Pleasure: The New Middle Class and Islam in Indonesian Popular Culture. In *Islam and Popular Culture in Indonesia and Malaysia*, ed. Andrew N. Weintraub, 76–98. London: Routledge. https://doi.org/10.4324/9780203829004.

Himawan, Karel Karsten, Matthew Bambling, and Sisira Edirippulige. 2018a. Singleness, Religiosity, and the Implications for Counselors: The Indonesian Case. *Europe's Journal of Psychology* 14 (2): 485–497. https://doi.org/10.5964/ejop.v14i2.1530.

Himawan, Karel Karsten, Matthew Bambling, and Sisira Edirippulige. 2018b. What Does It Mean to Be Single in Indonesia? Religiosity, Social Stigma, and Marital Status Among Never-Married Indonesian Adults. *SAGE Open* 8 (3): 1–9. https://doi.org/10.1177/2158244018803132.

Hoesterey, James Bourk. 2008. Marketing Morality: The Rise, Fall and Rebranding of Aa Gym. In *Expressing Islam: Religious Life and Politics in Indonesia*, eds. Greg Fealy and Sally White, 95–112. Singapore: ISEAS Publishing.

Hoesterey, James Bourk, and Marshall Clark. 2012. Film Islami: Gender, Piety and Pop Culture in Post-Authoritarian Indonesia. *Asian Studies Review* 36 (2): 207–226. https://doi.org/10.1080/10357823.2012.685925.

Ibrahim, Rozita. 2018. Never-Married Malay Muslim Women in Modern Malaysia: Gender, Identity and Agency. PhD Thesis, University of Aberdeen. https://ethos.bl.uk/OrderDetails.do?uin=uk.bl.ethos.794103.

Imtoual, Alia, and Shakira Hussein. 2009. Challenging the Myth of the Happy Celibate: Muslim Women Negotiating Contemporary Relationships. *Contemporary Islam* 3 (1): 25–39.

Jones, Carla. 2004. Whose Stress? Emotion Work in Middle-Class Javanese Homes. *Ethnos* 69 (4): 509–528.

Jones, Gavin W., and Bina Gubhaju. 2009. Factors Influencing Changes in Mean Age at First Marriage and Proportions Never Marrying in the Low-Fertility Countries of East and Southeast Asia. *Asian Population Studies* 5 (3): 237–265.

Jones, Gavin W., and Wei-Jun Jean. Yeung. 2014. Marriage in Asia. *Journal of Family Issues* 35 (12): 1567–1583. https://doi.org/10.1177/0192513X14538029.

Kailani, Najib. 2015. Aspiring to Prosperity: The Economic Theology of Urban Muslims in Contemporary Indonesia. PhD Thesis, School of Humanities and Social Sciences, UNSW Canberra, The University of New South Wales.

Khatkar, Perminder. 2011. The British Muslim Men Who Love "Both Their Wives". https://www.bbc.com/news/uk-15032947. Accessed 12 Dec 2020.

Kingdom of Saudi Arabia, General Authority for Statistics. 2020. The Saudi Youth in Numbers: A Report for International Youth Day 2020. General Authority for Statistics of Kingdom of Saudi Arabia. Available at: https://www.stats.gov.sa/sites/default/files/saudi_youth_in_numbers_report_2020en.pdf.

Livia, Klara. 2019. Ini 5 Perbedaan Jomblo dan Single, Kamu Termasuk yang Mana? https://www.idntimes.com/life/relationship/klara-livia-1/ini-5-perbedaan-jomblo-dan-single-kamu-termasuk-yang-mana/1. Accessed 18 Aug 2021.

Mahartika, Loudia. 2019. Dijual Seharga Rp. 2 Miliar, Ini 6 Potret Rumah Gadang Milik Dorce. Liputat 6. https://hot.liputan6.com/read/4111058/dijual-seharga-rp-2-miliar-ini-6-potret-rumah-gadang-milik-dorce. Accessed 18 Aug 2021.

Majah, Ibn. 2015. *Sunan Ibn Majah*. Riyadh: Daar al-Hadhoroh lin Nasar wat Tauzi.

MEMRI. 2017. Saudi University Lecturer: The Solution to the Problem of Single Women in Saudi Arabia Is Polygamy—Three Wives Per Man, and If That Works Out, He Gets One More MEMRI. https://www.memri.org/reports/saudi-woman-academic-calls-to-encourage-polygamy. Accessed 10 July 2020.

Merdekawan, Guntur. 2018. Transgender & Operasi Kelamin: Wanita Itu Bernama Dorce. *KapanLagi.com*. https://www.kapanlagi.com/showbiz/selebriti/transgender-38-operasi-kelamin-wanita-itu-bernama-dorce-930275.html. Accessed 18 August 2021.

Mernissi, Fatima. 1987. *Beyond the Veil: Male-Female Dynamics in a Modern Muslim Society*. Bloomington, Indiana: Indiana University Press.

Mohammed, Syma. 2012. Why British Muslim Women Struggle to Find a Marriage Partner. https://www.theguardian.com/commentisfree/belief/2012/jan/18/british-muslim-women-marriage-struggle. Accessed 18 Aug 2021.

Muhsin, Ilyya, Nikmah Rochmawati, and Muhammad Chairul Huda. 2019. Revolution of Islamic Proselytizing Organization: From Islamism to Moderate. *QIJIS (Qudus International Journal of Islamic Studies)* 7 (1): 45–70.

Murphy-Geiss, Gail. 2010. Islam and Motherhood. In *Encyclopedia of Motherhood*, ed. Andrea O'Reilly, 586–590. Sage. https://doi.org/10.4135/9781412979276.n295.

Nurjamal. 2016. Ustadz M. Fauzil Adhim: Pakar Parenting Islam dan Pendakwah dengan Segudang Karya. gomuslim. https://umma.id/article/share/id/12/194104. Accessed 18 Aug 2021.

Nurmila, Nina. 2016. Polygamous Marriages in Indonesia and Their Impacts on Women's Access to Income and Property. *Al-Jami'ah: Journal of Islamic Studies* 54 (2): 427–446.

Oh, Irene. 2010. Motherhood in Christianity and Islam: Critiques, Realities, and Possibilities. *Journal of Religious Ethics* 38 (4): 638–653.

Pappano, M Aziza. 2016. *Muslim Mothering: Global Histories, Theories and Practises*. Ontario: Demeter Press.

Peletz, Michael G. 1996. *Reason and Passion: Representations of Gender in a Malay Society*. Berkeley and Los Angeles: University of California Press.

Population, United Nations Department of Economic and Social Affairs. 2019. World Marriage Data 2019. Available at: https://population.un.org/MarriageData/Index.html#/home.

Rashad, Hoda, Magued Osman, and Farzaneh Roudi-Fahimi. 2005. *Marriage in the Arab World*. Population Reference Bureau Washington, DC.

Renaldi, Erwin. 2018. Female Circumcision: Culture and Religion in Malaysia See Millions of Girls Undergo Cut. https://www.abc.net.au/news/2018-11-13/female-circumcision-is-still-happening-in-malaysia/10473640. Accessed 18 Aug 2021.

Retnaningsih, Umi Oktyari. 2013. Indonesian Educated Unmarried Career Women: Gender Inequality, Discrimination, and Prejudices. *Asian Women* 29 (1): 5–25.

Rinaldo, Rachel. 2013. *Mobilizing Piety: Islam and Feminism in Indonesia*. Oxford and New York: Oxford University Press.

Rumah Ta'aruf MyQuran. 2021. Tentang Rumahtaaruf.Com. Rumah Taaruf MyQuran. http://www.rumahtaaruf.com/p/rumah-taaruf.html. Accessed Apr 2021.

Sabbah-Karkaby, Maha, and Haya Stier. 2017. Links Between Education and Age at Marriage Among Palestinian Women in Israel: Changes Over Time. *Studies in Family Planning* 48 (1): 23–38.

Sakai, Minako. 2012. Preaching to Muslim Youth in Indonesia: The 'Dakwah' Activities of Habiburrahman El Shirazy. *RIMA: Review of Indonesian and Malaysian Affairs* 46 (1): 9–31.

Sakai, Minako. 2019. Embracing Islam, Work and Family: Women's Economic Empowerment in Islamising Indonesia. *Intersections: Gender and Sexuality in Asia and the Pacific* 43 (July). http://intersections.anu.edu.au/issue43/sakai2.html#n18.

Sakai, Minako, and Amelia Fauzia. 2014. Islamic Orientations in Contemporary Indonesia: Islamism on the Rise? *Asian Ethnicity* 15 (1): 41–61. https://doi.org/10.1080/14631369.2013.784513.

Sakai, Minako, and Amelia Fauzia. 2016. Performing Muslim Womanhood: Muslim Business Women Moderating Islamic Practices in Contemporary Indonesia. *Islam and Christian-Muslim Relations* 27 (3): 229–249. https://doi.org/10.1080/09596410.2015.1114243.

Septiana, Ema, and Muhammad Syafiq. 2013. Identitas "Lajang" (Single Identity) dan Stigma: Studi Fenomenologi Perempuan Lajang di Surabaya. *Jurnal Psikologi Teori dan Terapan* 4 (1): 71–86.

Seta, Putra Dewangga Candra. 2018. Potret Sekolah Gratis Milik Dorce Gamalama untuk Yatim Piatu, Dhuafa & Lansia, Fasilitasnya Mumpuni. https://surabaya.tribunnews.com/2018/11/09/potret-sekolah-gratis-milik-dorce-gamalama-untuk-yatim-piatu-dhuafa-lansia-fasilitasnya-mumpuni. Accessed 10 Nov 2021.

Shehada, Nahda. 2008. Between Change and Continuity: Age and Marriage Trends in Gaza. *Hawwa* 6 (3): 315–350.

Siegel, James T. 2000. *The Rope of God*. Ann Arbor: University of Michigan Press.

Smith-Hefner, Nancy J. 2005. The New Muslim Romance: Changing Patterns of Courtship and Marriage among Educated Javanese Youth. *Journal of Southeast Asian Studies* 36 (3): 441–459. https://doi.org/10.1017/S002246340500024X.

Smith-Hefner, Nancy J. 2018. Courtship and Marriage in Indonesia's New Muslim Middle Class. In *Routledge Handbook of Contemporary Indonesia*, ed. Robert W. Hefner, 335–345. London and New York: Routledge. https://doi.org/10.4324/9781315628837-27.

Smith-Hefner, Nancy J. 2019. *Islamizing Intimacies: Youth, Sexuality, and Gender in Contemporary Indonesia*. Honolulu: University of Hawai'i Press.

Takariawan, Cahyadi. 2005. *Di Jalan Dakwah Aku Menikah*. Jakarta: Era Intermedia.

To, Sandy. 2015. *China's Leftover Women: Late Marriage Among Professional Women and Its Consequences*. London: Routledge.

Traboulsi, Karim. 2019. All the Single Ladies: The Arab World's 'Spinster Revolution'. https://english.alaraby.co.uk/english/society/2019/3/8/all-the-single-ladies-the-arab-worlds-spinster-revolution. Accessed 18 Aug 2021.

Utomo, Ariane J. 2014. Marrying Up? Trends in Age and Education Gaps among Married Couples in Indonesia. *Journal of Family Issues* 35 (12): 1683–1706.

van Doorn-Harder, Nelly. 2013. Polygamy and Harmonious Families: Indonesian Debates on Gender and Marriage. In *Gender and Islam in Southeast Asia: Women's Rights Movements, Religious Resurgence and Local Traditions*, ed. Susanne Schröter, 55–71. Leiden: Brill.

Vignato, Silvia. 2012. 'Men Come in, Men Go Out': Single Muslim Women in Malaysia and Aceh. *Social Identities* 18 (2): 239–257.

Wadud, Amina. 2006. *Reading the Sacred Text from a Woman's Perspective*. Oxford: Oxford University Press.

Weintraub, Andrew N. 2011. *Islam and Popular Culture in Indonesia and Malaysia*. New York: Routledge.

Wieringa, Saskia. 2003. The Birth of the New Order State in Indonesia: Sexual Politics and Nationalism. *Journal of Women's History* 15 (1): 70–91.

Young, Matt. 2017. Rising Number of Spinsters and Divorced Women in Saudi Arabia Leads to Polygamy Push. http://www.albiladdailyeng.com/rising-number-of-spinsters-and-divorced-women-in-saudi-arabia-leads-to-polygamy-push/. Accessed 18 Aug 2021.

Zainal, Humairah. 2018. Intersectional Identities: Influences of Religion, Race, and Gender on the Intimate Relationships of Single Singaporean Malay-Muslim Women. *Marriage & Family Review* 54 (4): 351–373.

Zuberi, Aliya. 2021. Azad Chaiwala's Secondwife.Com Is Making Headlines Again. Cutacut. https://cutacut.com/2021/04/22/azad-chaiwalas-secondwife-com-is-making-headlines-again/. Accessed 18 Aug 2021.

CHAPTER 5

Exemplifying Muslim Mompreneurs in Indonesia

Minako Sakai

Abstract This chapter presents the case studies of Pamela Sunardi Syahuri and Nurhayati Subakat: two middle-class Muslim mompreneurs in Indonesia. It examines the traits demonstrated by these prominent Muslim businesswomen, who are looked up to as new role models for mompreneurs. Following this examination, this chapter explores how Islamic study groups and social media interactions disseminate the influence of these role models. We argue that the fluid nature of Islamic authority enables women to present and share the interpretations of ideal womanhood, increasingly referring to Khadijah, the Prophet's first wife. Indonesian Muslim women are making use of business opportunities to strengthen their roles in family and community. Middle-class Indonesian Muslim women are currently pioneering the phenomenon of Muslim mompreneurs.

Keywords *Halal* business · Indonesia · Islamic authority · Khadijah · Middle class · Mompreneurs

M. Sakai and A. Fauzia, *Women Entrepreneurs and Business Empowerment in Muslim Countries*,
Gender, Development and Social Change,
https://doi.org/10.1007/978-3-031-05954-4_5

Introduction

This chapter will analyse case studies of middle-class Muslim mompreneurs in Indonesia. It will examine the traits demonstrated by these role models. Following this analysis, it will explore how such role models influence other middle-class women through Islamic study groups and social media interactions. This chapter will argue that the fluid nature of Islamic authority enables women to demonstrate and share the interpretations of ideal womanhood broadly in line with the government policies. This situation does not mean that middle-class Muslim women are passively accepting the situation. Rather, they are making use of this opportunity to strengthen their role in family and community by creating innovative interpretations of women's role in society.

As the previous chapters have highlighted the predicaments of educated career women who remain unmarried, marriage and raising a family continues to be a significant part of Muslim women's life. The life stories of two well-known Indonesian entrepreneurs, Pamella Sunardi Syahuri and Nurhayati Subakat, illustrate how these women have chosen to become Muslim mompreneurs, combining entrepreneurship and Islam to achieve their aspirations in life. Pamella Sunardi runs a popular local supermarket chain called Pamella Supermarket in Yogyakarta, Central Java. Based on her successful supermarket chain, which has eight shops, she has formed Pamella Group, consisting of petrol station businesses, a beauty shop, a construction warehouse, an indoor soccer (futsal) centre, and clothing shops.[1] Most of her shops cater for Muslim consumers' needs including halal products. Along with her Muslim preacher husband Sunardi Syahuri, they are a well-known Muslim couple in Central Java and are core members of Muhammadiyah and their women's wing Aisyiyah. She has raised her profile nationally through her business partnerships. On the other hand, Nurhayati Subakat is known as the CEO of Indonesia's top *halal* cosmetic brand, Wardah, under the holding group Paragon. Pamella Group has developed business collaborations with Wardah cosmetics and Paragon for her retail outlets and in view of shared similarities between them, the growth of mutual respect as Muslim mompreneurs is a natural consequence.

This chapter argues that the case studies of these two Muslim mompreneurs illustrate the processes of socio-economic changes, including the permeating influence of Islam among middle-class Muslims that has taken place as part of modernity in Indonesia. The new role models for middle-class women who are emerging in Indonesia distinguish themselves from the previous image of female traders who would maximise their profit driven by greed and desire for economic independence.[2] Thus, the role model Muslim mompreneurs make the effort to become an important family member as a caring wife and mother, and as a pious community member who contributes to the betterment of the community by Islamic charitable and devotional activities. These mompreneurs are pursuing a new womanhood, emulating Muslim women's role models, Khadijah and Aishah, the wives of the Prophet Muhammad. Mompreneurs are dedicated not only to running a family business but to ensuring a harmonious family life while maintaining their Muslim religiosity. This clearly separates them from the dubious morality associated with female traders in traditional markets.

The life story of the first case, Pamella Sunardi Syahuri, reflects the socio-religious context of Yogyakarta, which is built on trade by Muslims in the heartland of Javanese culture as symbolised by the Sultanate of Yogyakarta. Due to a strong market culture, Javanese women are particularly well known for their activities in small trades (Alexander 1998; Alexander and Alexander 2001). Pamella's Muslim mompreneur career demonstrates her successful upholding of local small businesses, which is assisted by government policies and thriving Islamic *halal* consumer opportunities. Before our analysis of her life story, an overview of Yogyakarta and its socio-religious context will be provided.

Socio-Religious Tradition in Yogyakarta

Yogyakarta, located in the Southern Central coastal area of the Island of Java, is the location of the residence of the Sultan of Yogyakarta. The Sultanate of Yogyakarta supported the establishment of the Republic of Indonesia as an independent nation, and during the Independence period, Yogyakarta became the temporary capital city of Indonesia. To acknowledge the political support for establishment of the Republic, the province of Yogyakarta was given special regional status (*Daerah Istimewa*) so that the reigning sultan could be appointed governor of the province without having to be elected. The sultanate is also the centre of Javanese cultural and religious tradition, which attracts domestic and international tourists. For example, the world's largest Buddhist temple, Borobudur, is only one hour's drive from Yogyakarta, which illustrates the influence of Buddhism in the area. The practice of shadow puppet theatre, known as *wayang kulit*, draws stories from Indian epics, reflecting the Hindu influence in the area. The more recent conversion of the majority of the local population to Islam did not completely erase the existing local culture and religious traditions. The Sultanate of Yogyakarta has embraced the influence of existing local traditions and is seen as the guardian of the practice of Islam, particularly syncretic Islam (Beatty 1999; Geertz 1976) as practised in Central Java.

The responses to the syncretic practice of Islam came from reformist Muslims. For example, Muhammadiyah is a socio-religious movement that was established by K. H. Ahmad Dahlan in Yogyakarta in 1912. He was born into a pious Muslim family who resided in Kauman, near the sultan's palace. Kauman was a residential area and home to pious Muslim families many of whom were traders. His father was an official of the Grand Mosque of the Palace (Peacock 1978: 25) and he was influenced by Islamic reformist ideas emerging in the Middle East at the time of his Muslim pilgrimage. Upon his return to Yogyakarta, he started a new Islamic Reformation movement with a focus on returning to the holy scripture through modern education and social activism in contrast to the worshipping practice of syncretic rituals that fused with local cultural tradition. As part of this newly established organisation, Muhammadiyah also founded an affiliated women's affairs organisation, Aisyiyah, to teach Islamic interpretations of matters affecting the lives of women and their families.[3]

Yogyakarta is known as a thriving market town that sells local sweats and handicrafts, including a renowned batik textile. Used and promoted as Indonesia's cultural heritage, and acknowledged by UNESCO, a wide range of textiles are produced in Yogyakarta and the surrounding areas in Central Java. These products are produced by family-owned workshops in which women are often shop owners and managers. In Java, a woman's ideal role is to manage her household, including the financial matters, while a man's job is to bring in an income (Sullivan 1994). It is considered to be culturally inappropriate if a woman shows she cannot make ends meet with the income generated by her husband. According to the interpretations of Islam and also the 1974 Marriage Law, the husband bears the responsibility of earning an income, so not earning enough to support his family indicates his incompetence. The best option for a household needing extra income is for the wife to engage in small income-generating activities such as the production of food items for sale. This is particularly important because married couples are expected to live independently from both side's parents, although the couple may choose to maintain close relations with them if it is suitable. Thus, the dynamics of patriarchy in Indonesia are often negotiated between a husband and wife, sanctioned by the perceptions of the surrounding community. As women generally go shopping at the market for their household's needs, it was, and still is, appropriate for them to sell their goods there to earn an additional income. As a result, traditional markets in Java have been run by female traders with a shop in the market. The Beringharjo market, located in the centre of the city, has been a buzzing trading place catering for the needs of Yogyakarta residents for a long time. At the market, women not only worked as shopkeepers, but also as female market porters known as *ibu gendong* or *buruh gendong*[4] who would carry heavy shopping items to assist customers. A recent study of gender-based work participation in Yogyakarta between 2012 and 2017 shows that women's workforce participation averaged 60% there, 10% higher than the national average of 50% (Sulistyaningrum et al. 2021).

Along with the emergence of nationalist movements in Indonesia during the pre-independence period, several educational movements were established and were based around Yogyakarta City. The Taman Siswa movement and Budi Utomo[5] are examples of such movements that brought young students to Yogyakarta. After independence, the Republic of Indonesia established its first national university, Gadjah Mada University (UGM). In 2019, Yogyakarta had 353 higher education institutions. It is known as the city of education.[6] With the constant presence of students and tourists, businesses involved in small food production and the production of souvenirs and those offering services such as accommodation, cooking and laundry have thrived, creating business opportunities for small business traders. A well-known practice of saving for an emergency and to provide for daily needs includes a rotatory credit and savings scheme called *arisan*. *Arisan* involves an informal group being set up to save a specific amount of money among its members and operates based on the social capital that members can trust each other to contribute a certain amount every month. Such funds can be used to run small businesses to earn an extra income for household needs.

Yogyakarta has one of the highest population density rates in Indonesia (Badan Pusat Statistik 2019). Both men and women use motorbikes as their main form of transport. They frequently get together for meetings and socialising, to share ideas and to study Islam. They also commonly live in clusters of those employed in specific trades. Gatherings designed specifically for sharing ideas and learning from each other are highly valued by the community. As a result of such meetings, social organisations, such as *paguyuban*, are formed to assist members. The notion of *paguyuban* is different from a mere cluster or a group, it is rather a group of people who feel embraced and supported as if the group is a family (Zaenuddin et al. 2003). Grassroots NGOs are also formed and based in the Yogyakarta region, availing themselves of the presence of students as well as activists who share a vision for the future (Hadiwinata 2003). In addition to the tradition of Islamic study groups known as *pengajian* (Islamic study group), women also regularly gather to run *arisan* on a regular basis (Abdullah 2016; Bowen 1986; van Doorn-Harder 2006). It is this socio-cultural context from which our case study examples are drawn and examined.

Pamella Sunardi Syahuri

One of the important sources of Pamella's thought on Islam, family and entrepreneurship derives from her biography, which is reconstructed based on her interviews with the author Widiyatno (2006). I was told by one of Pamella's sons, an academic who came to my conference keynote presentation in Indonesia on the topic of Islamic economy in 2016, that the biography was written because so many people wanted to know about her life and why she became a successful businesswoman in Yogyakarta.

Pamella was born in 1955 to an Islamic family with a strong background in trade. Based on her biography written by Widiyatno (2006) her maternal grandfather lived in a large house in K. H. Dahlan street, located in the heartland of a Muhammadiyah community of Kauman. Her grandmother ran a batik textile store in the Beringharjo market and also ran a *warung* (small eatery) near the newly built Muhammadiyah Hospital (Rumah Sakit PKU Muhammadiyah) in the centre of Yogyakarta City. Her maternal grandfather's siblings also ran different retail businesses. Pamella's parents were involved in the batik textile trade, even though her father worked as a teacher of Islam in a secondary school. Prior to becoming a teacher, her father studied in Pesantren Gontor[7] and also studied English literature at Gadjah Mada University (Widiyatno 2006: 16). Her father was an active member of Partai Amanat Nasional (PAN) and Pelajar Islam Indonesia (PII). Her family background represents a strong Muhammadiyah Muslim trade tradition that has continued in Yogyakarta, coupled with a secular education. As outlined in her biography, titled *With Harmonious Family (Keluarga Sakinah) God Blesses My Business* (Widiyatno 2006), Pamella grew up helping her extended family members run their businesses while also assisting in her own family's business. She helped her grandfather produce and sell handmade souvenirs for Muhammadiyah members attending the annual congress. Today she runs nine Pamella supermarkets and also has a *halal* beauty salon, and she involves some of her own children in managing her group of business.

Pamella's life changed drastically when her father died of cancer in 1970, leaving the family with a significant debt to the bank. She recalls that the debt amounted to Rp. 300,000. This is equivalent of Rp. 300 million rupiah in 2006. She thought the debt indicated her father's entrepreneurial bravery to develop his business, but she has learnt that caution needs to be balanced with risk (Widiyatno 2006: 22). Before her father's death, the bank borrowings were mostly spent on medical treatment. Consequently, the goods in her family shops were sold to pay off the debts to the banks.

As she was growing up, her extended family members taught her important skills essential to developing entrepreneurship and the essence of embracing Islam in her business development. She acquired essential business management skills and was paid to assist her maternal aunt's business, as her aunt did not have any children of her own. Her aunt ran a large clothing shop in Madiun, East Java and Pamella worked there in her school holidays. She learnt entrepreneurship and the foundational skills for running a shop while she was still at school. She uses these skills now to run her own businesses. She also learnt from her grandfather that businesses increase their profits by responding to the needs of the market quickly. This was learnt through her childhood experience of selling handicrafts when she was in the fifth grade (Widiyatno 2006: 46–49). She learnt that her papercrafts, used to decorate her grandfather's shop, were attractive to Muhammadiyah members who came to Yogyakarta for the annual congregation event. Her grandfather's shop was close to the convention venue used for the event. Her grandfather asked her to produce more in exchange for pocket money. He also gave her mother, who had sewing skills, a tailoring job. Pamella rode a bicycle to deliver the finished clothing to his shop and to bring home new material for sewing. Gradually Pamella started to sell her clothes in the rich neighbourhood of Kusumanegara Street after first selling batik from her uncle's shop. Later, her mother opened her own shop and asked Pamella to run and manage it. Eventually she was too busy to complete high school.

Pamella experienced the efficacy of *zakat* or almsgiving in assisting the community firsthand when she was faced with financial difficulty after her father's death. Her uncle, a maternal relative who owned an established Ramayana Batik shop, gifted her mother a total of Rp. 100.000 in *zakat*. The gift of *zakat* impressed Pamella. *Zakat* is beneficial for people in need and she reported wanting to increase her income so that she could give a larger amount of *zakat* to the poor (Widiyatno 2006: 37). Consequently, she incorporated providing assistance to social causes as part of her business (Widiyatno 2006: 150–155). Among the causes that Pamella donates to is the provision of free health clinic services for the community, which are often conducted by religious organisations. It is important to note that Islamic philanthropic activities have a long history in Indonesia (Fauzia 2008, 2013) and that since the 1990s these have gained wide support to address social problems such as poverty, which led to the growth of Islamic microfinance institutions (Sakai 2008, 2014). Muhammadiyah, for example, has systematically used *zakat* funds to run social programs through its own *zakat* collection institution, LAZISMU, Muhammadiyah's Institution of Zakat, Sedekah and Infak (Latief 2013), and is known for its activities, especially in Yogyakarta.

Following the Life of the Prophet's First Wife, Khadijah

As explained in Chapter 1, Khadijah, a wealthy female merchant who successfully ran a family business and used her wealth to support her husband, Prophet Muhammad, has held a special position as an exemplary Muslim woman across Muslim communities. Khadijah's life clearly influenced Pamella, as recounted in a book section titled *Meneladani Isteri Nabi* (Follow the Example of the Prophet's Wife) (Widiyatno 2006: 75–77).

Sunardi Syahuri, Pamella's husband, came from a pious Muslim family that ran a family business.He proposed to Pamella when she was 19 years old. He intended to become an Islamic preacher in the community, and he had completed a diploma (*sarjana muda*) in Islamic Law in Universitas Islam Indonesia (UII), Yogyakarta and also studied Islamic Law in the State Islamic Institute in Yogyakarta (IAIN Sunan Kalijaga), now known as UIN Sunan Kalijaga. When he proposed, he listed three conditions for

Pamella; she was to help him by earning an income for their household, she was to wear Muslim clothing when they were married and she was to accept that her husband would travel for his preaching duties.

In her book Pamella stated that she recalled the story of Khadijah when he brought up these conditions, and consciously agreed to follow this path. Yet, her reflection as recounted in this biography shows that using Islamic values to guide her life and her business development and her decision to be a Muslim mompreneur was a gradual process. She understood that her future husband wanted her to follow the example of the first wife of the Prophet Muhammad, Khadijah, who was independent, but offered tranquillity and security for her husband (Widiyatno 2006: 77). For her the concept of ***keluarga sakinah*** or harmonious family, was important even before this idea was formulated as an important program for members of Aisyiyah.[8] Her own taking of this idea, which underpins being a Muslim mompreneur, is summarised as below.

A Muslim Woman's Duty to Support Her Husband's Propagation of Islam

One of the major contributions made by the prophet's first wife Khadijah was supporting her husband's preaching activities using the family's wealth. She was the first person to convert to Islam and she supported her husband's mission to propagate Islam in the community. Through this, she represents an ideal Muslim woman, not only among Aisyiyah members but in Yogyakarta and the surrounding region. A good Muslim woman, according to Sunardi, would want to wear Muslim clothing and would support him travelling for his propagation activities as Khadijah did for the prophet. Pamella accepted the role of caretaker of their family while he was away with ease. Wearing Muslim clothing, however, was more of a struggle because, despite her strong Muhammadiyah background, the expectation of Muslimness was not closely associated with clothing in Indonesia until the 1990s.

Although secularisation theory pre-supposes that the relevance of religion diminishes as modernisation and rationalisation progress in society, the influence of Islam in contemporary Indonesia has gradually increased (Fealy and White 2008; Sakai and Fauzia 2014). The impact of Islamisation in Indonesia can be seen through the rising popularity of Islamic clothing and *halal* goods consumption as well as the gradual development of Islamic financial and charitable systems in society.[9] Pamella's life story demonstrates these significant changes that are associated with the process of Islamisation and the resultant increase in the importance of Islam among the middle-class in Indonesia.

During the 1970s in Indonesia, public servants were banned from wearing headscarves and Muslim piety was not exclusively expressed by wearing Muslim clothing. Gradually elite university female students started to wear headscarves to demonstrate their faith (Smith-Hefner 2007). Pamella's biography (Widiyatno 2006: 57) shows a picture of her at age 17, wearing a trendy mini skirt at her birthday party standing next to Sunardi and her mother who did not wear a headscarf. Pamella's wedding photos in 1975 show that even her family members, who were associated with Muhammadiyah, wearing an Islamic veil were not very common. She wore a wedding dress and a traditional Javanese wedding costume. Her husband's request that she wear Islamic clothing at the time of his marriage proposal was not common in Indonesia. Preacher's wives, however, were traditionally expected to wear loose Muslim clothing. Shortly after having their first child, Pamella wore long skirts and a short headcover when she went outside the house, but she did not always wear completely appropriate Muslim clothing when she was working in her shop. When her husband asked her about wearing non-compliant Muslim clothing at her shop, she insisted that because the shop was within her house, there was no need for her to be fully clad in Muslim clothing (Widiyatno 2006: 92). In Indonesia, it is customary for women who have made a pilgrimage to wear full Muslim clothing (Utomo et al. 2018). Yet Pamella admits that even after her first pilgrimage with her husband, she still struggled to wear a full Muslim outfit including headscarf.

It took until 1992 when the couple made their second obligatory pilgrimage (*haji*) that she started to wear entirely loose clothing. Just before their second pilgrimage, she received a gift from her friend, Ibu Hj. Manfluti, a hat that covered her ears and her hair. She felt ashamed for not wearing fully Muslim clothing and that she had compromised her husband's position as a preacher (Widiyatno 2006: 93).

It was only upon returning home that she learnt that the hat was in fact a gift from her husband. She also learnt that having a wife who did not wear fully covering Muslim clothing made her husband's life as a Muslim preacher difficult (Widiyatno 2006: 94). To set an example as a Muslim woman and to support her husband as a preacher, she then accepted her husband's will that she wear Muslim clothing. Pamella appreciates the fact that her role is to support her husband in leading and building a strong Islamic community.

Demonstrating a life of a Muslim Mompreneur

For women, combining work and raising a family is generally challenging because the demands of child-rearing often conflict with the expectations of the regular office-based employment that is inherent in modern professional careers. The example of Pamella, who gave birth to and raised five children, thus sheds light on a new way of finding compatibility between women's aspirations to participate in the economy and society while raising a harmonious family, which is the concept of ***keluarga sakinah*** and was promoted by Aisyiyah.

Pamella's case illustrates that a business career has been built on the existing strong tradition of women running home-based businesses in Indonesia to generate an income (Alexander 1987, 1998; Brenner 1998; Sullivan 1994). In other words, what separates her from the existing womenpreneurs in Indonesia is the fact that she has consciously implemented Islamic values in building her business while working to support her husband's Islamic propagation. The conscious use of references to Islamic values to support her husband's propagation activities has earned her respect from the Muslim community for her success as a wife, mother and entrepreneur and for following the footsteps of Khadijah. Pamella's experiences growing up in her extended family and helping to run family businesses meant that starting a business of her own to support her family came as second nature. In her narratives about her life, the key concept framing her as an exemplary Muslim mompreneur was her commitment to the use of Islamic ways of life to guide her family life and her businesses. In this sense, Pamella draws her understanding of Muslim mompreneurs from the Muhammadiyah circles in Yogyakarta, and her internalised Islamic practice occurred with the Islamisation that gradually spread across Indonesia from the 1980s onwards.

There are four elements in Pamella's life story that explain the making of contemporary Muslim mompreneurs. The first is that she continued running a small business—a widespread practice among Muslim traders in Indonesia—while consciously implementing Islamic values into her family life. She fully supports her husband's propagation activities because she can provide a stable income for her family. Her income facilitates her children's education and funds her family trips, thus maintaining a suitable middle-class family lifestyle. Her children usually find her at her shops, not at home, but she has always attended important social and religious functions as a wife and a mother. She has consulted with her husband on business decisions and appointed him as the Pamella Group board chair, while she is the CEO, running and managing the Pamella Group.

As was agreed at the time of their marriage, Pamella has had her husband's full support to develop her businesses. She has mentored one of her sons to be her successor in the business. She has given full credit to her husband who has offered to look after her family in a practical way. For example, the first chapter of her book is titled *Membentuk Keluarga Sakinah*, meaning, to establish a harmonious family (Widiyatno 2006: 3–9), in which she recounted an incident that took place within a month of the birth of her first baby. Because she was busy at her shop during the day, she had fallen asleep after she had put her baby down for a nap and did not realise that her baby had woken, crying because of a soiled nappy. Before she had woken, her husband had arrived home, and had changed the nappy and fed the baby without disturbing her. When she asked him if he had eaten dinner, he said he would eat later, not wanting to put pressure on her. He helped her continue her business when she was too busy to undertake domestic chores. He would look after their children at night if she was too busy running the business. In return, she tried to be as nice as possible, respected him as the head of the family and followed his advice. Pamella's economic gains did not come without taking her away from home, but she did manage to maintain a harmonious family. As her business grew, she admits that she could afford to rely on domestic assistance.

Pamella highlights the importance of a harmonious family supported by financial gains through her business, and contrary to the image of financially independent women entrepreneurs who operated in traditional markets, she is not drifting away from her family. Another chapter of her book is titled *Peran Keluarga*, which translates as 'the role of the family'. In this chapter she emphasises that family issues take priority over everything (Widiyatno 2006: 132–136). Supported by the success of her businesses, her family was able to enjoy trips away, including overseas holidays, which were then still a luxury especially for a middle-class family.

Secondly, the Islamic values Pamella and Sunardi embraced helped her to achieve harmony with her family. She explains the importance of Islam throughout her book. Pamella has grown her business based on Islamic ethics, raised their children and supported her husband in building a strong Muslim community. At the time of writing, she runs eight Pamella supermarkets in Yogyakarta.

To compete against larger international supermarket chains such as Carrefour and Indomaret, she has differentiated her business by adhering to Islamic ways of life in its development, in customer service and in ensuring her employees' social welfare and community engagement. She avoids charging *riba* (interest) and uses Islamic financing if she needs to borrow money. She became wary of commercial banks when they came to recoup the defaulted borrowing when her father died (Widiyatno 2006: 40–42), and only takes loans from Islamic financial institutions. She does not want her supermarket outlets to make profit from selling any products that would damage the community.

Ensuring she runs an ethical Islamic business also led to her decision in 2003 to stop selling tobacco, despite it being a very profitable product. Pamella did not want to contribute to the many illnesses smoking causes (DetikHealth 2014). Tobacco sales accounted for two per cent of her business. Her decision to stop selling tobacco, however, was made even before the Muhammadiyah's edict (known as a *fatwa*) regarding the harmfulness of smoking was issued in 2010. The Muhammadiyah also prohibited e-cigarette smoking in 2020 with decree No. 01/PER/I.1.E/2020 (TribunNews 2020). She worked closely with the city mayor of Yogyakarta and her husband to promote the message that smoking causes various illnesses and is deemed *haram*, prohibited in Islam. Her supermarkets do not sell alcohol because Muslims are not permitted to drink it. Other supermarkets, however, commonly sell at least beer to make profits.[10]

Pamella wants her business to profit, but only through ethical transactions and by selling products as cost-effectively as possible to also serve the community, which is her duty according to the teaching of Islam. In order to increase profits, she has chosen to sell high-turnover products, which reduces the cost of storage (Widiyatno 2006: 148). Her husband, who often accompanied pilgrims to Mecca, also established an executive pilgrimage (ONH Plus) and *umroh*[11] travel bureau called Husuna Tour (Widiyatno 2006: 133) as a not-for-profit social enterprise. To compensate her business losses and to serve the community further, the Pamella Group expanded to run a chain of gas stations and *halal* beauty salons in partnership with Wardah Islamic beauty products (Pamella Supermarket 2021a).

The third element is that contributing to the betterment of the community, particularly Muslims in the neighbourhood, has been an important influence on Pamella's decision-making. Her motto, as quoted in her CV, is (Widiyatno 2006: 190) 'to be useful to many people', which is closely linked with *rahmatan lil 'alamin* (Widiyatno 2006: 150–153). This Arabic term is from the Qur'an, surah Al-Anbiya verse 107 and means 'blessing for the universe' or 'mercy for all creation'. To implement her motto, when her businesses grew, she started to incorporate social engagement with the community using *zakat* funds raised from her business profit. Since 2006, to increase those funds, she has implemented a policy that a very small change (under Rp. 100) will be donated towards Pamella social funds. Instead of the buyer receiving a candy, she donates the small change to *zakat* funds that contribute to social programs in her business' neighbourhood. She has developed partnerships with Palang Merah Indonesia or (PMI or Red Cross Indonesia, https://www.pmi.or.id/) to offer such programs every month to coincide with the date of her business' establishment. She notifies the community the total of the funds collected and which social programs they have funded. Since the early 2000s, there was a call for transparency and accountability of the collected funds. This call came from the rising middle-class Muslims who were donating *zakat* to professionally managed modern *zakat* foundations such as the Dompet Dhuafa Foundation.

With her businesses, Pamella tries to create a strong Islamic community (Widiyatno 2006: 146–155). For example, to accommodate the devotional needs of her Muslim employees, her business allows workers to take time for compulsory Muslim prayers during their working hours and enables Muslim female employees to wear a headscarf as part of the uniform. She also provides a weekly Islamic study group (*pengajian*) session at work (Widiyatno 2006: 147). These allowances for the needs of Muslims and their devotional requirements in the workplace are very important but are rarely provided by employers (Sakai 2014).

As pointed out by scholars researching Muslim women traders (Alexander 1987; Brenner 1998; Sakai 2019), businesses are usually run to maximise profits at any cost. Pamella's example, however, illustrates a new way of conducting business that benefits of the whole of society. One of her motivations for running a business is to build a stronger Islamic community by undertaking various forms of Islamic charitable activities through her businesses.

The fourth element relates to when Pamella accepted her husband's marriage proposal; she made the point to negotiate patriarchy with the condition that he would only have one wife, despite the practice of polygamy being common for Islamic preachers. Her demand for a monogamous relationship to keep harmony in the family came from a program known as *Keluarga Sakinah*, which predates the Aisyiyah family program. This earlier program was launched in 1985 and states that five factors make a family calm and harmonious, an outcome for which women bear full responsibility. These factors include the family's practice of Islam, the family's education, a stable income, good health and harmonious relations (van Doorn-Harder 2006, 2013).[12]

By ensuring a stable income through her business, contributing to strengthening the Muslim community, and negotiating patriarchy by insisting on a monogamous relationship, it is fair to conclude that Pamella has embodied the ideal contemporary Muslim woman, thus supporting her husband's role as a preacher until his death in 2018.

Popularising *Halal* Beauty Products

Despite Indonesia having the largest Muslim population in the world, its popularity of *halal* consumer products is a relatively recent phenomenon. *Halal* certificates are not issued by a single universal Islamic certifier for the whole world. In the case of Indonesia, the certifier is, Majelis Ulama Indonesia (Indonesian Council of Islamic Scholars [MUI]), which was established in 1975 as a national Islamic organisation that represented prominent Islamic scholars in Indonesia. The MUI, along with other Islamic organisations, can issue *fatwa* on matters deemed important to guide the decisions of Muslims in Indonesia (MUI Digital). Ma'ruf Amin, the Vice President of Indonesia at the time of writing in June 2021, served as chair of the MUI between 2015 and 2020. One of the roles of the MUI is to issue *halal* certificates for consumption goods. Their role as the national *halal* certifier became increasingly important when the growth of urban-dwelling Muslims in the 1990s triggered an interest in *halal* products. Until 2019, the Food and Drug Research Institute of the MUI was directly involved in the examination of consumer goods and services in Indonesia. To facilitate this process of examination, the Ministry of Religious Affairs established the Halal Product Assurance Agency, which liaises with producers and sellers of goods and services in Indonesia (Medina 2019).

Wardah is a well-known beauty product brand used by Muslim women in Indonesia, particularly professional career women. Wardah, is a household name, favoured by Muslim fashionistas knowns as *hijabers* (Beta 2014), who boast of being fashionable, trendy Muslim women with Muslim clothing. However, the concept of a fashionable Muslim woman was non-existent in the 1990s. For example, in the mid-1990s my adopted Muslim sister from South Sumatra remarked that she was reluctant to wear nail colours, as the product is not *halal*. These remarks demonstrate the typical confusion and anxiety felt by Muslim women who adhered to Islamic teaching and undertook ritual prayers while renouncing their desire to look beautiful and trendy. It was as if following Islamic teaching was deemed inherently in conflict with a woman's desire to look attractive. Ten years later in the mid-2000s, a good Muslim friend of mine who worked as a lecturer at Sriwijaya University, a state university located in South Sumatra, started to wear a headscarf and Muslim attire. She also proudly showed me that using a Wardah beauty product is her way of keeping her life *halal*. I saw an advertisement for Wardah that showed a popular Muslim film star, *Inneke* Koesherawati, wearing full Muslim clothing and a headscarf, with glossy lipstick and eyeshadow, smiling sweetly and beautiful.[13] In 2013, Wardah also started to work with Dian Pelangi,[14] an internationally acclaimed Muslim fashion designer, in their advertisements. In one popular advertisement, Dian visited Paris wearing trendy Muslim clothing of her own, looking attractive and using Wardah cosmetics (WardahBeauty 2013). The consistent message from Wardah is that Muslim women can enjoy appearing beautiful using *halal* cosmetic products created by Wardah.

Wardah started in 1985 as a home industry producing *halal* shampoo for salons in Jakarta, and in 1995 started to sell products using the brand name Wardah. It has since grown to employ more than 10,000 people (Yulistara 2018). In 2018 Wardah became the number one cosmetic sales brand in Indonesia.

Nurhayati Subakat

The woman responsible for Wardah's growth is Nurhayati Subakat, who started the company in 1995, and is now the CEO of Paragon Group, the holding company. Her beginnings as a Muslim mompreneur were humble. She shared her life story with an audience at a seminar organised by a leading Muslim charitable organisation, the Dompet Dhuafa, during the fasting month in 2014. This public event was designed to enable the recipients of *zakat* funds to meet with donors to the Dompet Dhuafa Foundation, Jakarta. I met her then and remained in communication with her. We were able to have another discussion along with other Muslim entrepreneurs at UIN, Jakarta subsequently in 2017. As her business has grown, a number of media articles and videos have been released retelling her life story because of her high profile as a Muslim businesswoman (Fig. 5.1).[15]

Nurhayati was born in 1950 in Padang, West Sumatra and attended an Islamic boarding school, Pondok Pesantren Diniyyah Puteri. West Sumatra is another area of Indonesia that has historically received strong influence from modernist and reformist Islam including from Muhammadiyah. Later Nurhayati completed her bachelor's degree at one of the most prestigious Indonesian engineering universities, Bandung Institute of Technology (ITB) where she majored in pharmacy. She graduated

Fig. 5.1 Light of Ramadhan event organised by the Dompet Dhuafa (*Source* Photo by Minako Sakai)

as the best student in pharmacy in 1975 (Adi 2019). Her birthplace of West Sumatra is known for its strong adherence to, and practice of, Islam, particularly in support for Muhammadiyah. It is also a region of strong commitment to increasing knowledge (Salim 2013). Women hold the important position of inheritors of the land and traditional houses (Jendrius 2017). Because the local practice of matrilineal customary law practice among the Minangkabau ethnic groups in West Sumatra conflicts with Islamic law, several attempts to reform the practice of Islam took place in West Sumatra including conflicts such as the Padri War (1803–1837). The Minangkabau ethnic group is also known for its long tradition of diasporic migration and entrepreneurship (Effendi 1999). In summary the region is known for its strong adherence to Islam but also preservation of Minangkabau tradition.

Nurhayati's life has had much in common with the broad traits of being a Minangkabau woman (Nurdyansa 2016; Ngobi 2020; Waruwu 2019). After completing her university degree, she worked as a pharmacist in Padang and later moved to Jakarta where she took up a position in a well-known cosmetic company as a quality control officer. Working in an international company as a professional was certainly an achievement. Nurhayati also had social standing based on her academic career. Even though she was originally from a Minangkabau family known for ethnic entrepreneurship, it was natural for her to seek professional employment because that was what the government was promoting through its economic policy at the time. Indonesia focuses on offering high-quality education to create the best human resources and to attract direct foreign employment (Hill 2000). While she was working, Nurhayati married and had three children. In the 1980s she was with a group of friends from an Islamic boarding school. Knowing that she worked for a cosmetic company, they asked why there were no Muslim beauty products in Indonesia. She was shocked, and she agreed with the widespread view that beauty products caused anxiety among Muslim women, despite the fact that it was permissible for Muslim women to appear attractive.

With a new-found conviction, she started to produce a shampoo called Putri (which means daughter or princess) in a workshop space at home in Tangerang, an industrial area adjacent to Jakarta. Around this time, she also began to tire of commuting and the pressures of raising her young family and meeting the expectation of her professional work in the office. Due to these reasons, she left her well-paid work at the cosmetic company to produce new *halal* beauty products. She later promoted these products to all the beauty salons in Tangerang, Banten. Her products were well-received, and she established a new company, which she called PT. Pusaka Tradisi Ibu (Mother's Heirloom), and she hired a few employees to assist with production. However, her workshop burned down, leaving her in debt. She wanted to give up on her new enterprise, but she felt obliged to keep her employees. She recalls that she recommenced production the following day as she needed to keep her employees, who were financially dependent on her business, working. With their support and her family's backing, in 1995 she revived her company by pursuing product innovation, including developing *halal* beauty products under the Wardah brand (an Arabic word meaning rose). The name was suggested by one of her friends at the meeting that had originally suggested the need for *halal* products. In 1999, her company officially received a *halal* certificate from MUI and was the first *halal* cosmetic brand in Indonesia. She successfully rebranded Wardah in 2009 when the Muslim fashionista *hijabers* became popular. As a result, Wardah became the top *halal* beauty product company in Indonesia. She started to involve her children and her husband in undertaking innovations. With the rising interest in *halal* cosmetics, her factory moved from Cibodas to a new industrial location in Tangerang, where her family still lives. By 2019, Wardah was owned by a holding company, PT. Paragon, which also owns the Make Over, Emina and IX brands, all of which have a distinctive market in Indonesia.

Choosing to Become a Muslim Mompreneur

Nurhayati emphasised that the most important thing for her, as a Muslim woman, was to be able to multi-task. Becoming an entrepreneur by developing a *halal* beauty product was done to accommodate the needs of her family while pursuing her aspiration to develop useful beauty products. She uses *mau* (willing) and *bisa* (able) as her guiding principles (Kumparan 2019). She has the aspiration to meet both the needs of the marketplace and of her own family (Channel 2017). As beauty salons appreciated the quality of her shampoo, she received requests to develop other products for hair and facial treatments for Muslim women. Developing new products and marketing them, she found, was compatible with the demands of looking after her children. When she was working in the office prior to starting her own company, her children did not like to be left alone and she felt sad leaving them. To overcome this, she went to work after her children went to school. Her new role enabled her to control her own time with flexible working hours. Her decision to leave a well-paid job in an established company to start a cottage industry was contrary to the dominant preference of professional women who opt to be employed in their professional area with a large salary.

While in 1995, she launched the Wardah brand, it did not gain popularity immediately. She realised that *halal* and high-quality products alone did not attract consumers to her products. To build interest in her brand, she used a well-known Muslim actress, Inneke Koesherawati, to promote an image of beautiful Muslim women wearing Wardah. Between 1995 and 2003, her products gained support from consumers. Her daughter, Sari Chairunnisa, became a skin specialist, took up the position of Vice President of PT. Paragon, and has a leading role in product development.

Nurhayati is motivated to continue her business by her aspiration to assist the community. When her factory burned down in 1990, her husband was still employed and his income was sufficient to cover the costs. If she had thought of her own financial needs, it made sense to close her business (Channel 2017). However, she put the needs of her employees and their families, who were dependent on her business, above her own. She borrowed her husband's savings to pay her employees and endeavoured to revive her business. Her understanding of four marketing principles; products, prices, promotion and placement, is supplemented with another principle, that is *pertolongan* Allah (the help of God). Her business is based on this principle and through it, she strives to benefit as many people as possible. She values close family relations, not only among her own family but also among those of her employees. Nurhayati has involved all three of her children in running the company, but she emphasised that the company is not working for the benefit of her family alone, but for the benefit of the whole community. As a result, her daughter remarked that she saw working for the company as a Muslim religious duty or *ibadah* (KumparanWOMAN 2019). In other words, her work is an extension of Islamic propagation by action (*dakwah bil hal*).

Nurhayati and her husband continue to live where she started her business in 1985. Her office is part of her house so that she can be close to her family and save on commuting time. She bought the adjacent areas to build houses for her three children, and she enjoys being able to catch up with them on a daily basis as they share a common courtyard. To assist new employees, most of whom are not from Jakarta and often need family support, Nurhayati also bought boarding houses nearby. She feels that being close to her employees would enable her to offer any assistance they may need.

Another point that she emphasised was innovation. She has effectively used her children and their friends of the younger generation to share ideas and innovation. She hopes that her company will be a place where ideas are shared in an egalitarian way and that the concept of *bisa* means that she will continue to learn from and better understand the community. Her office does not impose an Islamic dress code for its female employees. In fact, Wardah uses Indonesian women without a headscarf in her advertisements. This shows her commitment to assist anyone who is willing to use *halal* and high-quality products.

Her egalitarian attitude and her aspirations to assist as many people as possible are shown by her willingness to partner with Islamic philanthropic organisations to promote the importance of *zakat* and other almsgivings. When we approached her to invite her to a discussion about Muslim womanhood, she immediately responded, being pleased to be a part of the project. Because of her commitment to benefiting the community through her business, she was listed as a successful CEO from Indonesia by Forbes (Dhana 2018) and is highly regarded as an innovative Muslim entrepreneur in Indonesia, who combines family values with running an innovative business.

Promoting Socially Engaged Inspiring Women

Nurhayati is keen that Wardah's advertising promotes an active role for women. Initially, in 2012 Wardah sponsored the Muslimah Beauty Contest under the Inspiring Beauty Movement (WardahBeauty 2012; Wardah 2021). Beauty pageant competitions are generally frowned upon by conservative Muslims (Balogun 2012) but Wardah has supported women displaying their inner and outer beauty through Muslimah beauty contests. In their campaign video, Muslim women were depicted as active from dawn, praying, but also playing guitar, tree climbing and riding bicycles (WardahBeauty 2012).

Concurrently, Wardah also started to use models without a veil to appeal to non-veil-wearing women in Indonesia. Some patrons of Wardah seemed to be disappointed (Fitriati 2013) but it was accepted as Wardah showing support for the concept of women's beauty not being based on a rigid Muslimness, but on piousness and being a socially active individual.

Just before Indonesia's Independence Day In 2018, Wardah further refined the image of a socially engaging Muslim woman by launching a new movement called 'Inspiring Movement', (as opposed to Inspiring Beauty) as part of their Corporate Social Responsibility (CSR) program. It was Wardah's intention to make the corporate mission visible through these programs. In Indonesia, the prominence of CSR-funded programs is rising (Phuong and Rachman 2017) and large companies work in partnership with many charitable foundations. The launching of this CSR campaign is thus not new in substance, but it redefined Wardah's mission to promote and define the beauty of women, not only through a woman's appearance but also through a woman's skill in facing up to life's challenges.

Wardah defines beauty as a movement with good intentions, and the programs encourage women to engage in initiatives in the fields of education, health, women's empowerment and the environment (waste4change 2018). Women are active teachers, looking after community health, and taking action to reduce waste by recycling. In 2020, to prevent the risk of COVID-19 infections in Indonesia, Wardah undertook a zoom meeting to encourage volunteers to undertake good deeds to help people in need because of the impact of the virus. This is important because the crowdfunding movement called Gerakan Baru Salingjaga (New Mutual Assistance) (Kitabisa.com 2020) was gaining popularity and people were increasingly wanting to volunteer to assist others in need at the time of the pandemic. For this event Wardah invited a medical doctor who had studied at Harvard University to be the speaker.

Wardah supports women taking an active role to change the world. These initiatives can include volunteering to help in the local community and many share their activities through social media to inspire others. Wardah's holding company, PT. Paragon, continues to work with established Muslim organisations such as Aisyiyah to encourage women to participate in the economy, through entrepreneurship (Sahlan 2019).

Since Muslim organisations do not specifically emphasise women's role in taking up entrepreneurship, working closely with Aisyiyah is a strategic move designed to influence a leading Muslim organisation to encourage Muslim women to become entrepreneurs. As previously stated, Aisyiyah's Harmonious Family program emphasises the importance of having a stable income, and the welfare of the family, through education of children and good health, as these are important elements for raising a harmonious family.[16]

Thus, through Wardah, Nurhayati has shared her ideas of how Muslim women can take an active role in making changes in society. In doing so, a common theme, also resonating with Pamella's experience, is their conscious use of Islamic teaching, particularly the undertaking of charitable activities, to guide their business decisions. As elaborated in detail elsewhere (Sakai 2019), successful entrepreneurial skills are viewed as morally dubious, as traditionally, entrepreneurial behaviour was loosely associated with maximising profit at any cost (Brenner 1998). As a result, these women are promoting a new role model based on their commitment to Islam and to supporting their family, and to do so with the full support of their husbands (Sakai and Fauzia 2016). Thus, their entrepreneurial activities are accompanied by their active displays of public piety. Behaving in this way, they are successfully becoming important role models for other middle-class Muslim women. Their conscious choices of Islamic philanthropic activities reflect the development of these modern activities as part of the growing interest in Indonesian society in using Islam as the guiding principle in life (Sakai 2010, 2014, 2018). In 2020, Nurhayati donated Rp. 40 billion towards equipment and medical devices needed in hospitals and clinics treating COVID-19 patients (Pinandu 2020).

Islamic Authority in Indonesia

To understand why these Muslim women are emerging as exemplary Muslim mompreneurs in contemporary Indonesia needs further explorations on the nature of Islamic authority and the role of Islamic study groups (*pengajian*) in Indonesia. Islamic authority in Indonesia has been diverse, as represented by the wide range of Muslim organisations found there. Apart from MUI, Muhammadiyah and Nahdlatul Ulama have both exerted influence over Indonesians through education and social activities since their inception prior to the declaration of Indonesian independence in 1945. They both encouraged informal Islamic study groups in communities, which resulted in the tradition of Islamic study groups commonly known as *pengajian* or *majelis taklim* in Indonesia (Winn 2012).

Muslim mass organisations may issue guidance on appropriate behaviours for Muslims when it is deemed appropriate and necessary. The decision to follow and subsequent adherence rests largely with individuals. Muslim men also support women studying Islam to deepen their understanding of Islamic teaching. Studying Islam has long been a grassroots community activity in Indonesia. As internet use grew, along with

Muslim preachers who had no official connection with existing Islamic organisations, people started to use it to seek guidance on personal matters (Hosen 2008). New preachers who do not have Islamic authority or connection to Islamic institutions became popular, heavily utilising social media, TV talk shows and Islamic activities, including philanthropic undertakings.[17] Female preachers are also popular on TV and, in social media as illustrated by the popularity of middle-aged female preacher, Mamah Dedeh (Damayanti 2020; Nurlaelawati 2020), and Oki Setiana Dewi, a young mother (Sakai 2019). These female preachers are becoming popular with Muslim women. Both received their education from the State Islamic University, Jakarta, under the Ministry of Religious Affairs. As Oki started her career as a Muslim actress and uses social media, she is popular with young women, particularly university students and younger middle-class women. In addition to these Indonesian Muslim organisations and the influence of new media, Islamic influences from Saudi Arabia and Egypt have also gained support in urban Muslim communities in Indonesia (Meuleman 2011; Rijal 2020). As a result, influences of Islam in the life of urban middle-class Muslims have increased, incidentally creating business opportunities for an Islamic economy.[18]

Along with this change, women's Islamic study groups, known as *pengajian* or *majelis taklim*, became popular. The state co-opted women's groups, such as Dharma Wanita and PKK (Pemberdayaan Kesejahteraan Keluarga, or Empowerment for the Welfare of the Family) and Muslim women's organisations such as Aisyiyah and Muslimat, to support government policies.[19] It was and is common for women to share their ideas among groups of other women. Women's education is considered an essential part of creating a strong Indonesia either through secular education or Islamic education. Indonesian Muslim women can become experts on Islamic law and jurisprudence in state Islamic universities and they can lead women's Islamic education, including in boarding schools. As a result, Muslim women are shaping Islam for women (van Doorn-Harder 2006).

Reflecting the dynamic social context surrounding Islamic expression, Indonesian Muslims can choose to follow their own guiding preachers or to follow existing local Islamic authorities (Sakai and Fauzia 2014). Younger generations now actively follow preachers through social media as part of Indonesian popular culture (Beta 2014; Nisa 2018; Sakai 2012; Slama 2018). Many see consumption of Islamic goods and media as a way of expressing their Muslim identity (Fealy 2008).

Women's Islamic Study Groups

Along with the fluid nature of Islamic authority, the vibrant practice of informal Islamic study groups contributes to the accommodation of a wide range of Islamic orientations associated with the organisers of each group (Winn 2012). *Majelis taklim* is an important socio-religious activity that indirectly prepares women to expand their social networks. *Majelis taklim* (or *majlis ta'lim*) is an Arabic phrase that is popularly used to refer to a gathering place where Muslims study religious instruction informally. Most of them are attended by women and are led by female teachers and preachers (Kusmana 2017; Marcoes 2002; Winn 2012). The practice of *pengajian* allows women to choose the content explored by their study group.

We highlight that three features of women's Islamic study groups—discussions, and social networks and trust—facilitate Muslim women's learning about exemplary Muslim behaviour, including being a mompreneur. *Pengajian* can consist of activities such as reading the Qur'an and discussing the application of particular Qur'anic verses or concepts that can be implemented in everyday life. Pamella (along with Sunardi before his death) is a popular guest speaker who has promoted her ideas through public speeches and harmonious family concepts. Through this she has also promoted her engagement in Aisyiyah and its activities, where she is regarded as a role model who would not separate business from the interpretations of Islam, as demonstrated by her refusal to sell tobacco products in her supermarkets. Furthermore, Pamella receives neither speaking fees nor transport fees when she talks at these Islamic study group meetings (Widiyatno 2006: 169–172).

I attended meetings of an Islamic study group attached to the Beringharjo market in Yogyakarta between 2008 and 2014 as part of my research into Islamic microfinance. This study group is called Dewi Khadijah, and the membership consists of women workers at the market, including women labourers. The study group offers moral guidance on how to become a good Muslim businesswoman. The female group leaders want female workers and shop owners to think beyond making an immediate profit and instead think about modelling themselves on the actions of Khadijah. I understood that the wider Central Javanese community believed that immorality was pertinent in markets where business activities were geared towards maximising profits, as observed by Brenner (2011). One of the sessions I attended was when the organisers invited Sunardi

Syahuri, the husband of Pamella Sunarid Syahuri, to offer discourses and interpretations of Islam that were modelled on Khadijah. The message of looking up to Khadijah as a role model is aimed at creating an entrepreneurial self, differentiated from the profit-driven motivations of traditional traders.

The popularity of emulating the wives of the prophet, Khadijah and Aishah, is also shown strongly in Indonesia. For example, the demands for books on both women are on the rise as the urban middle-class Muslims in Indonesia have shown a strong appetite for Islamic literature (Watson 2005). Along with this trend, books on Khadijah focusing on her life stories highlighting her roles in business management and support of her husband have become much in demand.[20] Similarly sermons on the life of Khadijah as an inspirational woman are also delivered on TV (Yufid.TV Pengajian and Ceramah Islam 2017). On its third anniversary, IPEMI (Indonesian Muslim Women Entrepreneurs Association) invited a speaker, Agus Yudhoyono, an aspiring Indonesian presidential hopeful and son of the former Indonesian President Susilo Bambang Yudhoyono. He remarked that Khadijah and Kartini are good examples for Muslim businesswomen in Indonesia to learn from (Keumala 2018), indicating the importance of nationalism and Muslim faith. The Indonesian government is aware of the popularity of Khadijah among Muslim businesswomen running small businesses and thus, in 2021, named a forum of Muslim women's small business networks Forum Khadijah to promote digitalisation and *halal* certifications of small businesses run by women (ISEF Indonesia 2021).[21]

The second factor is that attending Islamic study groups facilitates women traders to expand their social networks supported by the trust gained through their membership in the group (Sakai 2019; Winn 2012). Women's groups usually combine a rotary credit group known as *arisan* with an accompanying Islamic study group meeting where they recite Arabic texts and then engage in discussions about the interpretation of the text. Some groups are based locally while others form part of national Islamic study group networks, which enables women to learn beyond the teaching of Islam and to extend their social networks to develop businesses. Muslim women entrepreneur organisations, such as IPEMI and as discussed in Chapter 3, draw inspiration for the establishment of its organisation from *majelis taklim* of women led by Tuti Alawiyah.[22] Tuti Alawiyah was a famous female preacher who established and led the Badan Kontak Majelis Taklim (Majelis Taklim Contact Body [BKMT]) in 1998 when she was appointed Minister of Female Empowerment under the Suharto government. BKMT has an extensive national network across Indonesia and is suitable for networking.[23]

This network was supported by the government and led to the creation of the network of *majlis taklim* Al-Hidayah, organised at village level, especially in the Greater Jakarta area. Its potential for mobilisation and networking has been used to facilitate government campaigns on certain policies, such as family planning (Menchik 2014), and individual political campaigns for candidates for public positions, such as governors and heads of districts/cities. When Muslim women start microbusinesses, the *majelis taklim* can provide sales opportunities.

The development of Islamic study groups into business networking opportunities is estimated to have taken place in the late 1980s when Islamic mosque groups have become a suitable gathering venue to solve social issues with Islam (Thornton et al. 2012) and one of such outcomes include Islamic microfinance institutions (Hefner 2003; Sakai 2008, 2014). While there was development of Islamic finance and the heightened interest in *halal* consumer goods, Muslim entrepreneurs started to form Islamic study groups or training sessions to connect entrepreneurs.

For example, the Majelis Ta'lim Wirausaha (Islamic Studies Group of Entrepreneurship [MTW]) was formed in 2014. It is a network of Islamic study groups associated with mosques across Indonesia. This network plays an important role, allowing members to connect beyond the realms of Islamic study activities. This is because the founder Valentino Dinsi is a prominent Muslim businessman and a board member of the ICMI (Indonesian Association of Muslim Intellectuals). He also chairs the Indonesian Muslim Entrepreneurs Network, Jaringan Pengusaha Muslim Indonesia [JPMI] (@valentinodinsi). One of the aims of MTW is to build a generation of pious Muslim entrepreneurs. This *majelis* was established because 'there are many Muslim entrepreneurs who want to participate in training and business networks but do not have much funds' (Mustisany 2015). By utilising mosques and the networks of *majelis taklim*, MTW can organise exhibitions, and training workshops and can assist with establishing stores and cooperatives. The majority of its members are *mompreneurs*—as they are the main members of *pengajian*—though the gender composition of the founders and top leadership remains mostly male. MTW has chapters and branches in a number of regions in Indonesia, but mainly in strongly Islamic regions, such as West Java, as Fauzia observed in 2020.

The establishment of these entrepreneurial Muslim communities became popular as a result of the growth of an Islamic economy and because, in contemporary Indonesia, membership of such a community is seen as an Islamic propagation activity. These activities aim to transform the traditional Islamic study groups known as *pengajian* into *dakwah bil hal* (Sakai 2014, 2017). Thus, the Islamic study group network has become a significant incubator for Muslim women to gain more support in becoming mompreneurs.

Pamella Sunardi Syahuri is a key member of Yogyakarta's women's Islamic rotatory credit gatherings, which combine to function as an Islamic study group such as As-Sakinah and Yasmin. These women's groups draw their members exclusively from respected businesses. Thus, being allowed to participate in these gatherings attests that members are middle-class women entrepreneurs who can trust each other. These meetings are aimed at women's self-improvement (Rahmawati 2019) and also serve as a business and social networking venue for elite businesswomen. Nurhayati Subakat also frequently undertakes charitable activities in partnership with Islamic organisations including universities' advisory boards. For example, she was appointed to be a member of Majelis Wali Amanat ITB between 2019 and 2024. In 2018 she was awarded an honorary doctorate from ITB as a graduate who had established a well-regarded Islamic *halal* cosmetics company (Esqnews.id 2019). She gave a talk with ITB students titled Inspiring Talk with Nurhayati Subakat (Adi 2019). As illustrated, her company works with Islamic philanthropic organisations and she is often invited as an inspiring role model speaker to motivate people.

The duality of a Muslim mompreneur—who embraces Islamic value in developing a family business—is clearly shown in Pamella's statement in a Pamella Supermarket Instagram post about her business collaborations with Paragon-Wardah, 'Looking at Paragon, it is just like seeming myself in the mirror. My conviction is that family businesses can grow if managed well' (Pamella Supermarket 2021b).

What she intends is that she employs one of her sons, Wildan Zia Muhammad Dani and her youngest daughter, Himmatun Nafida Noor Afifa, to continue to run Pamella Group. In a recent video with her youngest daughter, which she released on Mother's Day in 2021, her daughter stated that she is now responsible for continuing this business for another 100 years to contribute to society (Pamella Supermarket 2021b).

Conclusion

This chapter has analysed the life history of two exemplary Muslim mompreneurs in contemporary Indonesia. The way they have internalised Islamic values and have successfully combined raising their family while being innovative and successful entrepreneurs illustrates the process of becoming a Muslim mompreneur. They are committed to Islamic values, personally as well as in their business dealings. Because these female entrepreneurs have not only demonstrated business success but also raised harmonious Muslim families and contributed to the building of Muslim communities and Indonesia's economy, they are now being seen as role models for influential and inspiring Muslim mompreneurs.

In reality, both women are building their businesses and their work requires them to be away from home. The majority of middle-class mompreneurs tend to rely on domestic assistance. Yet the delegation of such domestic chores to others has been tolerated for the sake of propagation. For example, since the early years of its formation in 1932, and through the use of its official magazine, *Suara Aisyiyah*, Aisyiyah has encouraged women to travel around and preach as they deem women's primary duty to be Islamic propagation, although spousal permission remains essential (van Doorn-Harder 2006: 119).

It is worth noting that Indonesians started to doubt the value of running small businesses as women gained access to higher education. The number of women with aspirations for a professional career has increased and the idea of running a small trading business—once the main thriving economic occupation for women—has begun to be seen as old-fashioned. Women have started to work in non-traditional areas such as paid factory work (Ford and Parker 2008; Warouw 2008). People with university degrees, irrespective of gender, generally aspire to work for the government or in other paid office work, while large supermarkets also compete against small traders (Watson et al. 1999). Yet as the next chapter shows, there is an emergent trend for Muslim women to see entrepreneurship as an alternative profession that allows them to balance work and family to exemplify an appropriate harmonious middle-class family. Having Khadijah as a role model of an ideal woman strongly appeals to middle-class Muslim mompreneurs. It aligns embracing Islam with running a business to contribute to the welfare of their family and the community, and establishes them as appropriate middle-class Muslims in Indonesia. Their actions distinguish them from lower-class traditional market traders who, because of their economic needs, had to work with maximising their profit at the forefront.

Notes

1. See her company website at http://pamellagroup.com/.
2. For example, female traders working in traditional markets are often perceived negatively because they are said to have an uncontrolled desire for sex and money (Brenner 1998: 161–166). Negative impressions are also applicable to IWAPI members as they were rumoured to have offered sexual favours to male bureaucrats in exchange for business and economic gains (Suryakusuma 1996: 116–117).
3. See Chapter 3 for Aisyiyah and their support for Muslim mompreneurs.
4. *Buruh gendong* or *endong-endong* refers to female porters in traditional markets in Central Java. They carry heavy loads of market commodities on their backs to assist buyers.
5. Budi Utomo was the first youth organisation established by Dr. Soetomo and STOVIA students on May 20, 1908. The organisation played a significant role in raising nationalism in Indonesia.
6. Thirty-four higher education institutions under the Ministry of Religious Affairs; and 319 higher education institutions under the Ministry of Education and Culture (Badan Pusat Statistik Propinsi D.I Yogyakarta 2019).
7. Pesantren Gontor is one of the most prominent Islamic boarding schools in Indonesia. It is located in East Java and was established in 1926.
8. See Chapter 3 for a detailed analysis of *keluarga sakinah.*
9. See Chapter 3.
10. Alcohol sales in Indonesia are regulated by Presidential Regulation No. 74 of 2013 on the Control and Supervision Alcoholic Beverages; and the Regulation of the Minister of Trading No. 20/M-Dag/Per/4/2014 of 2014 on the Control and Supervision of the Production, Distribution, and Sales of Alcoholic Beverages. It is rare for Muslims to serve drinks as part of entertainment events, but private consumption is common in Indonesia.
11. *Umrah* or *umroh* is a pilgrimage made by Muslims to Mecca. Compared to *hajj*, *umrah* is non-mandatory, has lesser rituals, and can be performed at any time.
12. See Chapter 3 for the details of the program related to women's entrepreneurship in Aisyiyah.
13. In 2018 Inneke's husband was arrested by KPK for corruption charges and Inneke's role as a Wardah brand ambassador seems to have been paused.

14. See Chapter 6 for Dian Pelangi.
15. The details of her life story used in this chapter are drawn from the published sources Nurdyansa (2016). Other Sources of her life history are Waruwu (2019), Channel (2017), Ngobi (2020) and Paragon Technology and Innovation (2016).
16. See Chapter 3.
17. There is a growing scholarly body of work in this area and our earlier work has examined these issues (Sakai and Fauzia 2014). Television is also frequently used for Islamic propagation, featuring shows with new preachers, such as AA Gym (Hoesterey 2008), who do not come from a traditional Islamic educational background.
18. See Chapter 3.
19. See Chapter 3.
20. For example, one of the popular internet bookshops, bukukita.com, lists 14 books for adult readers on the theme of Khadijah, while six books on Aishah have been listed (as of 17 November 2021), indicating a stronger interest from middle-class women willing to learn from Khadijah as a role model.
21. This forum receives support from the Bank of Indonesia, the Ministry of Cooperatives and Small Businesses, the Ministry of Religious Affairs, and the Ministry of Women's Empowerment and Children Protection.
22. See this chapter.
23. See Chapter 3.

References

@valentinodinsi '[Instagram Profile] Valentino Dinsi' Dinsi, Valentino. Instagram. Accessed April 2021.

Abdullah, Varatisha Anjani. 2016. Arisan Sebagai Gaya Hidup (Sebuah Kritik Terhadap Masyarakat Konsumtif Perkotaan). *Jurnal Komunikasi* 11: 17–28.

Adi, Permana. 2019. Cerita Nurhayati Subakat Dalam Menjalankan Bisnis Kosmetik. itbofficial. https://www.itb.ac.id/news/read/57275/home/cerita-nurhayati-subakat-dalam-menjalankan-bisnis-kosmetik. Accessed 4 November 2021.

Alexander, Jennifer. 1987. *Trade, Traders and Trading in Rural Java*. Oxford: Oxford University Press.

Alexander, Jennifer. 1998. Women Traders in Javanese Marketplaces. In *Market Cultures: Society and Values in the New Asian Capitalisms*, ed. Robert Hefner. Singapore: Institute of Southeast Asian Studies/Westview Press, Inc.

Alexander, Jennifer, and Paul Alexander. 2001. Markets as Gendered Domains: The Javanese Pasar. In *Women Traders in Cross-Cultural Perspective: Mediating Identities, Marketing Wares*, ed. Linda Seligmann, 47–69. Stanford: Stanford University Press.

Badan Pusat Statistik. 2019. 'Kepadatan Penduduk Menurut Provinsi, 2015–2019'. Available at: https://www.bps.go.id/indicator/12/141/1/kepadatan-penduduk-menurut-provinsi.html. Accessed 20 April 2021.

Badan Pusat Statistik Propinsi D.I Yogyakarta. 2019. 'Jumlah Perguruan Tinggi, Mahasiswa, Tenaga Pendidik (Negeri dan Swasta) Di Bawah Kementerian Riset, Teknologi Kabupaten/Kota Di Propinsi Di Yogyakarta, 2019'. Available at: https://yogyakarta.bps.go.id/statictable/2020/08/05/141/jumlah-perguruan-tinggi1-mahasiswa2-dan-tenaga-pendidik-negeri-dan-swasta-di-bawah-kementerian-riset-teknologi-dan-pendidikan-tinggi-kementerian-pendidikan-dan-kebudayaan-menurut-kabupaten-kota-di-provinsi-di-yogyakarta-2019-.html.

Balogun, Oluwakemi Monsurat. 2012. Contesting Nationalisms: Gender, Globalization, and Cultural Representation in Nigerian Beauty Pageants. PhD Thesis, UC Berkeley.

Beatty, Andrew. 1999. *Varieties of Javanese Religion: An Anthropological Account*. Cambridge, New York and Melbourne: Cambridge University Press.

Beta, Annisa R. 2014. Hijabers: How Young Urban Muslim Women Redefine Themselves in Indonesia. *International Communication Gazette* 76 (4–5): 377–389.

Bowen, John R. 1986. On the Political Construction of Tradition: Gotong Royong in Indonesia. *The Journal of Asian Studies* 45 (3): 545–561.

Brenner, Suzanne April. 1998. *The Domestication of Desire: Women, Wealth, and Modernity in Java*. Princeton, N.J.: Princeton University Press.

Brenner, Suzanne April. 2011. Private Moralities in the Public Sphere: Democratization, Islam, and Gender in Indonesia. *American Anthropologist* 113 (3): 478–490.

Channel, Jaktv Official. 2017. '[Video] Jatuh Bangun Nurhayati Subakat Memperkenalkan Kosmetik Halal'. YouTube. Available at: https://youtu.be/1fR4_tzJaB0.

Damayanti, Imas. 2020. Mamah Dedeh: Istri Para Nabi Juga Cari Duit. Republika. https://www.republika.co.id/berita/qg3wo9483/mamah-dedeh-istri-para-nabi-juga-cari-duit. Accessed 1 November 2021.

DetikHealth. 2014. Kisah Pamella, Pemilik 8 Supermarket Yang Sukses Meski Tak Jual Rokok. Detik. https://health.detik.com/berita-detikhealth/d-2589093/kisah-pamella-pemilik-8-supermarket-yang-sukses-meski-tak-jual-rokok. Accessed 18 August 2021.

Dhana, Atika. 2018. Wardah Bringing Halal Cosmetics to the World. *Go Trading Asia*. Retrieved from https://www.gotradingasia.com/tradingasia/1260-wardah-bringing-halal-cosmetics-to-the-world.

Effendi, Nursyirwan. 1999. Minangkabau Rural Markets: Their System, Roles and Functions in the Market Community of West Sumatra. Ph.D, Fakultät für Soziologie, Universität Bielefeld.

Esqnews.id. 2019. Nurhayati Subakat Wanita Pertama Penerima Gelar Doktor Kehormatan Dari Itb. Accessed 10 November 2021.

Fauzia, Amelia. 2008. Women, Islam and Philanthropy in Contemporary Indonesia. In *Indonesian Islam in a New Era: How Women Negotiate Their Muslim Identities*, eds. Susan Blackburn, Bianca J Smith, and Siti Syamsiyatun, 167–190. Clayton: Monash University Press.

Fauzia, Amelia. 2013. *Faith and the State: A History of Islamic Philanthropy in Indonesia*. Leiden: Brill.

Fealy, Greg. 2008. Consuming Islam: Commodified Religion and Aspirational Pietism in Contemporary Indonesia. In *Expressing Islam: Religious Life and Politics in Indonesia*, eds. Greg Fealy and Sally White, 15–39. Singapore: ISEAS Publishing.

Fealy, Greg, and Sally White, eds. 2008. *Expressing Islam: Religious Life and Politics in Indonesia*. Singapore: Institute of Southeast Asian Studies.

Fitriati, Afia R. 2013. Inspiring Beauty? A Critique of Wardah Cosmetics' Ad Campaigns. Muslimahmediawatch.org. http://www.muslimahmediawatch.org/2013/03/07/inspiring-beauty-a-critique-of-wardah-cosmetics-ad-campaigns/. Accessed 10 September 2021.

Ford, Michele, and Lyn Parker. 2008. *Women and Work in Indonesia*. Oxon and New York: Routledge.

Geertz, Clifford. 1976. *The Religion of Java*. Chicago: University of Chicago Press.

Hadiwinata, Bob S. 2003. *The Politics of Ngos in Indonesia: Developing Democracy and Managing a Movement*. London: Routledge.

Hefner, Robert W. 2003. Islamizing Capitalism: On the Founding of Indonesia's First Islamic Bank. In *Shari'a and Politics in Modern Indonesia*, eds. Azyumardi Azra and Arskal Salim, 148–167. Singapore: ISEAS Publishing.

Hill, Hal. 2000. *The Indonesian Economy*. Cambridge: Cambridge University Press.

Hoesterey, James Bourk. 2008. Marketing Morality: The Rise, Fall and Rebranding of Aa Gym. In *Expressing Islam: Religious Life and Politics in Indonesia*, eds. Greg Fealy and Sally White, 95–112. Singapore: ISEAS Publishing.

ISEF Indonesia. 2021. '[Video] Forum Khadijah PPUMI | the 8th ISEF 2021' ISEF *Forum Khadijah: Menuju Sejuta Sertifikasi Halal Gratis bagi UMKM*. YouTube. Available at: https://www.youtube.com/watch?v=lZPqRfCUI48.

Jendrius. 2017. *Women in Minangkabau Nagari Government: Gender, Negotiating, and Contesting Power at the Local Level*. Padang, Sumatera Barat: Penerbit Erka.

Keumala, Meuthia. 2018. Ahy: Khadijah R.A dan Kartini Adalah Panutan Tepat Bagi Para Muslimah Pengusaha. Kumparan. https://kumparan.com/meuthia-keumala/ahy-khadijah-r-a-dan-kartini-adalah-panutan-tepat-bagi-para-muslimah-pengusaha. Accessed 17 October 2021.

Kitabisa.com. 2020. Gerakan #Salingjaga Untuk Bantu Warga Melawan Corona. https://blog.kitabisa.com/gerakan-salingjaga-untuk-bantu-warga-melawan-corona/. Accessed 13 April.

Kumparan. 2019. [Video] #Theceo: nurhayati Subakat, Ibu Rumah Tangga Bawa Wardah Jadi Kosmetik Indonesia. YouTube. https://www.youtube.com/watch?v=DN-3MDEn9mA. Accessed 11 August 2021.

KumparanWOMAN. 2019. Spesial Hari Ibu Wawancara Sari Chairunnisa and Nurhayati Subakat. Kumparan. https://kumparan.com/kumparanwoman/spesial-hari-ibu-wawancara-sari-chairunnisa-and-nurhayati-subakat-1sVOFUr4TDE. Accessed 1 November 2021.

Kusmana (2017). "Contemporary Interpretation of Kodrat Perempuan: Local Discourse of Muslim Women's Leadership in Indonesia". PhD Thesis, Erasmus University.

Latief, Hilman. 2013. *Melayani Umat: Filantropi Islam dan Ideologi Kesejahteraan Kaum Modernis*. Jakarta: PT. Gramedia Pustaka Utama.

Marcoes, Lies. 2002. Women's Grassroots Movements in Indonesia: A Case Study of the Pkk and Islamic Women's Organisations. In *Women in Indonesia: Gender, Equity and Development*, eds. Kathryn Robinson, and Sharon Bessell, 187–197. Singapore: ISEAS Publishing. https://doi.org/10.1355/9789812305152.

Medina, Ayman Falak. 2019. Indonesia Halal's Law Takes Effect, Impacting Products and Services. https://www.aseanbriefing.com/news/indonesias-halal-law-takes-effect-impacting-products-services/. Accessed 11 August 2021.

Menchik, Jeremy. 2014. The Co-Evolution of Sacred and Secular: Islamic Law and Family Planning in Indonesia. *South East Asia Research* 22 (3): 359–378.

Meuleman, Johan. 2011. Dakwah, Competition for Authority, and Development. *Bijdragen Tot De Taal-, Land-En Volkenkunde/journal of the Humanities and Social Sciences of Southeast Asia* 167 (2–3): 236–269.

MUI Digital Sejarah Mui. MUI Digital. https://mui.or.id/sejarah-mui/. Accessed 21 April 2021.

Mustisany, Hafidz. 2015. Majelis Ta'lim Wirausaha (Mtw) Berjejaring, Bertumbuh, Berbagi. https://republika.co.id/berita/koran/dialog-jumat/15/11/20/ny3swa42-majelis-talim-wirausaha-mtw-berjejaring-bertumbuh-berbagi. Accessed 1 November 2021.

Ngobi. 2020. '[Video] Nurhayati Subakat|10 Fakta Unik Sosok Wirausaha Pendiri @Wardahbeauty' [video]. 03 January 2020. YouTube. Available at: https://www.youtube.com/watch?v=1mKQFG3wGCs.

Nisa, Eva F. 2018. Creative and Lucrative Daʿwa: The Visual Culture of Instagram Amongst Female Muslim Youth in Indonesia. *Asiascape: Digital Asia* 5(1–2): 68–99.

Nurdyansa (2016). Biografi Nurhayati Subakat, Kisah Sukses Perjalanan Pemilik Wahdah Kosmetik. Biografiku.com. https://www.biografiku.com/biografi-nurhayati-subakat.

Nurlaelawati, Euis. 2020. Muslim Female Authorities in Indonesia: Conservatism and Legal Notion of Women Preachers on Familial Issues. In *New Santri: Challenges to Traditional Religious Authority in Indonesia*, ed. Norshahril Saat and Ahmad Najib Burhani, 83–104. Singapore: ISEAS Publishing.

Pamella Supermarket. 2021a. [Video] Pamella Beauty House X Wardah: Success Story with Paragon. YouTube. https://youtu.be/M73SC8R6ojk. Accessed.

Pamella Supermarket. 2021b. '[Video] Yang Belum Tersampaikan: Antara Ibu dan Anak Tercinta (Spesial Hari Ibu)' Supermarket, Pamella. 26 February. YouTube. Available at: https://youtu.be/msEdOMn1Ef0.

Paragon Technology and Innovation. 2016. [Video] Company Profile PT Paragon Technology and Innovation. YouTube. https://youtu.be/115mtA UIsSg. Accessed 04 November 2021.

Peacock, James L. 1978. *Purifying the Faith: The Muhammadijah Movement in Indonesian Islam*. Menlo Park, California: Benjamin/Cummings Pub. Co.

Phuong, Thao, & Deva Rachman. 2017. Csr Landscape in Indonesia: The Past, Present and the Future. https://sustainablesquare.com/evolution-csr-landsc ape-indonesia/. Accessed 1 November 2021.

Pinandu, Ratih Wulan. 2020. Nurhayati, Bos Kosmetik Yang Beri Sumbangan Rp40m Untuk Tangani Corona. https://www.haibunda.com/moms-life/ 20200518122626-76-140793/nurhayati-bos-kosmetik-yang-beri-sumban gan-rp40-m-untuk-tangani-corona. Accessed 1 November 2021.

Rahmawati, Hilda. 2019. Pengajian Bangun Mental Spiritual Keagamaan Warga Godean. Local government of Sleman. https://mediacenter.slemankab.go. id/pengajian-bangun-mental-spiritual-keagamaan-warga-godean/. Accessed 1 November 2021.

Rijal, Syamsul. 2020. Following Arab Saints: Urban Muslim Youth and Traditional Piety in Indonesia. *Indonesia and the Malay World* 48 (141): 145–168.

Sahlan, M. 2019. Kolaborasi Lazismu dan Wardah, Pemberdayaan Perempuan dan Bangun Masjid. https://www.jurnas.com/artikel/61863/Kolaborasi-Laz ismu-dan-Wardah-Pemberdayaan-Perempuan-dan-Bangun-Masjid/. Accessed 1 November 2021.

Sakai, Minako. 2008. Community Development through Islamic Microfinance: Serving the Financial Needs of the Poor in a Viable Way. In *Expressing Islam:*

Religious Life and Politics in Indonesia, ed. Greg Fealy, and Sally White, 267–286. Singapore: ISEAS publishing. https://doi.org/10.1355/9789812308528.

Sakai, Minako. 2010. Growing Together in Partnership: Women's Views of the Business Practices of an Islamic Savings and Credit Cooperative (Baitul Maal Wat Tamwil) in Central Java, Indonesia. *Women's Studies International Forum* 33 (4): 412–421. https://doi.org/10.1016/j.wsif.2010.02.015.

Sakai, Minako. 2012. Preaching to Muslim Youth in Indonesia: The 'Dakwah' Activities of Habiburrahman El Shirazy. *RIMA: Review of Indonesian and Malaysian Affairs* 46(1): 9–31.

Sakai, Minako. 2014. Establishing Social Justice through Financial Inclusivity: Islamic Propagation by Islamic Savings and Credit Cooperatives in Indonesia. *TRaNS: Trans-Regional and-National Studies of Southeast Asia* 2(2): 201–222.

Sakai, Minako. 2017. *Kacang Tidak Lupa Kulitnya: Identitas Gumay, Islam, dan Merantau Di Sumatra Selatan*. Jakarta: Yayasan Pustaka Obor Indonesia.

Sakai, Minako. 2018. *Penggiat Bisnis Syariah: Muslimah, Kewirausahaan dan Pemberdayaan Masyarakat*. Jakarta: Dompet Dhuafa.

Sakai, Minako. 2019. Embracing Islam, Work and Family: Women's Economic Empowerment in Islamising Indonesia. *Intersections: Gender and Sexuality in Asia and the Pacific* 43 (July). http://intersections.anu.edu.au/issue43/sakai2.html#n18.

Sakai, Minako, and Amelia Fauzia. 2014. Islamic Orientations in Contemporary Indonesia: Islamism on the Rise? *Asian Ethnicity* 15 (1): 41–61. https://doi.org/10.1080/14631369.2013.784513.

Sakai, Minako, and Amelia Fauzia. 2016. Performing Muslim Womanhood: Muslim Business Women Moderating Islamic Practices in Contemporary Indonesia. *Islam and Christian-Muslim Relations* 27 (3): 229–249. https://doi.org/10.1080/09596410.2015.1114243.

Salim, Delmus Puneri. 2013. Islam, Politics and Identity in West Sumatra. *Journal of Indonesian Islam* 7 (1): 96–118.

Slama, Martin. 2018. Practising Islam through Social Media in Indonesia. *Indonesia and the Malay World* 46 (134): 1–4. https://doi.org/10.1080/13639811.2018.1416798.

Smith-Hefner, Nancy J. 2007. Javanese Women and the Veil in Post-Soeharto Indonesia. *Journal of Asian Studies* 66 (2): 389–420. https://doi.org/10.1017/S0021911807000575.

Sulistyaningrum, Eny, Budy P. Resosudarmo, and Anna T. Falentina. 2021. Can the Internet Buy Working Hours of Married Women in Micro and Small Enterprises? Evidence from Yogyakarta, Indonesia.

Sullivan, Norma. 1994. *Masters and Managers: A Study of Gender Relations in Urban Java*. Crows Nest, NSW: Allen & Unwin.

Suryakusuma, Julia I. 1996. The State and Sexuality in New Order Indonesia. In *Fantasizing the Feminine in Indonesia*, ed. Laurie J. Sears, 92–119. New York: Duke University Press.

Thornton, Alec, Minako Sakai, and Graham Hassall. 2012. Givers and Governance: The Potential of Faith-Based Development in the Asia Pacific. *Development in Practice* 22 (5–6): 779–791. https://doi.org/10.1080/09614524.2012.685864.

TribunNews. 2020. Fatwa Pp Muhammadiyah Rokok Elektrik Hukumnya Haram Sebagaimana Rokok Konvensional, Ini Alasannya. https://www.tribunnews.com/nasional/2020/01/24/fatwa-pp-muhammadiyah-rokok-elektrik-hukumnya-haram-sebagaimana-rokok-konvensional-ini-alasannya. Accessed 10 August 2021.

Utomo, Ariane, Anna Reimondos, Peter McDonald, Iwu Utomo, and Terence Hull. 2018. Who Wears the Hijab? Predictors of Veiling in Greater Jakarta. *Review of Religious Research* 60 (4): 477–501.

van Doorn-Harder, Nelly. 2006. *Women Shaping Islam: Indonesian Women Reading the Qur'an*. Urbana: University of Illinois Press.

van Doorn-Harder, Nelly. 2013. Polygamy and Harmonious Families: Indonesian Debates on Gender and Marriage. In *Gender and Islam in Southeast Asia: Women's Rights Movements, Religious Resurgence and Local Traditions*, ed. Susanne Schröter, 55–71. Leiden: Brill.

Wardah. 2021. Wardah Inspiring Movement. Wardah. https://inspiringmovement.wardahbeauty.com/. Accessed 7 July 2021.

WardahBeauty. 2012. '[Video] Wardah for World Muslimah Beauty 2012 Windri Marieta Modest Song' WardahBeauty. 26 September. YouTube. Available at: https://www.youtube.com/watch?v=FEg3lVlWWcI.

WardahBeauty. 2013. '[Video] Wardah TV Commercial: Scentsation - Dian Pelangi in Paris'. 16 July 2013. YouTube. Available at: https://www.youtube.com/watch?v=0fAzrduOarY.

Warouw, Johannes Nicolaas. 2008. Industrial Workers in Transition: Women's Experiences of Factory Work in Tangerang. In *Women and Work in Indonesia*, eds. Michele Ford and Lyn Parker, 104–119. London and New York: Routledge.

Waruwu, Christ Bastian. 2019, 30 July 2019. Sejarah Berdirinya PT Paragon Technology and Innovation Hingga Sukses. *IDN Times*. Retrieved from https://www.idntimes.com/life/career/christ-bastian-waruwu/sejarah-pt-paragon-c1c2/4.

waste4change. 2018. The Launching of Wardah Inspiring Movement (August 15, 2018). https://waste4change.com/blog/launching-wardah-inspiring-movement/. Accessed 2 July 2021.

Watson, Conrad William. 2005. Islamic Books and Their Publishers: Notes on the Contemporary Indonesian Scene. *Journal of Islamic Studies* 16 (2): 177–210.

Watson, Sue, Sletske Waslander, and Martin Strathdee. 1999. *Trading in Futures: Why Markets in Education Don't Work.* UK: McGraw-Hill Education.

Widiyatno, Eko. 2006. *Pamella Sunardi Syahuri: Dengan Keluarga Sakinah Membangun Bisnis Barokah.* Yogyakarta: Matan.

Winn, Phillip. 2012. Women's Majelis Taklim and Gendered Religious Practice in Northern Ambon. *Intersections: Gender and Sexuality in Asia and the Pacific* (30): 1–15. http://intersections.anu.edu.au/issue30/winn.htm.

Yufid.TV Pengajian and Ceramah Islam. 2017. 'Kajian Umum: Kisah Penuh Inspirasi Khadijah Binti Khuwailid—Ustadz Dr. Firanda Andirja, M.A'. 12 December 2017. Available at: https://youtu.be/-E36RIkaXSM.

Yulistara, Arina. 2018. Kisah Bos Wardah, Dari Usaha Rumahan Hingga Masuk Forbes Asia. CNBC Indonesia. https://www.cnbcindonesia.com/profil/20180603113724-41-17627/kisah-bos-wardah-dari-usaha-rumahan-hingga-masuk-forbes-asia. Accessed 18 August 2021.

Zaenuddin, Dundin, Rusydi Syahra, and Nina Widyawati. 2003. *Modal Sosial untuk Penguatan Masyarakat Sipil di Era Otonomi Daerah.* Jakarta: Lembaga Ilmu Pengetahuan Indonesia, Puslit Kemasyarakatan dan Kebudayaan (PMB-LIPI).

CHAPTER 6

To Be or Not to Be a Muslim Mompreneur in Indonesia

Minako Sakai

Abstract How do Muslim women become mompreneurs? This chapter focuses on the perceptions of younger Muslim women in Indonesia to explore what motivates them to or hampers them from becoming mompreneurs. This chapter shows becoming good Muslim mompreneurs following their role model of Khadijah is a way to balance work and family, and to make social contributions among middle-class women. The increased emphasis on entrepreneurship education at university and the rapid spread of digital marketplaces are further facilitating this social trend. Yet due to the need for an education and technological and digital competence to operate a business, the opportunity to become a mompreneur is largely limited to middle-class women.

Keywords Digital entrepreneurship · Education · *Halal* business · Indonesia · Mompreneurs · Muslim women

M. Sakai and A. Fauzia, *Women Entrepreneurs and Business Empowerment in Muslim Countries*,
Gender, Development and Social Change,
https://doi.org/10.1007/978-3-031-05954-4_6

Introduction

In this chapter attention turns to the lived experiences of aspiring younger Muslim women regarding becoming mompreneurs. Indonesian state policy and patriarchal norms influenced by Islamic teaching place the responsibility of raising the family heavily on Muslim women (Chin 2018). This chapter examines the process of becoming a Muslim mompreneur to identify the enabling factors found in Indonesia. It will also analyse why becoming a mompreneur has emerged as a possible and appropriate choice for middle-class women. However, taking up an entrepreneurial opportunity naturally entails financial insecurity, as it is deemed more volatile than the office-based employment or public service that is generally preferred by university graduates.

This chapter concludes that Muslim women are carefully carving out multiple roles for themselves in an Islamising Indonesia. As Muslim mompreneurs, they are achieving their career aspirations and framing the significance of their economic role to obtain a middle-class lifestyle. They also advocate that they are building a stronger Indonesia while nurturing a harmonious family life in line with Islamic principles, national policies and societal expectations. By doing so they are becoming new role models, quietly negotiating to change assumed gender roles by expanding female contributions to the community. This chapter draws on case studies in Indonesia to support our argument.

From Career Woman to Muslim Mompreneur

The first case study we explore is that of Dian Pelangi. She is an internationally renowned Muslim fashion designer at only 30 years old. Born in 1991, Dian was originally from Palembang, Indonesia. She began her career in her early 20s, and once identified herself as a Muslim woman who wanted to stand up on her own two feet.[1] Her popularity can be seen through her followers, known as *hijabers*, who are young Muslim fashionistas in Indonesia. Her Instagram followers number a phenomenal 5.1 million (as of 4 May 2021). Because of her Muslim fashion business success, young Indonesian Muslim women admire her entrepreneurial skills as well as her stylish Muslim fashion. She grew her fashion design business while being a brand ambassador for an Indonesian dairy company, Hilo, which advertises milk products for young Muslim women under the name of Soleha (meaning obedient Muslim women in Indonesian). In partnership with Hilo, in 2016 Dian offered fashion workshops at Sekolah Menengah Kejuruan (SMK), a vocational school. She acknowledged that she was a graduate of SMK and wanted to inspire fellow students to succeed and follow in her footsteps (Novia 2016).

It is worth noting that she was only 20 years old when she married her first husband, Tito Harris Prasetyo in 2011. There was a rumour that she had married on the condition that her husband would not pressure her to start a family immediately after their marriage, as is generally expected in Indonesia. It was understood that she was prioritising the growth of her fashion business. Dian is an active user of Instagram and her Instagram self-identification during the first marriage included fashion designer, entrepreneur, travel blogger and brand ambassador, without any mention of the word wife. While the usual Muslim definition of a wife is closely associated with the role in the family home, Dian focused on her international business travel and associated blogging through Instagram postings. In the meantime, her husband resigned from his job at an international petrol company to assist Dian's business by running a fashion magazine (Fitriadi 2018).

In 2016, criticism mounted when Dian's marriage ended in divorce and without any children (Entertainment News 2016). Subsequently, her public esteem declined somewhat. One year later, her ex-husband married another woman while Dian remained single, pursuing her career as a fashion designer, until her second marriage in 2019. Her divorce from Tito is attributed to her firm views of being a financially independent woman. Her Instagram posting summarises her appreciation of being able to generate an income for herself:

> If you have a job, pay your bills, work hard on your own, and manage to live comfortably before you commit to a relationship or any friendship, understand that you want Loyalty, not money. Somebody else's money will never excite an independent woman/man.

This post has received over 42,000 likes and it is fair to say her opinion is supported by certain segments of Instagram users. However, while this view is generally aligned with Western feminism, secular and individualistic in its nature, and advocates gender equality, it is in conflict with a patriarchal and Islamic gender norm widely promoted in Indonesia. This is because earning a livelihood is the official responsibility of a husband in Indonesia, as stipulated in the Marriage Law of 1974, while a woman's role is defined as being a mother and a wife (Robinson 2009: 84–86). As discussed in Chapter 3, Muslim women's organisations promote a concept of raising a harmonious family. Dian's statement above clearly undermines the expectations of socially accepted gender relations. Post-divorce comments from internet users urged her to place her priority on marriage and raising a family and curtail her solo overseas trips in order to avoid being sinful (Syaukani 2016).

Dian spent three years as a divorcee, known as *janda* in Indonesian. *Janda* are viewed in a derogatory way because they are stereotyped as having uncontrolled sexuality (Parker 2016). A woman who is referred to as *janda* is generally viewed as one who has failed to raise a family and who may bring bad luck to their community (Salim and Souisa 2020). Despite the fact that some women are divorcees as a result of being victims of domestic violence or unintended polygamy, the negative image prevails in Indonesia (Parker 2016).

A drastic change took place when in November 2019 Dian married for a second time. Her new husband, Sandy Nasution, was a businessman, in multimedia, from Malaysia (Purnomo 2019). To keep her followers updated, Dian regularly posted on Instagram about significant events in her life including her marriage ceremony, and her *umroh*—honeymoon trip, pregnancy and family life.

What is worth highlighting is the number of likes she has received from her followers. Two postings that have received the highest number of likes are related to the announcement of her pregnancy (298,000 as of 26 December 2019) and the first photo of her daughter after her birth (311,000 as of August 2020). These postings received more likes than her wedding photos and her previous posting on women's independence (Fig. 6.1).

Her pregnancy announcement posting includes a video clip in which Dian and Sandy are both anxiously waiting for the digital pregnancy kit test result in a hotel where the couple were undertaking an *umroh* immediately after their wedding in November. Her test kit showed a yes surrounded by a love heart mark (Fig. 6.2). Upon knowing the result, Dian sobbed with joy and appreciation to God, as her English text in the posting indicates, while her husband was delighted and could not stop laughing. Her pregnancy results immediately after their marriage, revealed during their honeymoon—*umroh* trip, clearly shows that Dian wanted to have a family with this marriage, clearly different from her first marriage. Her choice of words, her posts about dreaming of having a family, being

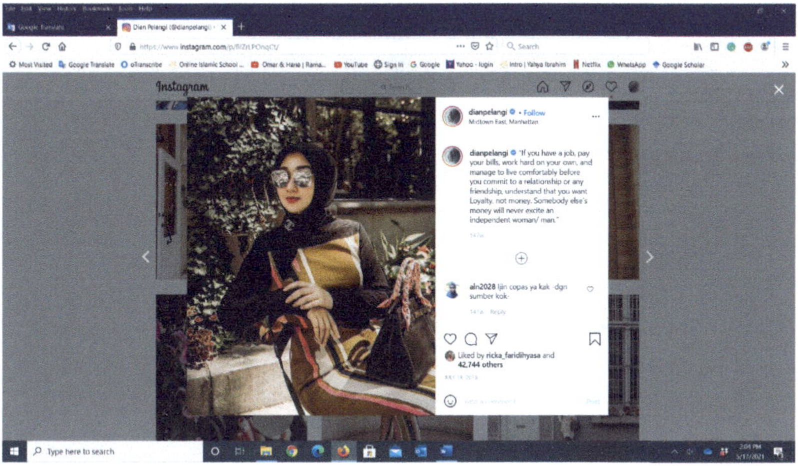

Fig. 6.1 Dian's statement in her Instagram about woman's independence in 2018 (*Source* Dian Pelangi Instagram @dianpelangi [2018])

blessed with God's power, all while she is wearing white prayer clothing and lying with her head against her husband is a perfect image. It shows the world that Dian is a good Muslim wife who has already made her husband happy, and that she is on her way to becoming a mother.

Dian's photo as shown in Fig. 6.2 attracted nearly 300,000 likes from her followers. The arrival of her daughter, Rumi, was announced on 18 August 2020, one day after the annual Indonesian Independence Day. Dian posted a photo of her baby daughter wrapped in a baby pink cloth, and she wrote, 'This is by the grace of my Allah. *Alhamdulillah*.. *Assalamu'alaikum* world. Please say *salaam*[2] to baby Rumi ♡😘'.

Since the birth, Dian's posts include family photos with her husband and her baby daughter. She dresses her baby with a headband in the shape of a ribbon. Her posts feature Dian dressed in her stylish Muslim clothing line, holding her baby dressed cutely in matching colour tones. The popularity of the birth of Dian's daughter is also seen by the level of media coverage it received. The YouTube account of Muslimahdaily.com (2020) at the time of writing in June 2021, showed a clip with the announcement of the birth of Dian's daughter had received 3900 views. This is a significant contrast to the usual number of views of less than 500 for

Fig. 6.2 Dian Pelangi Instagram announcing her pregnancy on 26 December 2020 (*Source* Instagram of @dianpelangi [2019])

clips about Muslim propagation programs, indicating the popularity of the news surrounding the arrival of Dian's baby.

Since the birth of her baby, Dian's Instagram profile has added two key words: wife and mom in addition to her original profession of entrepreneur as shown in Fig. 6.3.

We highlight that Dian's new Instagram profile epitomises her newly acquired identity as a Muslim mompreneur. Her recent Instagram postings include such images as her cooking in the kitchen, a family trip to IKEA to show her harmonious happy family life and photos of business meetings at trendy cafés with other Muslim ladies. She has emphasised her identity as a wife and a mother ahead of being a businesswoman. We argue that through her Instagram posts she is now widely promoting an image of a young Muslim mompreneur or a contemporary version of Khadijah to her fellow Muslim women. This is because her identity transition reflects the widespread views among her follower *hijabers*.[3]

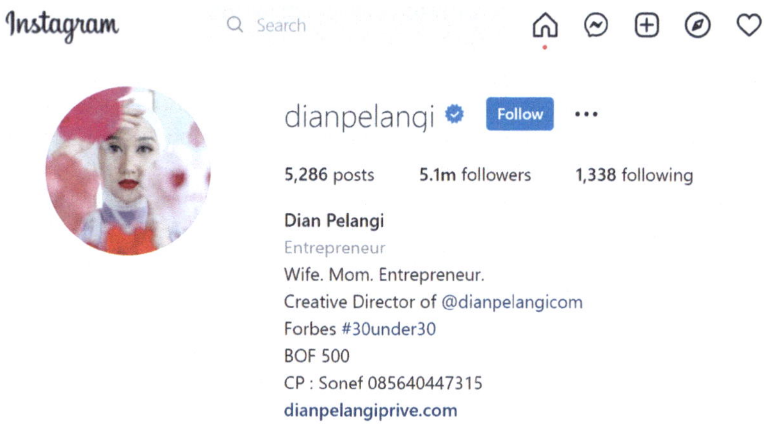

Fig. 6.3 Dian Pelangi Profile as of 4 May 2021 (*Source* Dian Pelangi Instagram account [@dianpelangi])

Pathways to Becoming a Muslim Mompreneur

Contrary to Dian Pelangi's case, however, our research shows that for most Indonesian Muslim women the decision to become an entrepreneur is made out of consequence rather than being their first choice of career. Most women, particularly the educated middle-class women we met, chose office work as their first preference. Large established companies such as Telkomsel, an Indonesian telecommunication giant, banks or state-owned companies offer a substantial and regular income with attractive welfare provisions. As a result, obtaining a job with one of these established companies is deemed to be extremely prestigious in Indonesia if one is not seeking a job in the public service.

The decision to become an entrepreneur is, therefore, a choice that women often eventually make only after having attempted to pursue a formal career involving long hours in an office away from their home. Examples of this being the case are illustrated elsewhere (Sakai 2019) through the experiences of Diajeng Lestari, a prominent online fashion brand owner, Hijup, the wife of the digital commerce entrepreneur, and Achmad Zaky, a co-founder of Bukalapak, one of the most successful digital market places in Indonesia. Diajeng started her online shop after completing her degree at the University of Indonesia, one of the most prestigious universities, and working for a large company, and only made the choice to become a mompreneur because her office work conflicted with her role as a mother and a wife.

The findings through these cases that women's choice to take up entrepreneurship as a solution to this problem supports the findings of other recent literature analysing women's entrepreneurship. Highly educated women are less likely to start their business in middle or high-income countries (Global Entrepreneurship Monitor 2019: 26–28). Furthermore, according to Solesvik et al. (2019), women's motivations to take up entrepreneurship differs from men's in the sense that women are driven more than are men by also seeking to make a social impact. With these scholarly debates as our base, we will explore empirical cases in Indonesia to analyse if women seek out entrepreneurship opportunities over office work as a way to allow them to run both a family and a business.

Finding a Solution in Muslim Mompreneurship

Noor Rafita's case illustrates the emergent trend of educated middle-class women choosing entrepreneurship as a solution. Rafita lives in Bogor city in West Java, which is often used as a residential base for people who work in offices in Jakarta. Having a strong Muslim community, Bogor city has been promoting *halal* tourism and a *halal* economy as one of the city's development policies.[4] The city's main mall, Botani Square, received an award for being Indonesia's best Muslim tourist-friendly mall in 2016 from the Ministry of Culture and Tourism (Sufa 2016). This mall is equipped with appropriate prayer facilities for Muslims and sells only *halal* food. Even though Indonesia has the largest Muslim population in the world, for a long time upper middle-class luxurious hotels and malls did not offer such exclusive Muslim prayer rooms or *halal* culinary outlets. These facilities are relatively new in Indonesia (having emerged since the year 2000) along with the emergence of middle-class Muslims who consume Islamic and *halal* commodities (Fealy 2008). The popularity of *halal* consumption is also found among growing middle-class Malaysian communities (Fischer 2011) (Fig. 6.4).

Since Law No. 33/2014 for *Halal* Product Certification (UU tentang Jaminan Produk Halal) passed in 2014, consumer goods in Indonesia must now be certified with the official *halal* certificate by the Majelis Ulama Indonesia (MUI) or Council of Islamic Scholars. This has further

Fig. 6.4 Rafita Bakery in Bogor, West Java (*Source* Photographed by Minako Sakai)

strengthened the demands of *halal* food popular among the middle class. In October 2021 the government launched a new business network called Khadijah Forum to facilitate the implementation of *halal* certifications to women-owned SMEs that play a key role in realising this law (ISEF Indonesia 2021).

Bogor city has been promoting *halal* foods using their own regional agricultural products, and taro chiffon cake known as *kue talas* has also been promoted widely as a local food product from Bogor (Khairunnisa 2020).

The profile of Rafita from Bogor city attracted my attention, as she was the owner of a *halal* birthday cake store and the producer of jackfruit cakes (*kue nangka*) (Hen 2014). I visited her bakery in 2017 in person for the first time and continued our meetings in my subsequent visits to Indonesia. I also followed her social media posts.

Noor Rafita, (known as Rafita) is in her late 30s. When I met her for the first time in December 2017, she was dressed like a university lecturer, and in fact, she has bachelor's and master's degrees in agricultural business attained at Bogor Agricultural University (IPB), which is in Bogor city. It is the most renowned state agricultural university in Indonesia. Upon finishing her study, she became a lecturer at Universitas Pakuan Bogor, a private university in Bogor. She enjoyed teaching, particularly as she likes sharing useful information with students. Her challenge, however, came after she started her family. She found it difficult to balance her work and family obligations, particularly when she had to teach and examine a student's thesis at the university at the same time as her own child happened to fall ill. She had to go to work as she could not cancel the examination of the thesis presentation with no notice. She felt guilty, though, about failing to be a good mother according to the expectations of herself, her husband and her society. Furthermore, she also had the sad experience of having a miscarriage while she was working as a lecturer. She was torn between her career aspiration to be an academic and her desire to be a good mother and wife. Seeing her distress, her husband supported her in resigning from her job as a university lecturer in 2008 (Hen 2014) (Interview, 30 September, my translation).

As she was very active in her workplace, she started to feel empty and bored while staying home. One day she received a lot of jackfruit as a gift from her neighbours. Jackfruit are very large and can be one metre long when whole. She was at a loss about what to do with it but thought of making a jackfruit cake. This was the beginning of the production of her specialty cake nicknamed Kue La Nang (abbreviation from kue lapis nangka). *Lanang*, from the Malay language, means a boy or male and she designed a character for her brand promotion based on an image of a jackfruit. Rafita enjoys making cakes and sweets and she started making birthday cakes using only *halal* ingredients. She posted some cake photos on her Facebook page. Then a lot of her friends asked that she make one for them to celebrate occasions such as major family events and children's birthdays. She felt that Indonesian consumers love cakes but at that time she could not find anyone else who specialised in selling *halal* cakes suitable for special occasions. She started taking orders as a hobby, as she was able to do this work all from her home kitchen. Her business started in 2012 with an initial investment of five million rupiah to hire a few assistants. Her business, *kue nangka*, grew initially through her social media contacts who lived in Bogor and surrounding areas (Oktavian 2015) (Fig. 6.5).

In April 2014, in the main street of Bogor, Jalan Pandu Raya, Rafita opened her bakery/café as pictured (Fig. 6.4). Her décor imitates some

Fig. 6.5 Children's *Halal* Birthday Cake from Rafita Bakery (*Source* Photographed by Minako Sakai)

of the atmosphere of a café in Paris. She explained that some clients want to sit and eat her fresh cakes after shopping and going on outings.

To promote her bakery business, she worked in partnership with Bogor city, which supports the growth of creative industries with a focus on *halal* food. This is because Bogor city has a vision to promote *halal* local products in line with the national strategy and Rafita's *halal* products are ideal for this aim (News 2015). She regularly participated in training opportunities provided by local government agencies and promoted her products through government-sponsored expos. She also received support to legalise her business and in 2014 received a *halal* certificate from MUI as the first *halal* cake shop in Indonesia. The acquisition of the MUI *halal* certificate made her business even more popular among middle-class consumers seeking *halal* foods to suit their lifestyle needs.

To grow her business and contribute to making Bogor a thriving business town, she feels that it is important that she encourages fellow businesspeople in Bogor. She feels that having one well-known shop will not entice much tourism from other areas. If Bogor offers a wide range of attractive products, people are more likely to spend a few days in Bogor for their holidays and the local communities will benefit from the increased economic activity this would bring. With this vision in mind, in early 2017 she co-founded a weekly business-mentoring program called Bogor Berdaya, which means Bogor Empowers (meaning Bogor empowers the Bogor city). It is a business-mentoring program with a subtheme expressed as 'meet, grow and share', supported by like-minded local businesspeople, both men and women, and used for them to share their experiences of starting up and growing their businesses. People of any faith, gender or location can attend their sessions for free and meet successful entrepreneurs for inspiration. The organisers attempt to bring highly successful national businesspeople, such as the general manager of McDonald's, as role models to the group as speakers who can share successful tips for growing businesses. This local business-mentoring program has inspired like-minded businesspeople in Jakarta to form Jakarta Berdaya (Jakarta Empowers), which also draws together start-ups and aspiring SME owners in Jakarta.

Rafita's view about taking an active role in Bogor Berdaya is that entrepreneurship enables her to engage and share knowledge with more people than she could when she was a university lecturer. Although her business focuses on *halal* cakes, she was comfortable with the inclusive nature of Bogor Berdaya's membership. In addition to her involvement in Bogor Berdaya, she also mentors her own employees to acquire new business skills. Every year she offers a full package of *umroh* as an annual award to her best employee to motivate her employees to work hard.

Rafita remarked, 'When I left my job as a lecturer, I was sad as I had lost the opportunity to learn and share. In hindsight, I can now share more with like-minded businesspeople through my business. I can fund my family's pilgrimage with my business profit, share experiences with successful people and contribute to the growth of the economy in Indonesia. I did not expect that.' (interview 30 September 2017)

She also stated that her husband is happy with her business. She feels that her business is compatible with her lifestyle and family needs, she is supported by the local government agencies, and she feels she can contribute to the community in a much more significant way than she could in her role as a lecturer. She is also committed to growing her business as well as assisting her fellow Bogor business owners in growing their businesses through the Bogor Berdaya movement. Instead of working for a university, she has become a role model mompreneur who would inspire fellow entrepreneurs and contribute to the community by sharing her knowledge. Although she did not use the word Khadijah in our communication, it is obvious that she is undertaking her business to become a good mother and a wife who funds Muslim religious obligations and can contribute to the strengthening of the community with her expertise and business profits.

So far, we have presented profiles of married women choosing to take up entrepreneurship as a compromise in order to achieve their career aspirations, while having the flexibility necessary to be able to care for their family and to contribute to the community. What about single women who are freer to engage with start-ups or to pursue their entrepreneurial career path before they marry and start a family? Do they see start-ups as their preferred pathway on their journey to be good Muslim women?

Existing scholarly literature highlights that the enabling factors that trigger entrepreneurship are influenced by the social context and cultural embeddedness of this way of life surrounding gender norms (Morrison 2006; Yousafzi et al. 2018). Empirical studies show that the growth of digital entrepreneurship in Indonesia is supported by having a good education (Sutarjo and Raharja 2020). Indonesia, though, still has poor digital infrastructure that is in need of greater support and investment from the government, compared with other advanced digital economies, such as that of Singapore (Erh 2021). With this literature providing our framework, the next case study shows how a young Muslim woman decided to remain an employee despite having the potential to develop financially insecure digital entrepreneurship, as she prioritises job security for her long-term family needs.

Putting Entrepreneurship on Hold

In 2016, when I was undertaking desk research trying to find Muslim female tech start-up figures, Anita Rahmawati caught my attention. The article I found in an Indonesian local newspaper reported she was a graduate of Institut Teknologi Sepuluh Nopember (Sepuluh Nopember Institute of Technology [ITS]) majoring in chemical engineering. She was also a graduate of Manchester University and was the recipient of the George Davis Prize in 2015, the annual award granted to the best graduate from the master's course. The article reported that she was about to launch an application with her friends, Anisa Zaskia and Fahmi Hidayatullah from Balikpapan. She was smiling sweetly and wearing a headscarf to reflect her Muslim identity. In 2016, her team won first prize in a social digital competition that sought the best application designed to solve social problems (Lomba Socio Digi Leader). The competition was sponsored by the Indonesian telecommunication giant, Telkomsel (Nurdin 2016).

Telkomsel was aware that most of the Indonesian population was moving away from landlines to mobile phones, particularly to smartphones and it was interested in developing a new market to accommodate this change. It thus continued searching for young and bright Indonesians who could develop this emergent digital technology and associated services by sponsoring this type of competition (DetikNews 2017).

Contacting Anita turned out to be easy as one of my then Ph.D. students, now Dr. Bhirawa Anoraga, knew her through his wife, as they had all received a prestigious Indonesian government scholarship called Lembaga Pengelola Dana Pendidikan (LDPD) or the Indonesia Endowment Fund for Education scholarship. They were all connected through Facebook. I met Anita later in the year in Jakarta and again for this research on 27 September 2017 to ask her about her entrepreneurial pursuits designing digital applications.

In late 2016 she was about to launch a new application named Tukangpedia. The naming consisted of an Indonesian word *tukang*, meaning tradesperson and *pedia*, an abbreviation of encyclopaedia in English. She was keen to do something to save her hometown, Balikpapan, from further economic decline, which has already deprived tradespeople of their jobs. Her dream app was intended to enable locals who needed services to find appropriate tradespeople through her Tukangpedia application. She thought it would be beneficial to connect people and to create job opportunities using a digital app.

Anita had long had a vision to use her knowledge for the improvement of people's lives. When I asked about her choice of study, she stated that she was determined to study a subject that would be useful for the Indonesian community. She was born in Madiun, Central Java, but grew up in Balikpapan, East Kalimantan, where oil and gas exploration through mining provided the bulk of the livelihoods. Her mother worked as a secretary in a multinational oil company after her divorce from her husband. Anita felt that her job security would have been stronger if her mother had been an engineer. That triggered her interest in science, mathematics and English and she studied hard to excel in these subjects.

With her hard work, Anita won academic competitions in multiple areas during her secondary schooling. She became the head of the Organisasi Siswa Intra Sekolah (OSIS) or High School Student Association. Subsequently, she was awarded a provincial scholarship to study at ITS, a technology-focused university in Surabaya, East Java, renowned for its engineering and science programs. She majored in chemical engineering, which she thought would be important in the mining and oil sector. She believed she had a future in this sector in East Kalimantan. It was after that that she then obtained an LPDP scholarship to study at Manchester University, in the UK, finishing her master's degree there in 2015. On receiving the George Davis Prize at graduation, she became the first Indonesian woman to win the award. Her mother was delighted to see Anita's achievements in the UK and attended the graduation ceremony in person. Upon Anita's return to Indonesia, she got a job at a leading Japanese engineering company in Jakarta, but her mother fell ill unexpectedly. Anita resigned from her job to be home to look after her mother, who had supported her all her life.

What Anita saw when she returned to Balikpapan in 2016 was an economic decline because of mining company closures. The impact of environmental damage and reckless operations that risked workers' safety resulted in closures of mining companies in East Kalimantan. For example, 10 coal mining companies shut down in 2015 in East Kalimantan Province alone (Wibisono 2015).

As mining companies employed locals as cleaners, gardeners and caterers, the closure of these mining companies resulted in high local unemployment. Since there was no provision for tradespeople to advertise their services locally, people who wanted to find cleaners, gardeners and other tradespeople were at a loss as to how to find them. The competition organised by Telkomsel was timely for Anita, Balikpapan and Telkomsel. Anita was idle at home, after returning to Balikpapan to look after her mother, tradespeople were in search of jobs, and Telkomsel needed refreshing ideas about how to make its business more relevant when many people were moving away from landlines to databased mobile phones.

Indonesians enjoy being connected online and offline. In 2013, 48 million people in Indonesia were using Facebook (Kemp 2013). In January 2021, 345.3 mobile connections were recorded, which was an increase of four million over the previous year (Kemp 2021b). The rapid growth of internet and smartphone use in Indonesia is creating a supportive ecosystem for the digital economy. For example, in 2020 Indonesians aged between 16 and 64 years old spent an average of 8.52 hours on the internet per day, ranking Indonesians as the eighth highest internet users in Asia with the Philippines ranking first with 10.56 hours. The same report ranks Indonesians as the ninth highest users of social media in the same survey (Kemp 2021a: 90). With the increased use of digital applications on smartphones, it is natural that middle-class Indonesians want to use applications such as Tukangpedia to find tradespeople.

Anita was not able to do the coding necessary to develop the Tukangpedia application herself and so her friends who supported her idea undertook this task for her as a team. During our meeting, she showed me a short promotional video featuring what Tukangpedia can do (Telkom Indonesia Official 2017). Tukangpedia was obviously aimed at being a digital Yellow Pages, used to connect tradespeople looking for work with the people who need their services. Her mother taught Anita an important life principle, '*Rezeki itu untuk berbagi, jangan buat sendiri*', meaning that people's livelihood should be for the greater good and not be self-centred. This life principle motivated her to create the Tukangpedia application for smartphones.

In 2016 Anita's team was Telkomsel's first Socio Digi Leaders Competition winner. As such, they were invited to the Silicon Valley to visit Stanford University and the tech giant Google. After she returned to Indonesia, her mother's health improved and Telkomsel offered Anita a position as a product development apprentice. She took up this position to further advance her career in Jakarta. However, this posed some significant challenges for her in finalising the production of Tukangpedia while also fulfilling her work commitments at Telkomsel. None of her team had the time to bring this project to fruition due to conflicting commitments.

Being a single Muslim woman in Indonesia is not ideal. Anita was engaged to marry in the following year. Her fiancé's family owns a business, which he is involved in. Usually, married couples in Indonesia are expected to live on their own and start a family soon after their marriage. Anita then would be expected to start her family shortly after her wedding. In Indonesia working for a large company like Telkomsel, offers various welfare benefits in addition to financial stability. Anita herself was educated at a good private school, generously funded by her mother's established employer in Balikpapan. Large companies generally offer other benefits, such as health care for an employee's family and access to a range of recreation and educational facilities. Subsidised housing schemes are also common. For an engaged Muslim woman like Anita, choosing to become an entrepreneur would pose immediate challenges as she needed to accommodate the demanding hours of her work for the start-ups, while also preparing to start a family. The more family-friendly policy and provisions the employer offers to working mothers, the fewer motivations working mothers develop. Recent scholarly work (Agnihotri and Bhattacharya 2020) on Indian women also attests to this point by qualitative research on working women.

In September 2017 Anita was working full-time for Telkomsel, leaving very little time for her digital start-ups, as she also spent time with her new husband. Soon after our meeting, the couple were blessed with the arrival of their baby. Tukangpedia was finally launched in 2017, but it was not as popular as expected. The difficulty in promoting Tukangpedia is attributed to two factors. We argue that competition from the better resourced Gojek app that offers a variety of household services has intensified.

Gojek, founded in 2010, achieved brand recognition by enabling independent ride service drivers across Indonesia to register with Gojek as partners. With their bright green uniforms and helmets, what were seen as seedy motorbike riders began to be recognised as a credible ride service. Initially, Gojek specialised only in short ride services, but it has expanded the services covered by the platform to include couriers, food delivery and miscellaneous payment and shopping services associated with the needs of businesses and households (Gojek, n.d.). Gojek was developed by a young entrepreneur, Nadiem Makarim, a highly educated young Indonesian man who uses creativity to promote businesses and entrepreneurship in line with the Indonesian government's current policy. Nadiem was appointed to serve as the Minister of Education under the Widodo government in 2020. In April 2021, the news report that Gojek and Tokopedia, two e-commerce giants in Indonesia, were finalising a merger deal with the total assets of the merged company being estimated at US$18 billion. Facing this type of competition from Gojek, a single-purpose application such as Tukangpedia has been outpaced by the resources these tech giants have access to.

Further, access to these apps is limited to smartphones and tablet users, the majority of which are from the urban Indonesian middle class. Data from internet service provider APJII in 2018 shows that 74.1% of the urban population use the internet compared to 61.6% of the rural population. Data also shows that internet use is also more prominent among the highly educated population. For instance, 100% of those who have studied at the tertiary level use the internet while only 18% of those who have never had schooling use the internet. 63.5% of those who have had at least nine years of education use the internet (Annur 2019).

In addition to having the necessary digital literacy, the cost associated with using mobile phones and data downloads is a matter of great concern for people on low incomes. Many street vendors do not and cannot afford to own smartphones. Their knowledge about digital devices is also generally quite limited. They understand simple texts and messaging services and they are happy to receive orders by phone. Smartphones and more complex apps often require them to have an email account, which they may not. In addition, smartphones use data, which also adds to the financial burden imposed on users. This digital divide makes it difficult for average tradespeople without much education to use the Tukangpedia platform effectively.

Digital marketing, however, is becoming popular in Indonesia. For example, GAPURA Digital, a Google subsidiary business in Indonesia, often runs free Women Will (Women Will, n.d.) training sessions for women. Gapura stands for Gerakan Pelatihan Usaha Rakyat (Gapura) Digital, meaning Digital Small Business Training Campaign. The training focuses on how to use Google My Business features to strengthen a business's online presence. The session I observed in Yogyakarta in September 2019 had approximately 100 female participants, and most of the people participating were aged over 50 years old and came to the training session with younger female participants, often their relatives or daughters who were familiar with the use of smartphones.

Participation in this training session was free and open to any women, with the only condition being that all the participants were expected to bring a smartphone and have an email account for their business. The training was held in the Hotel Aston, a modern upmarket hotel in Yogyakarta. By the end of the session, the participants gained important knowledge about how to register their businesses using Google My Business, making their enterprise visible online. They also learnt directly from the experiences of the trainers who run digital business platforms. Participants heard stories about how their increased digital presence as a result of using this platform has increased the prosperity of businesses. What remains unclear is how the pool of experienced small business owners and inexperienced university-educated women can work in partnership to enable them to balance work and family through entrepreneurship. To explore this issue, the next section will focus on the ways in which youth entrepreneurship and the gig economy are merging to create a new form of female entrepreneurship in Indonesia.[5]

Youth Entrepreneurship and the Gig Economy

The promotion of youth entrepreneurship has been an important focus of Indonesian government policy in recent times.[6] Since 2009, the Yudhoyono government has been promoting the growth of creative industry and entrepreneurship, particularly targeting university graduates. As a result, becoming an entrepreneur is gaining popularity among the middle class and university students. These university graduates once aspired to secure work in the public sector in offices or schools. It was understood that this type of work would provide financial security. But because such jobs are hard to find, the government encouraged universities to include entrepreneurship courses in their electives. University management encouraged students' interest by creating competitions or offering small grants to reward entrepreneurship. These businesses may be linked with the course specialisation or majors that the students are studying. For example, a student majoring in biology started a mushroom growing business and negotiated a contract to regularly supply local restaurants as mushrooms are a popular delicacy. Universitas Negeri Yogyakarta (Yogyakarta State University), once known as Teachers' College or Institut Keguruan dan Ilmu Pendidikan (IKIP) in Yogyakarta, was one of the universities with a compulsory one-semester entrepreneurship course for undergraduate students studying to be teachers.[7] The university management understood that securing a full-time teaching position may take longer than graduates thought and so they needed to be prepared to support themselves through entrepreneurial activities in the meantime. As a result, the university held an annual International Conference on Educational Research and Innovation (ICERI) in 2016 and the conference focused on creativity and entrepreneurship as an outcome of the application of knowledge (Institute of Research and Community Service 2016). Indonesian universities are expected to make social contributions to the community through teaching and research and Lembaga Penelitian dan Pengabdian kepada Masyarakat (LPPM) or the Institute for Research and Community Services is an important integrated institution to oversee the university activities.

I was invited to give a keynote speech in person in 2016 for ICERI and online in 2020 for their annual research and social engagement conferences, and other research-related discussions frequently took me to their campus. In 2018 I was invited by the Department of Religious Affairs on the topic of social engagement and community services by state Islamic universities in Indonesia and observed the displayed reports on activities of university social engagements.

While on campus at the Yogyakarta State University in 2016, I witnessed thriving pilot businesses run by the students. The university runs a series of lectures for undergraduate students taking the entrepreneurship course. Undergraduate students receive lectures and participate in workshops on how to develop their disciplinary knowledge into a product for a business. As the university offers a wide range of subjects, entrepreneurship lectures try to connect disciplinary knowledge with commercial or applied products to develop business opportunities and ideas.

It is not only state universities, but also private business schools fostering interest among their students in becoming their own bosses, instead of working for someone else. The red jacket in Fig. 6.6 is symbolic of the change of mindset occurring in Indonesia. Usually, company uniforms advertise the name of the company. Instead, these shirts say 'Sorry we're entrepreneurs! (not working for anyone)' indicating that the wearer is their own boss. The Umar Usman Business School run by the Dompet Dhuafa Foundation, Jakarta, is a for-profit wing of the foundation's educational institution. In 2017, the board displayed at the entry to the campus stated 'If after one year of studying, you would like to be able to become an entrepreneur. This is the campus!'.

Ojek Syariah Women-Only Transport Business

An example of an emergent student-led business initiative utilising a pool of casual female workers is Ojek Syariah (*halal* motorbike ride service)

Fig. 6.6 Umar Usman Business School's advertisement (*Source* Photographed by Minako Sakai)

popularly known as Ojesy. This is a service in which women transport women in line with Islamic jurisprudence. This start-up was created by a female Muslim university student named Evilita Adriani. It has made use of the growing interest in the *halal* economy, combining the use of social media and mobile phones to grow a business. It also reflects an emerging trend of entrepreneurship among the youth in Indonesia, starting businesses that utilise middle-aged women who seek more flexible employment conditions as a labour force.

Our findings here demonstrate that the development of this start-up reflects the reality of 'single' women, who are divorced or widowed and have the financial responsibility of providing for themselves and their dependents. We argue that the development of increased instances of female-owned or run small businesses in contemporary Indonesia indicates that women are challenging patriarchy and that this challenge is not limited to negotiating with male guardians and husbands. Having the permission of one's husband is not only the precondition for achieving a work–family life balance for women, accommodating the perceptions of one's community is also necessary. Having one's neighbours embrace those who aspire to combine their motherhood and their economic role in the family is essential.

Along with the rising interest in entrepreneurship among university students, it is not surprising that Evilita, popularly known, as *Mbak* Lita (Miss Lita) was an undergraduate at Universitas Pembangunan Nasional (National Development University), or commonly known as UPN, in Surabaya, East Java in 2015 when she started a new bike ride service that was shariah-compliant for Muslim women called Ojek Syariah or Ojesy. We met for the first time in December 2016 in Surabaya with her business partner and Ojesy co-founder, Reza Zamir, a male Muslim student. We continued our meetings online and in person over some years so that I could learn about her challenges as a young entrepreneur in Indonesia.

Lita told me that her business idea emerged while she was working as a bike rider to support herself while studying at university in Surabaya. She read from published reports that women were being sexually abused when using public transport. She said the report she read stated that 70% of the women interviewed about the sexual abuse said that they would feel safer if they could use single-sex public transport. In addition, as a bike rider, she did not feel comfortable giving a ride to a male stranger. So, she had an idea. Why not create a transport service for Muslim women? She shared her idea with her friend Reza, who was studying Islamic propagation in Surabaya.

Initially they started with only Lita as the driver and Reza as the marketing officer (interview, 2 December 2017). He advertised the service through Facebook. Through their posts on Facebook, they attracted two business partners with much-needed resources. A gentleman who had been running BMT NU-Syah for eight years, developed five chapters of his own BMTs and was keen to invest in Ojesy. Another investor who lived in Jakarta but heard about Ojesy offered his programming service to run their call centre, which processes orders from clients and allocates them to suitable drivers. As the majority of female bike riders did not actively use apps, a phone system for ordering was essential. They moved their call centre to Bojonegoro, a local town away from Surabaya, East Java, to reduce costs so they could employ six receptionists to manage ride bookings.

The initial investment was only Rp. 15,000 or AUD 1.50 and this paid for petrol and data use for their mobile phones. Within a year, they raised Rp. 60 million through investment and they registered their business, with Lita as the CEO and Reza as Chief Marketing Officer. Lita and Reza gradually developed Ojesy as a platform to support Muslim women by offering a system of mutual support and educating community members about the importance of creating an inclusive and supportive society. As a student of Islamic communication, Reza thought that Islamic propagation and marketing of *halal* services have much in common.

They stated that Ojesy received great support from the community, not only from clients but female riders who wanted to join Ojesy. In 2016 the Surabaya office employed 40 riders as casual workers who were between 30 and 45 years old. In December 2017, we met Dwi and Santi, female drivers who worked for Ojesy. Both were in their mid-30s and were divorced with a child. Their former husbands had remarried and no longer provided financial support for their children. Renouncing the payment of child support by default is a common practice in strongly Muslim regions, as found in the study of West Java (van Huis 2010: 15), and women work to make ends meet and often receive support from their own parents.

Prior to joining Ojesy, Dwi, already a divorcee, worked in a call centre full-time but her child often protested at being left alone. Dwi had completed a diploma in taxation from one of the most prestigious Indonesian state universities, Universitas Airlangga in Surabaya but had never had a job in a relevant field. Santi was teaching Islam full-time at school, but she had not had the chance to finish her degree. Both were single parents and needed to work to support themselves but they felt they were not able to fully care for their children or be good mothers if they had to go to work. Both learnt about job opportunities at Ojesy from Facebook messages. Santi said, 'My child often protested that I should not work. ... Now I work for Ojesy, I feel less sinful as a mother'. Dwi said, 'Surely my income is less than before when I was working for the office, but I am prioritising my time to see my child anytime. I can work while they are at school' (interview, 4 December 2017).

By the end of 2016, Ojesy's business had expanded to operate in 22 cities including Surabaya. Their business only operates until 7 p.m., so that women drivers can finish their shifts before dark as a safety precaution for their employees and their clients. The Surabaya operation employed approximately 40 Muslim drivers on a casual basis. Not everyone was a single mother, some were simply making use of their free time after their children went to school to earn additional income.

The challenge faced by these female drivers was the public perception of their occupation as female bike riders. *Tukang ojek* or motorcycle taxi drivers, are predominantly male, and are often seen as untrustworthy because they overcharge clients or take a longer route than necessary to inflate the fare. Some female clients worried about using this kind of transport service, as they were worried for their safety during the ride. Gojek, lessened these safety concerns to some degree by making the identity of their drivers visible to clients through their app. This increased the credibility and public perception of these types of services (Silalahi et al. 2017).

The female drivers we spoke with said being called *tukang ojek* had negative connotations for them about their occupation, particularly because they were women. Public perceptions are that good Muslim women should not sit close to unrelated men. As a result, the chief marketing officer, Reza invented a new name for them to indicate that these drivers were 'transport friends' or *sahabat pengendara*, meaning transport companion. These female drivers are not only providing a transport service to female clients, but they are a companion in the pursuit of their Islamic way of life.

Dwi said, 'I am often invited to have breakfast with my clients. I am treated like their relative.... I also take their clients' children to various lessons such as piano lessons and English or school at Kumon. My clients are like my relatives'.

On this point Reza said their clients usually treat drivers with respect. This close relationship, based on the notion of a family known as *kekeluargaan*, is deeply appreciated in Indonesia's daily interactions, as it is not based on monetary transactions but affinity and affection (Hermawan and Loo 2019). Many employers such as Wardah, emphasise kekeluargaan or a sense of family as one of the most important elements of social capital in developing their enterprises. Santi revealed, 'I have an experience of receiving Rp. 100,000 while the tariff was only Rp. 25,000, the balance was for my child, my client said. My client treated me just like her relative' (interview, 4 December 2017).

Their clients usually wanted to use a bike ride service to go to regular Islamic study groups (*pengajian*) or rotatory credit meetings (*arisan*), two common pastimes for Muslim women. Sometimes the destination was a crowded urban area with narrow roads, which made it impossible to get to by car. Relying on a family member to give them a ride was also sometimes difficult. A lack of transport can mean that a woman cannot attend Islamic study group meetings. Ojesy thus offers not only a transport service but a companion with whom to attend the Islamic study group. The drivers often attend the Islamic study groups together.

Santi said, 'I joined the Islamic study group, so we go together, study together, and go home together. The usual fares are Rp. 60,000 but I was offered Rp. 100,000 and my client says I can have the change, and I am often asked to eat with the clients. These clients sometimes buy me clothes, we are just like my family, and I feel very comfortable and happy.'

Despite these positive experiences, drivers can face challenges, particularly from their community and relatives. Dwi said, 'People say I have a good education, and they [my relatives] are surprised that I am working as a motor bike driver' (interview, 4 December 2017).

The drivers' relationships with clients mirror a well-documented social patronage system widely practised across Indonesia (Pelras 2000), which plays a key role in creating an informal social security system (O'Neill et al. 2019; Pauwelussen 2016). Because Ojesy drivers do not meet with other co-workers as part of their daily work, once a month Ojesy organises an Islamic study group in the Baiturrozaq Mosque, located in the area of Surabaya Industrial Estate Rungkut, Surabaya. This mosque is located next to the lake, which offers a beautiful soothing scene from the mosque. The female drivers are expected to attend monthly meetings where they can learn about various facets of life, such as the difficulties of managing a family and how to manage jealousy, as part of their self-development. The management team also attends these groups to meet their employees.[8]

A challenge for Ojesy also comes from fierce competition with e-commerce giants that also offer a wide range of services through their highly sophisticated applications. Users of large internet platforms can order deliveries of food, arrange a ride home, pay for utilities and buy goods online through the use of a single application. The economic shutdown of the pandemic in 2020 suspended the ride services for the safety of the passengers and riders. Ojesy instead offered online Islamic study lessons using female Islamic teachers (personal communication 10 June 2020). However, not all the former riders were able to take up an opportunity to teach Islam online using a new digital start-up of Ojesy. ShariHub and Ojesy collaborated with an Islamic philanthropic organisation to raise funds to assist the female riders who had lost their livelihood during the COVID-19 pandemic (Nabila 2020). While the impact of COVID-19 has been extraordinary, the adversity Ojesy workers faced illustrates the challenges posed to start-up businesses because of the volatile working conditions of people involved in the initiatives (Fig. 6.7).

Not to Be a Digital Mompreneur

Finally, we will turn our attention to the owners of small businesses who remain hesitant to get involved in social media-based marketing and entrepreneurship development. This reluctance is strongest among

Fig. 6.7 Ojesy advertising lady driver services (*Source* Ojesy)

middle-aged Muslim women who do not have higher education and yet work to support their families running small businesses that range from catering with home-made food, running a kiosk from home and selling clothes. Most of these enterprises are micro, small and medium-sized enterprises, and they are set up by poor households out of financial necessity. In other words, these jobs are not a chosen career path, but rather the consequence of their financial insecurity and need to produce a secondary or a third source of income (Tambunan 2017). The majority of these women who have little education start a small informal business to generate an income (AIPEG 2017). As we demonstrate next, these women are not part of the emergent middle-class women who could seek their employment in an office.

In Yogyakarta, these small traders form the basis of the local economy, as can be seen in the bustling Beringharjo market located in Malioboro Street (Idid and Arif 2005; Iskandar et al. 2021). One of my long-term research contacts, Siti Fitri,who runs a small street food kiosk with her husband located in one of the main streets, Merdeka Street in Yogyakarta, remarked that she did not understand how to use smartphones and applications. Her daughter understands how to use these things, but she was too busy with her own family and could not help Siti Fitri use Google My Business or smartphones. Siti Fitri does not own a smartphone. On missing the training event by Women Will held in Yogyakarta on 8 September 2019, she remarked, 'I am good at making very tasty seafood dishes, but digital application matters are beyond me. I can send texts and some customers send me orders by texts, that is enough, isn't it? What is the application for? I can cook food well, and I am just happy with receiving text orders'.

Siti Fitri continued, 'The other day, one official from a bank came. He said, please put this on your stall. He gave me this sticker. He said customers could pay me by using this application. Looks complicated, doesn't it. I need cash to pay for my daily transactions. Why not use cash?'. She was referring to an application called Boost, promoted by one of the state-owned banks, Bank Negara Indonesia, commonly known as BNI (Fig. 6.8).

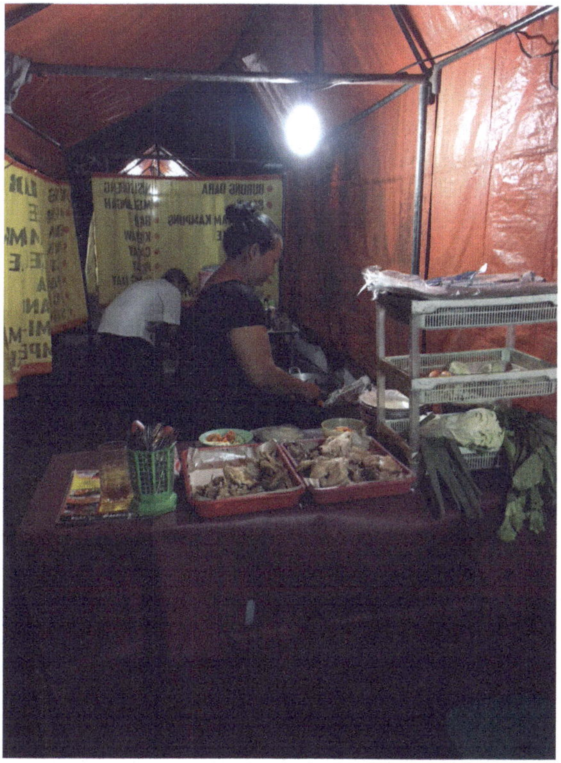

Fig. 6.8 Siti Fitri cooking with her husband in Yogyakarta (*Source* Photographed by Minako Sakai)

As the Indonesian government decided to promote the digital economy and entrepreneurship, a new financial institution called Otoritas Jasa Keuangan (Financial Services Authority [OJK]) was established in 2012. The government promotes support for financial inclusion. One of the areas the government targets to increase financial inclusion is in encouraging people to have a bank account so they can access financial services that meet their needs (OJK 2016). According to the World Bank report (2016), in 2011, only 41% of adults in developing countries had a bank account. That number increased to 54% in 2014. In the case of Indonesia, 51% of the Indonesian population aged 15 years or older do not have an account with a financial institution (Demirgüç-Kunt et al. 2017). In 2011, 80% of the adult population did not have a bank account. People with lower levels of education, who usual run small businesses, are less likely to have a bank account. For example, the World Bank Global Findex in 2017 shows that 66% of the population with only primary education or less do not have an account with a financial institution (Demirgüç-Kunt et al. 2017).

To promote entrepreneurship and the digital economy in Indonesia, the government has encouraged digital start-ups to use e-money by providing a promotional discount for the use of digital money instead of using cash. Users are enticed to open a digital wallet (account) with the application provider to increase familiarity with financial technology. For a small trader like Siti Fitri, e-money linked to financial products is beyond her comprehension. She has been using a credit system as a member of the street vendors' cooperative for more than 15 years, but she has never used a bank. She often said, 'I do not understand it. It is convenient to receive cash. I need cash to buy my groceries for my business every morning. Anyway, I put the sticker from the bank officer on the table, but I do not know how it works and no-one uses it here'. When asked about the recently implemented legal requirement on *halal* certification, she was confident that her food preparation meets the standard (MUI 2021). She said, 'An official from the cooperatives came and Yanto (my husband) and I attended training. They said that is enough at the moment. Fortunately, we do not have to obtain a certification from MUI, we don't have the money for that anyway.' (interview, 8 September 2019)

During her business hours, she pays in cash for access to electricity and water and makes daily repayments for her credit through the cooperative. This process of payment has been a steady feature of everyday life, which I have witnessed since 2008. For these small traders, the idea of using applications and digital financial transactions remains foreign and strange and creates uncertainty about cash flow. Because the BNI office is located near the Kauman district of Yogyakarta, most of the small eatery outlets had a sticker on display as the photo in Fig. 6.9 shows, but in reality, shop owners preferred to be paid cash daily. They need cash to pay for ingredients, vegetables and to pay for utilities. The use of credit cards or digital wallets is limited to people familiar with smartphones and digital financial transactions.

In August 2019, when the Greater Jakarta area was struck with a blackout that lasted for 48 hours, the people who suffered most were urban middle-class office workers. They were ordering food, shopping online and arranging their commutes using an application and without using cash. Some of them joked that they would die from hunger because they had little cash on them and had no access to their money.

Fig. 6.9 Boost sticker for digital transactions (*Source* Photographed by Minako Sakai)

Conclusion

This chapter has analysed the emergent social contexts in which Muslim women are capitalising to develop their businesses. The first example, the case of Dian Pelangi, shows the transition from being a career-driven businesswoman to becoming a successful middle-class Muslim mompreneur during her second marriage. Being a social media user, she is well supported by her five million fans who admire her as a fashion icon. Her popularity is increasing due to her new role as wife and mother. Her case shows that being a Muslim mompreneur is the key to becoming a successful middle-class Muslim businesswoman in Islamic Indonesia. Her second marriage sends a loud message that Muslim women can have it all.

The second case, that of Rafita, the owner of a *halal* bakery, illustrates a common scenario by which middle-class Muslim women choose entrepreneurship as a solution to accommodating their demands as mothers and wives while pursuing their desire to share skills and knowledge with other people. Rafita's commitment to becoming a good mother while also contributing to the community is widely respected by her family and the local business community. Her case illustrates a common pathway to becoming a Muslim mompreneur as a respectable middle-class woman.

The third case, that of a younger Muslim woman, Anita, shows that some find entrepreneurship riskier than office work, despite having some success in digital enterprises. The last case, being that of female-only transportation that aligns with Islamic law of gender segregation, is an appealing concept in the Islamising Indonesian modern economy. Nonetheless, competition between digital start-ups is fierce and can be off-putting for some pursuing entrepreneurship despite the image of entrepreneurs receiving positive attention from the public. Becoming a mompreneur is not yet the first choice among middle-class women, yet it is a way to negotiate career and family aspirations after marriage.

The trend of becoming a Muslim mompreneur is taking place alongside the Indonesian government's policy of fostering entrepreneurship among the middle class and includes digital entrepreneurship. The case of Siti Fitri shows the confusion and marginalisation of traditional small business owners who do not ride the wave of digital entrepreneurship. These older sole-traders account for a significant proportion of female-owned small businesses in Indonesia and provide services to the middle class. Siti Fitri's example demonstrates that in becoming a mompreneur one will naturally be assumed to have digital literacy and familiarity, thus making this pathway to success available mostly to privileged highly educated middle-class Muslim women.

While the growth in Muslim mompreneurship is a welcome trend as a strategy to support women in their pursuit of career and family aspirations, we see a potential risk. Women might become trapped in the pitfall of the gig economy where their employment is not statistically visible and may receive little attention from policymakers. If women do not legalise their businesses, they may face becoming hidden by the gig economy in the future (Sakai and Anoraga 2020). While the gig economy has the potential to create jobs for those who need them, potential risks associated with the precarious nature of the market and insecurity in the livelihood of workers have been identified in the research (Graham et al. 2017). The fragility of needs-based employment became apparent when the economic shutdowns during the COVID-19 pandemic were in place. Moreover, women are among the groups who were most severely affected by the pandemic. They carry the burden of unpaid work and this has been multiplied during the COVID-19 crisis (Setyonaluri and Samudra 2020). The lack of financial assistance from the government for affected but unregistered small businesses owned by women has worsened their situation (Ramdlaningrum et al. 2020).

Notes

1. The analysis of Dian Pelangi's first marriage was originally published in Sakai (2019).
2. *Salaam* is an informal spelling of an Indonesian term *salam*, meaning greetings. The text was written in English.
3. Beta (2021: 7) states that young *hijabers* are inspired to take up entrepreneurship by the example of Khadijah, a good Muslim woman who was a mother and a wife and used her wealth to assist her husband, the prophet, in propagating Islam.
4. This is aimed at boosting its local economy. See Chapter 3 for the impact of regional autonomy and the growth of Islamic lifestyle and *halal* businesses.
5. Gig economy is defined as 'a way of working that is based on people having temporary jobs or each paid separately, rather than working for an employer' (Cambridge Dictionary, n.d.).
6. See Chapter 3.
7. See Chapter 3 for the Indonesian government's policies related to entrepreneurship.

8. The incorporation of Islamic ethics in company management has become popular in Indonesia as promoted by Ari Ginanjar (Rudnyckyj 2009) and other popular Muslim preachers such as Abdullah Gymnastiar.

References

@dianpelangi Pelangi, Dian. Instagram.

@dianpelangi. 2019. Dian Pelangi Announcing Her Pregnancy' Pelangi, Dian *'This is by the grace of Allah. When two lost souls, longing for the same thing, dreaming the same dream, hoping the same hope for a very long time, and only put their hope in Allah, then if Allah wills it to be, it will be. At the very right time, for the very right reasons.'* December 26. Instagram.

Agnihotri, Arpita, and Saurabh Bhattacharya. 2020. Drivers of Mompreneurship: Evidence from India. *Society and Business Review* 15 (4): 373–396. https://doi.org/10.1108/sbr-01-2020-0016.

AIPEG. 2017. *Women's Economic Participation in Indonesia: A Study of Gender Inequality in Employment, Entrepreneurship, and Key Enablers for Change.* The Australia Indonesia Partnership for Economic Governance (AIPEG), The Australian Department of Foreign Affairs and Trade (DFAT), Center for Development Economics and Sustainability (CDES). Available at: https://www.monash.edu/business/cdes/research/publications/publications2/Womens-economic-participation-in-Indonesia-June-2017.pdf.

Annur, Cindy Mutia. 2019. Survey APJII: Penetrasi Penggunaann Internet di Indonesia Capai 64.8%. *Kata Data.* https://katadata.co.id/sortatobing/digital/5e9a51915cd3b/survei-apjii-penetrasi-pengguna-internet-di-indonesia-capai-648. Accessed Apr 2021.

Beta, Annisa R. 2021. Out of Thin Air: Emerging Muslim Fashion Entrepreneurs and the Spectre of Labour in Indonesia. *Continuum*: 1–14.

Cambridge Dictionary. n.d. Gig Economy. Cambridge University Press. https://dictionary.cambridge.org/dictionary/english/gig-economy. Accessed Apr 2021.

Chin, Grace V.S. 2018. State Ibuism and One Happy Family: Polygamy and the "Good" Woman in Contemporary Indonesian Narratives. In *The Southeast Asian Woman Writes Back: Gender, Identity and Nation in the Literatures of Brunei Darussalam, Malaysia, Singapore, Indonesia and the Philippine*, eds. Kathrina Mohd. Daud and Grace V.S. Chin, 89–106. Singapore: Springer Nature Singapore. https://doi.org/10.1007/978-981-10-7065-5_6.

Demirgüç-Kunt, Asli, Leora Klapper, Dorothe Singer, Saniya Ansar, and Jake Hess. 2017. *The Global Findex Database: Measuring Financial Inclusion and the Fintech Revolution.* Washington, DC: The World Bank Group.

DetikNews. 2017. Telkom Kembali Gelar Kompetisi Socio Digi Leaders. https://news.detik.com/adv-nhl-detikcom/d-3509362/telkom-kembali-gelar-kompetisi-socio-digi-leaders. Accessed 1 Dec 2020.

dianpelangi. 2018. Independent Woman' Pelangi, Dian *"If you have a job, pay your bills, work hard on your own, and manage to live comfortably before you commit to a relationship or any friendship, understand that you want loyalty, not money. Somebody else's money will never excite an independent woman/ man"*, July 19. Instagram. Available at: https://www.instagram.com/p/BlZrLPOnqCt/.

Entertainment News, Net. 2016. [Video] Dian Pelangi Menjalani Sidang Kasus Perceraiannya dengan Tito Haris, September 10. YouTube. Available at: https://www.youtube.com/watch?v=8HyTuWobJfc.

Erh, Joey. 2021. Assessing Digital Economy Policies in Six Southeast Asian Countries ISEAS. https://www.iseas.edu.sg/articles-commentaries/iseas-perspective/2021-50-assessing-digital-economy-policies-in-six-southeast-asian-countries-by-joey-erh/.

Fealy, Greg. 2008. Consuming Islam: Commodified Religion and Aspirational Pietism in Contemporary Indonesia. In *Expressing Islam: Religious Life and Politics in Indonesia*, eds. Greg Fealy and Sally White, 15–39. Singapore: ISEAS Publishing.

Fischer, Johan. 2011. *The Halal Frontier: Muslim Consumers in a Globalized Market*. New York: Palgrave Macmillan.

Fitriadi. 2018. 5 Tahun Menikah, Artis Cantik Dian Pelangi Tega Ceraikan Suaminya Demi Ini. *BangkaPos.com*. https://bangka.tribunnews.com/2018/03/14/5-tahun-menikah-artis-cantik-dian-pelangi-tega-ceraikan-suaminya-demi-ini. Accessed 18 Aug 2021.

Global Entrepreneurship Monitor. 2019. *Gem 2018/2019 Women's Entrepreneurship Report*. London, UK: Babson College, Smith College, and the Global Entrepreneurship Research Association (GERA). Available at: https://www.gemconsortium.org/report/gem-20182019-womens-entrepreneurship-report.

Gojek. n.d. Gojek's Products. https://www.gojek.com/en-id/products/. Accessed 7 Apr 2021.

Graham, Mark, Isis Hjorth, and Vili Lehdonvirta. 2017. Digital Labour and Development: Impacts of Global Digital Labour Platforms and the Gig Economy on Worker Livelihoods. *Transfer* 23 (2): 135–162. https://doi.org/10.1177/1024258916687250.

Hen. 2014. Berawal dari Oleh-Oleh, Wanita Ini Raup Rp 30 Juta/Bulan dari Lanang Bogor. *Detik Finance*. Retrieved from https://finance.detik.com/solusiukm/d-2727892/berawal-dari-oleh-oleh-wanita-ini-raup-rp-30-jutabulan-dari-lanang-bogor.

Hermawan, Marko S., and Mark K. Loo. 2019. The Construction of Kekeluargaan as an Indonesia's Organizational Culture. *Humaniora* 31 (1): 1–13. https://doi.org/10.22146/jh.42851.

Idid, Syed Z-Sholinah, and B. Arif. 2005. The Role of Informal Street Activities in the Context of Conserving Urban Cultural Entity. Case Study: Malioboro Street, Yogyakarta, Indonesia. In *VIII International Conference of the APSA (Asian Planning Schools Association)*.

Institute of Research and Community Service. 2016. International Conference on Educational Research and Innovation (ICERI) 2016. Yogyakarta National University. http://en.lppm.uny.ac.id/news/international-conference-educational-research-and-innovation-iceri-2016. Accessed 8 Oct 2018.

ISEF Indonesia. 2021. [Video] Forum Khadijah PPUMI the 8th ISEF 2021. ISEF *Forum Khadijah: Menuju Sejuta Sertifikasi Halal Gratis bagi UMKM*. YouTube. Available at: https://www.youtube.com/watch?v=lZPqRfCUI48.

Iskandar, Budiawati Supangkat, Johan Iskandar, Dede Mulyanto, Rahman Latif Alfian, and Suroso Suroso. 2021. Traditional Market, Social Relations, and Diversity of Edible Plants Traded in Beringharjo Market, Yogyakarta, Indonesia. *Biodiversitas Journal of Biological Diversity* 22 (4).

Kemp, Simon. 2013. Digital 2013: Asia Social Media Statshot March 2013. Data Reportal. https://datareportal.com/reports/digital-2013-asia-social-media-statshot-march-2013. Accessed 10 July 2020.

Kemp, Simon. 2021a. Digital 2021: Global Overview Report. We Are Social and Hootsuite. https://datareportal.com/reports/digital-2021-global-overview-report. Accessed 18 Aug 2021.

Kemp, Simon. 2021b. Digital 2021: Indonesia. We Are Social and Hootsuite. https://datareportal.com/reports/digital-2021-indonesia. Accessed 18 Aug 2021.

Khairunnisa, Syifa Nuri. 2020. Resep Bolu Lapis Taro Kukus, Oleh-Oleh Khas Bogor Yang Mudah Dibikin. https://www.kompas.com/food/read/2020/07/11/140700075/resep-bolu-lapis-taro-kukus-oleh-oleh-khas-bogor-yang-mudah-dibikin-?page=all. Accessed 10 Dec 2020.

Morrison, Alison. 2006. A Contextualisation of Entrepreneurship. *International Journal of Entrepreneurial Behavior & Research* 12 (4): 192–209. https://doi.org/10.1108/13552550610679159.

MUI, LPPOM. 2021. Regulasi Halal Di Indonesia/Halal Regulation in Indonesia. http://www.halalmui.org/mui14/main/page/regulasi-halal-di-indonesia-halal-regulation-in-indonesia. Accessed 17 July 2021.

Muslimahdailycom. 2020. [Video] Selamat! Dian Pelangi Melahirkan Putri Pertama, August 19. YouTube. Available at: https://www.youtube.com/watch?v=az11xc17eic.

Nabila, Marsya. 2020. Pelajaran tumbangnya Ojesy dan Menatap Peluang Bisnis Syariah Online. https://dailysocial.id/post/pelajaran-tumbangnya-ojesy-dan-menatap-peluang-bisnis-syariah-online. Accessed 10 Oct 2021.

News, Antara. 2015. Local Industries Should Boost Creativity to Design Halal Products: VP. *AntaraNews.com*. https://en.antaranews.com/news/163508/local-industries-should-boost-creativity-to-design-halal-products-vp. Accessed 18 Aug 2021.

Novia. 2016. Dian Pelangi, Berbagi Pengalaman Dunia Fesyen. http://majalahpeluang.com/dian-pelangi-berbagi-pengalaman-dunia-fesyen/. Accessed 5 Nov 2019.

Nurdin, Wahid. 2016. Sempat Diremehkan Saat Kuliah Di Inggris, Anita Berhasil Ciptakan Aplikasi Tukangpedia. https://www.tribunnews.com/techno/2016/09/25/sempat-diremehkan-saat-kuliah-di-inggris-anita-berhasil-ciptakan-aplikasi-tukangpedia. Accessed 11 Nov 2020.

OJK. 2016. International Best Practices on Policies and Regulation in Financial Inclusion. *OJK*. https://www.ojk.go.id/id/berita-dan-kegiatan/publikasi/Documents/Pages/Materi-OJK-PROKSI-2016/12.%20Endo_WB_Financial Inclusion(3.16.16).pdf. Accessed 18 July 2020.

Oktavian, Muhammad Rizal. 2015. Rafita's Cake, Dari Hobi Jadi Usaha Menggiurkan. *Bogor Today*. https://bogor-today.com/2015/12/rafitas-cake-dari-hobi-jadi-usaha-menggiurkan/. Accessed 18 Aug 2021.

O'Neill, Elizabeth Drury, Beatrice Crona, Alice Joan G. Ferrer, and Robert Pomeroy. 2019. From Typhoons to Traders: The Role of Patron-Client Relations in Mediating Fishery Responses to Natural Disasters. *Environmental Research Letters* 14 (4): 045015.

Parker, Lyn. 2016. The Theory and Context of the Stigmatisation of Widows and Divorcees (*Janda*) in Indonesia. *Indonesia and the Malay World* 44 (128): 7–26. https://doi.org/10.1080/13639811.2015.1100863.

Pauwelussen, Annet. 2016. Community as Network: Exploring a Relational Approach to Social Resilience in Coastal Indonesia. *Maritime Studies* 15 (1): 1–19.

Pelras, Christian. 2000. Patron-Client Ties Among the Bugis and Makassarese of South Sulawesi. *Bijdragen tot de Taal-, Land-en Volkenkunde* 156 (3): 393–432.

Purnomo, Sapto. 2019. Dian Pelangi Menikah Lagi, Ini 5 Fakta Tentang Suaminya Sandy Nasution. *Liputan 6*. https://www.liputan6.com/showbiz/read/4113415/dian-pelangi-menikah-lagi-ini-5-fakta-tentang-suaminya-sandy-nasution. Accessed 7 Apr 2021.

Ramdlaningrum, Herni, Fiona Armintasari, Cut Nurul Aidha, and Dwi Rahayu Ningrum. 2020. The Impact of Covid-19 on Women-Led MSMEs. Maftuchan, Ah. 2020/11/30/, 1–4. Jakarta: Perkumpulan

PRAKARSA. Available at: https://responsibank.id/media/496521/policy-brief-26-english-the-impact-of-covid-19-on-women-led-msmes.pdf.

Robinson, Kathryn. 2009. *Gender, Islam, and Democracy in Indonesia*. Oxon and New York: Routledge.

Rudnyckyj, Daromir. 2009. Spiritual Economies: Islam and Neoliberalism in Contemporary Indonesia. *Cultural Anthropology* 24 (1): 104–141. https://doi.org/10.1111/j.1548-1360.2009.00028.x.

Sakai, Minako. 2019. Embracing Islam, Work and Family: Women's Economic Empowerment in Islamising Indonesia. *Intersections: Gender and Sexuality in Asia and the Pacific* 43 (July). http://intersections.anu.edu.au/issue43/sakai2.html#n18.

Sakai, Minako, and Bhirawa Anoraga. 2020. Education, Digital Enterprise and Islam in the Indonesian Modern Embedded Economy. In *Muslim Women in the Economy: Development, Faith and Globalisation*, eds. Shamim Samani and Dora Marinova, 214–228. Oxon and New York: Routledge. https://doi.org/10.4324/9780429263194.

Salim, Natasya, and Hellena Souisa. 2020. Janda di Indonesia Masih Menghadapi Stigma dan Anggapan Miring Terutama di Wilayah Pedesaan. *ABC News*. https://www.abc.net.au/indonesian/2020-11-17/bagaimana-stigma-mempersulit-kehidupan-janda-di-indonesia/12891420. Accessed 18 Aug 2021.

Setyonaluri, Dianhadi, and Rachmat Reksa Samudra. 2020. In indonesia, the Covid-19 Pandemic Hurts Poor Women Most. *The Conversation*. https://theconversation.com/in-indonesia-the-covid-19-pandemic-hurts-poor-women-the-most-145694. Accessed 7 Apr 2021.

Silalahi, Shilvia L. Br., Putu W. Handayani, and Qorib Munajat. (2017). Service Quality Analysis for Online Transportation Services: Case Study of Go-Jek. *Procedia Computer Science* 124: 487–495. https://doi.org/10.1016/j.procs.2017.12.181.

Solesvik, Marina, Tatiana Iakovleva, and Anna Trifilova. 2019. Motivation of Female Entrepreneurs: A Cross-National Study. *Journal of Small Business and Enterprise Development* 26 (5): 684–705. https://doi.org/10.1108/JSBED-10-2018-0306.

Sufa, Theresia. 2016. Bogor Recognized for Muslim Tourist-Friendly Shopping Mall. *The Jakarta Post*. Retrieved from https://www.thejakartapost.com/news/2016/10/31/bogor-recognized-for-muslim-tourist-friendly-shopping-mall.html.

Sutarjo, S., and Sam'un Jaja Raharja. 2020. Entrepreneurial Spirit in Economic Development: A Study of Two Digital Start-Up Companies in Jakarta, Indonesia. *Review of Integrative Business and Economics Research* 9: 220–231.

Syaukani, Abdul Rahman. 2016. Dian Pelangi Gugat Cerai Suami, Netizen: Jangan Terlalu Gila Kerja dan Traveling Mbak! *TabloidBintang.com*, August

11. Available at: https://www.tabloidbintang.com/berita/gosip/read/44706/dian-pelangi-gugat-cerai-suami-netizen-jangan-terlalu-gila-kerja-dan-traveling-mbak. Accessed 7 Apr 2021.

Tambunan, Tulus. 2017. Women Entrepreneurs in MSMEs in Indonesia: Their Motivations and Main Constraints. *Journal of Women's Entrepreneurship and Education* 1–2: 56–86.

Telkom Indonesia Official. 2017. '[Video] Tukangpedia (1st Winner of Socio Digi Leaders 2016)' Indonesia, Telkom. YouTube. Available at: https://www.youtube.com/watch?v=g6VmBFJgRj0. Accessed 10 Nov 2021.

van Huis, Stijn Cornelis. 2010. Rethinking the Implementation of Child Support Decisions-Post-Divorce Rights and Access to the Islamic Court in Cianjur, Indonesia. https://warwick.ac.uk/fac/soc/law/elj/lgd/2010_1/vanhuis/. Accessed 7 Apr 2021.

Wibisono, Kunto. 2015. Gubernur Kalim Tutup 10 Perusahaan Tambang Batubara. https://www.antaranews.com/berita/535769/gubernur-kaltim-tutup-10-perusahaan-tambang-batu-bara. Accessed 7 Apr 2021.

Women Will. n.d. Women Will Indonesia. Google. https://www.womenwill.com/indonesia/. Accessed 7 Apr 2021.

World Bank. 2016. Women Entrepreneurs in Indonesia: A Pathway to Increasing Shared Prosperity. World Bank. https://openknowledge.worldbank.org/handle/10986/24751. Accessed 7 Apr 2021.

Yousafzi, Shumaila Y., Adam Lindgreen, Saadat Saeed, and Colette Henry. 2018. *Contextual Embeddedness of Women's Entrepreneurship: Going Beyond a Gender Neutral Approach*. New York: Routledge.

CHAPTER 7

Negotiating Patriarchy as Contemporary Khadijah and Aishah

Minako Sakai

Abstract The concluding chapter emphasises that Muslim mompreneurs are disseminating a new message that a good Muslim woman as wife and mother requires more than just raising a harmonious family. Their activities of contributing to the community are an important part of their gender role. Following the wives of the Prophet Muhammad as their role models, women intend to embody a form of propagation by action. This is an effective local strategy to foster gender equality and negotiate patriarchy within the framework of Islam. Their quiet challenge enables men to side with this important social transformation to build an inclusive society.

Keywords Gender roles · Islam · Role models · Women entrepreneurs · Work and family balance

M. Sakai and A. Fauzia, *Women Entrepreneurs and Business Empowerment in Muslim Countries*,
Gender, Development and Social Change,
https://doi.org/10.1007/978-3-031-05954-4_7

Introduction

Are Muslim mompreneurs a reality? With a focus on Indonesia this book has shown that middle-class Muslim mompreneurs are emerging and that becoming a Muslim mompreneur is both a response to modernity and a strategy to achieve gender equality in Muslim-dominant countries. Modernity for the Muslim middle class is different, yet women negotiate their desired careers alongside family needs by following in the steps of the wives of the Prophet Muhammad. This runs counter to secularisation and individualism in the Western countries. They increase their economic roles and social engagements, but they do so alongside their husbands, while wearing sophisticated Muslim clothing and serving tasty cakes catered by *halal* bakeries to celebrate important Islamic ceremonies. Their economic aim is to assist in raising a harmonious family and to contribute to the community, their career path is not framed solely by individual life goals, at least not so in public.

Following the discussions of modernity, Islam and the middle class, Chapter 1 has shown that the educated urban middle class are turning to Islam as a reference point to lead their life. In this process Khadijah and Aishah, the wives of the Prophet Muhammad, have received much attention among Muslims and new interpretations and imaginations about them as ideal Muslim women have been circulated. Because Muslims are increasingly faced with the needs to generate an income to maintain their consumer lifestyle, middle-class women are looking beyond a conventional office work appropriate for the middle class. Thus, becoming a good Muslim woman who can raise a harmonious family while working to support their middle-class lifestyle through a respectable income-generating job, has become an important issue. In this context the meaning of mompreneur has been framed as a way of being a good middle-class Muslim woman, and as distinct from traditional women traders who worked out of economic necessities.

Chapter 2 has explored the interplays among state economic policies and women's work participation and education attainments in the Muslim-dominant countries of the Middle East, South Asia and Southeast Asia. It further examined how Islamic authority has responded to changing gender norms. The analysis of the profiles of pioneering middle-class Muslim businesswomen from each region shows how these socio-economic contexts have affected the emergence of Muslim mompreneurs. They are emerging strongly in business sectors associated with female needs, but also expanding into new areas availing themselves of the presence of digital commerce.

In Chapter 3 the focus has shifted to Indonesia and how state economic policies and the rise of middle-class Muslims have created *halal* consumerism and markets from which Muslim mompreneurs have benefited. The Muslim women's organisations have endorsed the economic contribution of women as an essential part of raising a harmonious and healthy family. These organisations endorse Muslim mompreneurs as role models.

Chapter 4 has identified that marriage and becoming a mother remains an important social norm for Muslim women. Because of this, the narratives of single, never-married professional Muslim women in Indonesia reflect strong societal opposition and disapproval.

Chapters 5 and 6 have presented an in-depth analysis of Indonesian Muslim women's attempts to balance their career aspirations with their ideal of Muslim womanhood. Most of these women are a mother and a wife, while growing their business enterprise and giving back to their community when feasible. In balancing these roles, they frame their actions and motivations to become mompreneurs by emulating two exemplary Muslim women: the first wife of the Prophet Muhammad, Khadijah who could run a business to support her husband while raising their children, and the prophet's youngest wife, Aishah, who was bright and brave in her support of her husband's propagation to establish an Islamic community. Of importance is the fact that Khadijah has achieved rising popularity as a role model for the middle-class Muslim women of contemporary Indonesia (1990s onwards). We argue that the possibility of raising a harmonious middle-class family increasingly depends on socio-economic conditions of the household, and subsequently has an impact on and affects the understanding of what ideal Muslim modern womanhood entails.

Carving Out the Societal Role of Muslim Women

Following these new role models of Muslim women suggests that Muslim mompreneurs are disseminating a new message in society. Muslim mompreneurs present their role as one which adheres to God's expectations of human beings. This supports their active roles in family and community. They do not attempt to directly change patriarchy or criticise the state-endorsed husband's position as the head of their household.

However, they are expanding their own role in society by associating their activities with Khadijah and Aishah, both of whom have the undisputable reputation of ideal Muslim women. As Islamisation of the middle class deepens with lifestyle increasingly influenced by the desire to become a good Muslim (Latief 2017; Sakai 2018), Indonesian Muslim women do not feel comfortable being labelled feminist or seen to be ascribing to feminism as these terms could be seen as 'culturally inauthentic or, worse, a form of Western imperialism' (Rinaldo 2013: 8). By modelling themselves on the wives of the prophet and contributing to the betterment of their society, their approach is much more strategic than is taking up a Western feminist approach that appears to focus on pursuing individual aspirations. Muslim women see that the role-modelling approach has the potential to enhance the chances of women's empowerment or assist them in realising aspirations. By working to generate an additional source of income to support the household, their family would be able to enjoy a suitable lifestyle in the middle class. This harnesses and attests to women's ability to manage their households.

Throughout my research in Indonesia, I had regular discussions with Indri, a successful Muslim businesswoman in Yogyakarta, who happily allowed me to use her photo on the front cover of my book (Sakai 2018). We first met in 2008 in one of the business training sessions run by BMT Beringharjo for their clients' business development. She was introduced to me as one of the most hard-working BMT clients who had grown her business from a tiny kiosk at home and also managed to undertake charitable activities for her employees and the local neighbourhood (Sakai and Fauzia 2016).

The BMT's business development seminar was titled 'the Management of the Heart', which encouraged BMT clients to run their businesses motivated by compassion and empathy for the disadvantaged, and not by greed. It was intended that this compassion would translate into concrete charitable activities or business development, thus the BMT clients would be willing to pay almsgivings to relevant *zakat* institutions in Indonesia, including the charitable wing of the BMT enterprise (Sakai 2010). In the training session, the audience watched a film featuring two Muslim siblings from a financially disadvantaged family. They were alone in Yogyakarta for their schooling away from home. The elder sister was a university student wearing a headscarf. She was working part-time to feed her younger brother. She worked long hours as a shop assistant, but her wages were small. She regularly bought fried rice for dinner for both of them. Her brother was disappointed with fried rice for dinner, but she was not able to buy a more expensive option such as rice with meat. Seeing her brother disgruntled, she felt ashamed and was tempted to take up sex work to generate additional income so she could feed her brother better food. This film alludes to the fact that poverty may derail Muslims from their faith if the poor are not assisted. The film ended without a concrete outcome, and the trainer appealed to the viewers to give alms to Muslim philanthropic organisations including the philanthropic wing of the BMT Beringharjo. I heard many viewers sobbing while watching this film. They clearly felt that pursuing commercial benefit alone should not be the aim of growing their businesses. Indri and I met for the first time after this video training session and I could see she was emotionally moved.

While running her own business, Indri also completed her bachelor's degree and a master's degree in management to enhance her managerial skills. Her husband was a long-time member of Muhammadiyah and had been an emotional support for her, but he suffered from ill health. She ran rental car businesses, two grocery shops and also a cafe where her sons worked. She was a daughter of a successful businessman but her father's business collapsed when she was a child. She told me that she inherited an entrepreneurial spirit from her father, and after she had given birth to her twin boys, she started a small kiosk in her home initially using capital received from her family, including her in-laws. She successfully grew her business and was also actively involved in Muhammadiyah's women's organisation, Aisyiyah. Through her activities at Aisyiyah she expanded her networks and learnt about women's roles. She was able to undertake activities together with well-respected Muslim women, including Pamella. As her network expanded, she was asked to run sessions to mentor junior members who needed guidance from organisations or individuals.

In November 2018 when I was in Yogyakarta, I attended a training session where Indri was giving a lecture to students who were studying to become primary school teachers. I was a casual observer as I had an appointment to have lunch with Indri afterwards. But suddenly I was asked to introduce myself and speak about how I came to know about her and what I thought of her role. This was not unexpected in Indonesia. After my short talk, Indri added that she felt she had learnt from me as a senior academic from Australia. She added that she was lucky enough to have learnt from a host of established and respected international academics she has met through me. The participants looked happy and impressed as they listened to me—from Australia but originally from Japan—speaking in fluent Indonesian appreciating their role model, Indri. The message to her audience that day was that it is important to learn from a role model to become better and to share by disseminating key messages as a teacher to their students. Being a mompreneur creates upward mobility in society, expanding connections and outlooks beyond locality.

As her business grew, Indri started to run a monthly Islamic study group, which met in her cafe on Sunday mornings. She gives donations to children who need help. She also invites novice businesspeople to learn about entrepreneurship and business skills. I often asked why she continued to expand her businesses when she had become so busy, and what she felt about her role as the primary income earner for her family. Was she influenced by international development frameworks such as the Sustainable Development Goals, especially those related to gender equality.

Indri felt her husband, who stays home, was her bedrock. Her husband is always there to support her emotionally. She used her husband's devotional needs as motivation to grow her business and placed this ahead of any materialistic desire to renovate her house. She alone funded her husband's pilgrimage in 2003 and made her own pilgrimage in 2005 (Muttaqin et al. 2011: 40). She saw the concept that Muslim men must be the leader and head of the household, and she thought it was essential for her husband to undertake his religious obligations. Thus, she felt proud to be able to assist her husband by running a successful business. I often probed into her thinking about women supporting their husband financially while Islam designates men as the provider for families. Her response was rather philosophical. She felt that while she was the one who was able to grow the business, he was the foundation of her family. Becoming a wife, a mother and a businesswoman was what God intended for her and she was simply responding to this mandate. As is expected among middle-class Indonesian Muslim women, in everyday life she delegates the main domestic chores such as cooking or cleaning. No one questions if the wife is actually the one at home cooking or not. What is important is the ability to host home gatherings. Whether the food is home-cooked or catered is not a token of a wife's ability. I have been invited to dinner at Indonesian middle-class houses and have lived in such households throughout my research since the mid-1980s. All the households rely on domestic assistance for basic household chores such as shopping, cleaning and cooking, although the degree of assistance varied.

Recently catering for social functions has become so popular that new catering businesses are emerging in urban areas. Thus, being a wife and mother among middle-class Indonesian women does not necessarily mean that women are undertaking domestic tasks on their own.

This privileged lifestyle enables them to engage with community matters. For example, Indri sits on a local school board and assists the activities of Aisyiyah. Indri said:

> It is not suitable for Muslim women to present their individualistic career goals as the sole driver of Muslim women's life. People and the community would not approve of such behaviour, and she would be seen as egoistic. She would not be accepted in our community. Would that make women lonely? No friends? No respect? If so, what is the aim of working? Working so hard and then being marginalised? It is great to see that women can contribute to community and give and share as much. It is a much better use of time undertaking almsgiving than wasting time. (interview, 16 November 2018)

Her remarks resonate with subtle criticisms made by the public about Dian Pelangi, a successful Muslim fashion designer, after her divorce in 2016. Her recent reinvention of her identity as a wife, mother and entrepreneur (Chapter 5) summarised in the word mompreneur, is a tacit and effective way to negotiate the existing pattern of patriarchy in contemporary Indonesia. Muslim mompreneurs, the middle-class Muslim women who can rely on domestic assistance or can make full use of popular digital online applications to order food or catering for family gatherings, are in fact expanding their economic roles and creating new role models for Muslim women by disseminating the new lived experiences of Muslim women.

Women's Work and Role Modelling in Islam

What do the findings of this book indicate on the issue of Islam and women's participation in work? This book has focused on Islamisation processes since the late 1980s, processes which have affected the way middle-class Muslims have embraced Islam as part of modernity. Throughout this research, discourses on Islam were presented with a strong inclination to orthodox Islam, which illustrated the Islamic orientations taking place among middle-class Muslims in Southeast Asia.

Syncretic Islamic practices associated with bringing prosperity—such as *ziarah*, or a visit to sacred site (Quinn 2008)—have not been mentioned. On the contrary, Islam as practised among middle-class women regulates and guides their life. Their participation in Islamic study groups demonstrates their status and class, and their embracing of Islam, as this book has demonstrated. Kartini was a well-known national female figure who became a symbol as a pioneer to gender empowerment as an outcome of politics of gender representations (Bijl and Chin 2020). However, because the portraits of Kartini depict her in typical formal Javanese dresses without a headscarf, there is little connection between her and the role models of today's Muslim women.

Although Kartini became a mother, she died immediately after the birth of her first child thus losing the opportunity to show concrete examples of motherhood. Her letters, which were written in Dutch, have little connection to the current middle-class Muslim population, who endeavour to read Arabic to enhance their understanding of Islam and the Qur'an through Islamic study group activities, while studying English for professional or business needs. Islam has been taught through school education as a reference point to guide their life amid a growing inclination to Islamic orthodoxy alongside the increased influence of Middle Eastern Islam in Indonesia. An Acehnese Muslim female fighter from North Sumatra born in the nineteenth century, Cut Nyak Dhien, does not seem to appear to be an appropriate role model as a Muslim woman because she mingled with men on battlefields and led the troops as a widow (Taylor 2020: 187).

Imagining the lives of Khadijah and Aishah and emulating them illustrates the efforts of Indonesian middle-class women to find a new role model that suits their subjective Muslim identity. It mirrors the nature of Islamisation processes felt strongly among the middle-class Muslims in Indonesia over the last 30 years. The stories of Khadijah and Aishah as embodied and emulated by Muslim mompreneurs are enhanced by the state-endorsed womanhood, which promotes raising a harmonious Indonesian family as the basis of the nation. Muhammadiyah's women's organisation Aisyiyah, is named after the prophet's youngest wife. This embeddedness of socio-cultural gender norms is certainly fostering middle-class Muslim women to turn to entrepreneurial businesses and charitable activities. As a result, the public roles of middle-class Muslim mompreneurs are expanding, although the scope of activities is facilitated by available domestic assistance, which was once provided only to the privileged class of women, such as Kartini (Taylor 2020: 183). Emulating Khadijah and Aishah is a way for women to propagate Islam by action or *dakwah bil hal*. Muslim men, in supporting this action, demonstrate their agreeance that with modernity so comes gender empowerment.

The findings of this book also highlight that feminised sectors, such as retail and services involving food and clothing, are where mompreneurs and Muslim women entrepreneurs are most visible. On the other hand, the other case studies have highlighted that women are breaking into new areas of work such as transport and digital application development. Manufacturing involving science-based research for beauty products is another area of significance, particularly for mompreneurs with a background in science research. As the number of women choosing to study such specialisations increases, new possibilities of developing a business are likely to increase. Yet difficulties in accessing the necessary funds to develop a business, coupled with the requirement of advanced knowledge of the business area, makes it problematic for any start-ups with limited funding and networks.

Towards Gender Equality in Muslim-Dominant Countries

What do our findings say about achieving gender equality? The findings of this book emphasise the need to explore localised strategies for achieving gender equality. The case study of Indonesia, representing a type of patriarchal society with husbands holding the power, has shown that obtaining the husband's endorsement is essential for a woman wanting to expand her economic role. The Indonesian Muslim women profiled in this book represent new ideal Muslim women known as Muslim mompreneurs. They are contributing to the building of a strong community while raising a pious family. As the findings of Chapter 4 show, remaining unmarried can create grave unhappiness for Muslim women. Women themselves naturally seek happiness in raising a family and contributing to their communities, as is shown in Chapters 5 and 6. Subsequently, to gain more decision-making power in their work choices, well-educated Muslim women are consciously seeking out opportunities to run their own or family-operated businesses. These successful Muslim women consciously do not emphasise their individual career aspirations as the driving force for starting a business. Rather, they are seeking happiness in managing their family and businesses and sharing the benefits with the community. The Muslim women we interviewed did not feel that their single career-oriented life was satisfying, even though these options would be endorsed by Western feminists.

It is worth noting that even in the advanced Western economies such as that of the USA, a recent survey shows that 50% of women with children under 18 years old prefer staying home rather than working outside the home (Brenan 2019). This does not mean that women do not want to work, rather it highlights the difficulty of balancing paid work and parental responsibilities. Thus, developing a policy to foster mompreneurs would work for women across the globe.

This book demonstrates that Muslim mompreneurs are increasing opportunities for women more generally by quietly contesting patriarchal norms and increasing female agency in society. Indonesian Muslim women's organisations and government policies have strengthened women's ability to run small businesses and develop entrepreneurship. The growth of the economy in Indonesia and the rise of the Muslim middle class have offered opportunities for Islamic businesses to grow. The combined effects of these changes have made Indonesia one of the most successful environments for women's entrepreneurship to flourish despite its strongly Islamic context. Our findings show that utilising key Islamic concepts or a local socio-cultural framework to support gender equality in aligning with development goals endorsed by the relevant development agencies and the national government is crucial to triggering a quiet social transformation across Muslim-dominant countries. Our research findings will address the research gap surrounding the paucity of empirical case studies and life histories of successful women entrepreneurs in developing countries, as indicated by recent scholarly research (Alom et al. 2016). Challenges faced by mompreneurs from Muslim-dominant countries will inform the scholars, policymakers and aspiring entrepreneurs about the motivations and enablers to help foster women's entrepreneurship.

Our empirical findings concur with an emergent new research focus by Bano (2017, 2019) that highlights the importance of external conditions including women's employment opportunities, education and media access. Accelerating access to all of these aptly supports women's work and family balance rather than the efforts to reform Islamic gender norms. The rise of Muslim mompreneurs in Indonesia is certainly conditioned by the fluid and diverse nature of Islamic authority and the long-standing tradition of women studying Islam on their own. The limited family-friendly provisions offered by employers and family support for small businesses also entice Muslim women to take up entrepreneurship to balance their work and family.

We conclude this book with directions for further research into the efforts to advance gender equality in patriarchal societies. Firstly, the choice of becoming a Muslim mompreneur is exclusive to the urban middle-class women who can rely on the availability of affordable domestic assistance. These helpers can take the burden of their domestic chores. The use of domestic helpers is commonly practised, predominantly in Southeast Asia and Muslim-dominant countries. In other words, poor working women remain invisible and work to support these middle-class women's households. We both contemplated the injustice and inequality embedded in middle-class women's lifestyle choices. Intersectionality within Muslim women remains to be addressed.[1] Yet, as strong patriarchy shapes and moulds gender norms and expectations of Muslim women, middle-class Muslim women's role in creating a new role model warrants an important step to trigger social transformation to achieve wholistic gender equality over the course of time. We certainly envisage a research direction to examine intersectionality in gender equality within Muslim-dominant countries.

Further, the COVID-19 pandemic has had an impact on female-owned businesses (Gesund 2021). However, anecdotal evidence from Indonesia suggests that women were forced to accept more financial responsibility because their husbands had lost employment.[2] There are emerging reports that COVID-19 has shifted the patterns of shopping for middle-class Indonesians from in-person to online shopping (Septalisma 2020). Subsequently, this has created new opportunities for women in start-ups. Although we are alarmed by the aforementioned World Bank briefs (Gesund 2021) and UN reports (United Nations 2020) of the negative impact on female-owned businesses due to the increased burden of domestic chores being demanded of women, it is also important to note that the impetus arising from the pandemic has also created new online business opportunities and start-ups for women. Whether these new businesses will continue to grow after the pandemic remains to be seen.

Finally, the new economic and social blueprint in the Gulf states, such as Saudi Arabia's Vision 2030, would provide an important area to examine. Vision 2030 identified the key role of women in the new economy. Further investigation into how Muslim women in the Gulf states could contribute to a new economic direction would help understanding the changing gender norms in Muslim-dominant countries. In addition, Indonesian Muslim mompreneurs are certainly expected to take part in creating a new Khadijah and Aishah in their endeavour to fight against the existing patriarchal norms and conservative interpretations of Islam. How this role modelling would facilitate the negotiation to achieve gender equality in Muslim-dominant countries remains to be seen.

Notes

1. Recent research (Beta 2021; Khan 2019) shows that booming ethical fashion industries to cater for middle-class consumption rest upon the labour exploitation of unskilled female workers.
2. See Indonesian articles that show women are taking up new businesses during the COVID-19 pandemic to look for a new livelihood at and Setuningsih (2021) and Wijayanti (2020).

References

Alom, Fardous, Moha Asri Abdullah, Abdul Rashid Moten, and S.M. Ferdous Azam. 2016. Success Factors of Overall Improvement of Microenterprises in Malaysia: An Empirical Study. *Journal of Global Entrepreneurship Research* 6 (1): 1–13.

Bano, Masooda. 2017. *Female Islamic Education Movements: The Re-Democratisation of Islamic Knowledge*. Cambridge: Cambridge University Press.

Bano, Masooda. 2019. Religion and Female Empowerment: Evidence from Pakistan and Northern Nigeria. *Canadian Journal of Development Studies/Revue Canadienne D'études Du Développement* 40 (2): 163–181.

Beta, Annisa R. 2021. Out of Thin Air: Emerging Muslim Fashion Entrepreneurs and the Spectre of Labour in Indonesia. *Continuum* 35 (6): 824–837.

Bijl, Paul, and Grace V.S. Chin. eds. 2020. *Appropriating Kartini: Colonial, National and Transnational Memories of an Indonesian Icon*. Singapore: ISEAS-Yusof Ishak Institute.

Brenan, Megan. 2019. Record-High 56% of U.S. Women Prefer Working to Homemaking. Gallup. https://news.gallup.com/poll/267737/record-high-women-prefer-working-homemaking.aspx. Accessed 24 Oct 2021.

Gesund, Jessica. 2021. How Is Covid-19 Affecting Women's Employment? Evidence from the World Bank's Gender Innovation Labs. *World Bank Blogs*. World Bank Blogs 22 June 2021. Available at: https://blogs.worldbank.org/jobs/how-covid-19-affecting-womens-employment-evidence-world-banks-gender-innovation-labs.

Khan, Rimi. 2019. 'Be Creative' in Bangladesh? Mobility, Empowerment and Precarity in Ethical Fashion Enterprise. *Cultural Studies* 33 (6): 1029–1049.

Latief, Hilman. 2017. Marketizing Piety through Charitable Work: Islamic Charitables and the Islamization of the Middle-Class Families. In *Religion and the Morality of the Market*, eds. Daromir Rudnyckyj and Filippo Osella, 196–216. Cambridge: Cambridge University Press.

Muttaqin, A., R.M. Amtsar, Nuri Mashril, and A. Pratiwi. 2011. *Perempuan yang Menginspirasi: Kisah Sukses Mitra BMT Beringharjo*. Yogyakarta: BMT Beringharjo.

Quinn, George. 2008. Throwing Money at the Holy Door: Commercial Aspects of Popular Pilgrimage in Java. In *Expressing Islam: Religious Life and Politics in Indonesia*, eds. Greg Fealy and Sally White, 63–79. ISEAS Publishing.

Rinaldo, Rachel. 2013. *Mobilizing Piety: Islam and Feminism in Indonesia*. Oxford and New York: Oxford University Press.

Sakai, Minako. 2010. Growing Together in Partnership: Women's Views of the Business Practices of an Islamic Savings and Credit Cooperative (Baitul Maal Wat Tamwil) in Central Java, Indonesia. *Women's Studies International Forum* 33 (4): 412–421. https://doi.org/10.1016/j.wsif.2010.02.015.

Sakai, Minako. 2018. *Penggiat Bisnis Syariah: Muslimah, Kewirausahaan dan Pemberdayaan Masyarakat*. Jakarta: Dompet Dhuafa.

Sakai, Minako, and Amelia Fauzia. 2016. Performing Muslim Womanhood: Muslim Business Women Moderating Islamic Practices in Contemporary Indonesia. *Islam and Christian-Muslim Relations* 27 (3): 229–249. https://doi.org/10.1080/09596410.2015.1114243.

Septalisma, Bisma. 2020. Belanja Online Naik 400 Persen Saat Musim Corona. CNN. https://www.cnnindonesia.com/ekonomi/20200707172450-92-521925/belanja-online-naik-400-persen-saat-musim-corona. Accessed 10 Feb 2021.

Setuningsih, Novianti. 2021. Suami Kena PHK, Pinkan Mambo Sempat Berencana Buka Warung Kopi di Kampung. Kompas. https://www.kompas.com/hype/read/2021/08/07/161148066/suami-kena-phk-pinkan-mambo-sempat-berencana-buka-warung-kopi-di-kampung. Accessed 10 Sept 2021.

Taylor, Jean Gelman. 2020. Afterword. In *Appropriating Kartini: Colonial, National and Transnational Memories of an Indonesian Icon*, eds. Bijl Paul and V.S. Chin Grace, 175–190. Singapore: ISEAS—Yusof Ishak Institute. https://doi.org/10.1355/9789814843928-010.

United Nations. 2020. Policy Brief: The Impact of Covid-19 on Women. United Nations. Available at: https://www.un.org/sexualviolenceinconflict/wp-content/uploads/2020/06/report/policy-brief-the-impact-of-covid-19-on-women/policy-brief-the-impact-of-covid-19-on-women-en-1.pdf.07 November 2021.

Wijayanti, Endah. 2020. Suami Terkena PHK, Aku Membuka Usaha Kuliner dengan Modal Rp.100 Ribu. Fimela. https://www.fimela.com/lifestyle/read/4397380/suami-terkena-phk-aku-membuka-usaha-kuliner-dengan-modal-rp100-ribu. Accessed 02 Nov 2021.

Glossary

Aishah: The youngest wife of the Prophet Muhammad

Aisyiyah: Women's division of Muhammadiyah

***akhirat*:** Life after death

***arisan*:** A rotary credit or saving association established mainly by a group of members to meet on a regular basis to give the total savings amount to the members in sequence, often used as a saving method in Indonesia

batik: Indonesian traditional fabric dyed with a special technique using hot wax

***dakwah bil hal*:** Dakwah is propagation and dakwah bil hal is a propagation strategy using real examples or deeds to demonstrate good Muslim acts

Dharma Wanita: An organisation for civil servants' wives formed by the Suharto government

***ekonomi kerakyatan*:** People's economy, an economic concept used to support small businesses in Indonesia

Fatayat: Younger women's component of Indonesian Islamic organisation Nahdlatul Ulama

***fatwa*:** Non-binding legal opinion issued by ulama (qualified person(s) or scholars in Islamic knowledge) on social issues

***hadith*:** The sayings and actions of the Prophet Muhammad

M. Sakai and A. Fauzia, *Women Entrepreneurs and Business Empowerment in Muslim Countries*,
Gender, Development and Social Change,
https://doi.org/10.1007/978-3-031-05954-4

***halal*:** Matters that are permitted according to Islamic law
***haram*:** Matters that are forbidden according to Islamic law
***hijab*:** A type of Muslim women's veil that covers the head and chest
***hijabers*:** Muslim women who wear the *hijab* and stylistic but modest Islamic clothing in Indonesia
***ibadah*:** Worship; Islamic devotional acts
***ibu*:** Indonesian for mother
***ijtihad*:** Independent reasoning or judgement in interpretation of Islamic law
***infaq (infak)*:** A type of charity in Islam that is recommended and voluntary
***izin suami*:** Husband's approval
***janda*:** Widow; divorced woman
***jodoh*:** A match that is believed to be determined by God's will
***jomblo*:** A slang word for single men or women and those who are not in a relationship
***keluarga maslahah*:** A concept of family proposed by Nahdlatul Ulama in which the family is able to provide for its own basic primary needs. It literally means healthy family.
***keluarga sakinah*:** A concept of harmonious family originally proposed by Aisyiyah and Muhammadiyah
Khadijah: The first wife of the Prophet Muhammad, known to be a wealthy businesswoman
***kodrat wanita*:** The notion of woman's biologically ordained role
***majelis taklim*:** Islamic study group
mompreneur: Businesswomen who are also mothers; a hybrid English word deriving from mom and entrepreneur
Muhammadiyah: A modernist Muslim organisation established in Yogyakarta, Indonesia in 1912
Nahdlatul Ulama (NU): The Revival of Religious Scholars; the largest traditionalist Muslim organisation in Indonesia, founded in 1926
Nasyiatul Aisyiyah: Younger women's organisation of Aisyiyah, affiliated with Muhammadiyah
***ojek*:** Motorcycle taxi
Pancasila: Indonesian national philosophy, consisting of five principles
***pengajian*:** Islamic study group
***perawan tua*:** Literally means old virgin; a negative way to refer to unmarried older women
***pesantren*:** Islamic boarding school

***rahmatan lil alamin*:** Blessing for the universe; a concept of peaceful Islam mentioned in the Qur'an
***rezeki*:** Gifts from God in the form of livelihood
***salafi*:** An adherent of salafism; Muslims who endeavour to purify Islam by following the teachings of the Prophet Muhammad and the three generations following him
***santri*:** Islamic boarding school student
***ta'aruf*:** Islamic courtship or a period when a man and woman try to get to know each other before deciding whether to marry
***umi*:** Term of address for one's mother
***umroh*:** Lesser pilgrimage to Mecca
Wahhabism: Islamic revivalist movement associated with Muhammad ibn Abd al-Wahhab, known for its orthodox and puritanical approach to Islam
***warung*:** A small kiosk that usually sells groceries
***zakat*:** Almsgiving, one of the five pillars of Islam

Index

M. Sakai and A. Fauzia, *Women Entrepreneurs and Business Empowerment in Muslim Countries*, Gender, Development and Social Change,
https://doi.org/10.1007/978-3-031-05954-4

The manufacturer's authorised representative in the EU is Springer Nature Customer Service Centre GmbH, Europaplatz 3, 69115 Heidelberg, Germany. If you have any concerns regarding our products, please contact ProductSafety@springernature.com

Printed and bound by CPI Group (UK) Ltd, Croydon, CR0 4YY
30/09/2026
02225492-0002